D0208429

David
Hume
and the Problem of Reason

David Hume

and the Problem of Reason

Recovering the Human Sciences

John W. Danford

Yale University Press   New Haven and London

Designed by Sonia L. Scanlon.

Set in Bulmer type by The Composing Room of Michigan, Inc. Printed in the United States of America by BookCrafters, Inc., Chelsea, Michigan.

Library of Congress Cataloging-in-Publication Data

Danford, John W.

 David Hume and the problem of reason: recovering the human sciences/John W. Danford.

   p.   cm.

 Includes bibliographical references.

 ISBN 0-300-04667-7

 1. Hume, David, 1711–1776—Contributions in concept of reason. 2. Reason. I. Title.

 B1499.R4D35   1990

 121—dc20   89-29104

                                                       CIP

The paper in this book meets the guidelines of permanence and durability of the Committee on Production Guidelines for Book Longevity of the Council on Library Resources.

10 9 8 7 6 5 4 3 2 1

For Karen

Contents

Acknowledgments

I have incurred numerous debts, both intellectual and other, during the years I have worked on this book. I began writing it while the beneficiary of a Faculty Development Leave from the University of Houston in 1983–84. I am indebted to the Social Studies Faculty Centre of Oxford University, which provided me with office space, access to libraries, and a congenial atmosphere for writing. In particular I am grateful to Zbigniev Pelczynski of Pembroke College for his generous support and encouragement and to Mary Oxford of the Faculty Centre for her courteous assistance. I would also like to thank Enders and Jane Ann Wimbush, then of Charlbury, England, for excessive hospitality.

I am indebted to the National Endowment for the Humanities, from which I received a Senior Fellowship for Independent Study in 1986–87, which gave me the time to complete the study. I am grateful to Liberty Fund, of Indianapolis, Indiana, for excellent conferences that gave me the opportunity to try out some ideas and to meet colleagues from other universities with similar interests.

Many individuals have contributed in one way or another. In particular I am grateful to Joseph Hamburger, Tom Pangle, David Brady, Donald Lutz, Darrell Dobbs, Tony Sirignano, Nick Capaldi, David Miller, and John Gray. John Ackerman suggested judicious revisions that improved the early chapters. Donald Livingston, who read the manuscript for Yale

University Press, offered extremely helpful comments which led to some improvements in the study. None of these individuals agrees with everything I say, here or elsewhere, even though I have tried to show each the error of his ways. All the mistakes and infelicities are mine alone.

I would like to express my gratitude to Stacey Mandelbaum of Yale University Press, whose perspicacious editing improved my prose, and to three of my students—Bob Lichenstein, Nancy Oliver, and Katie Traverse—who generously helped with the proofreading.

Parts of this book have already appeared in print. Chapter 9 originally appeared as "'The Surest Foundation of Morality': The Political Teaching of Hume's *Dialogues concerning Natural Religion*," *Western Political Quarterly* 35 (June 1982). Parts of chapters 7 and 8 appeared in the same journal as "Hume on Development: The First Volumes of the *History of England*" 42 (March 1989). Adapted by permission of the University of Utah, copyright holder.

Finally, I want to acknowledge the unfailing assistance and encouragement of my wife, Karen Pawluk Danford, who time and again interrupted her own studies to help an impossible husband (not to mention bearing and raising two children). For a debt quite simply beyond measure, this book is dedicated to her.

Works Cited in the Text

Unless I have noted otherwise, all works are by Hume and are cited by page.

Abstract   *An Abstract of a Treatise of Human Nature*, ed. J. M. Keynes and P. Sraffa. Hamden: Archon, 1965.

D   *Dialogues concerning Natural Religion*, ed. Norman Kemp Smith. London: Thomas Nelson and Sons, 1947.

E   *Essays, Moral, Political, and Literary*, ed. Eugene F. Miller. Indianapolis: Liberty, 1985.

EHU
ECPM   *Enquiries concerning Human Understanding* [EHU] *and concerning the Principles of Morals* [ECPM], ed. L. A. Selby-Bigge. 3d ed. rev. P. H. Nidditch. Oxford: Clarendon, 1975.

EL   Thomas Hobbes, *The Elements of Law*, ed. Ferdinand Tönnies. London: Frank Cass, 1969. (Cited by part, chapter, and paragraph, respectively.)

Essay   John Locke, *An Essay concerning Human Understanding*, collated and annotated by Alexander Campbell Fraser. New York: Dover, 1959. (Cited by book, chapter, and paragraph.)

H   *The History of England: From the Invasion of Julius Caesar to the Revolution in 1688*, based on the

Edition of 1778, with the Author's Last Corrections and Improvements. 6 vols. Indianapolis: Liberty, 1983. (There is no critical edition, and this recent edition is the only one widely available. Cited by volume and page.)

Letters   *The Letters of David Hume*, ed. J. Y. T. Greig. 2 vols. Oxford: Clarendon, 1932. (Cited by volume and page.)

Leviathan   Thomas Hobbes, *Leviathan*, ed. C. B. Macpherson. Harmondsworth, England: Penguin, 1968. (Cited by either chapter or chapter and page.)

NHR   *The Natural History of Religion*, ed. H. E. Root. Stanford: Stanford University Press, 1957.

PHK   George Berkeley, *A Treatise concerning the Principles of Human Knowledge*, ed. Colin M. Turbayne. Indianapolis: Bobbs-Merrill, 1957. (Cited by part and paragraph.)

T   *A Treatise of Human Nature*, ed. L. A. Selby-Bigge. 2d ed. with text revised and variant readings by P. H. Nidditch. Oxford: Clarendon, 1978.

1 Introduction

What can justify another book-length study of the writings of David Hume? Many justifications could be offered: the abysmal state of our understanding of how economics is related to human nature, contemporary ignorance about the nature, power, and political importance of religious faith, widespread interest in the foundations of natural science—to name only three possibilities. On these subjects, and many more, Hume has a great deal to teach. But his importance is more fundamental. This book is about Hume, but it is also about a problem. The problem has been implicit in modernity since the epistemological revolution of the seventeenth century but has surfaced as what one might call a social problem only during the twentieth century. Not only was Hume's one of the greatest minds ever to reflect on what I call the problem of reason, but these reflections were, in my judgment, at the core of his entire philosophic life.

At the fundamental level, the problem of reason involves the claims about knowledge and its foundations which were made by such founders of modern natural science as Thomas Hobbes and René Descartes. But the surface manifestations of the problem are familiar even to the general population. They are probably most evident to teachers who confront daily the wholesale relativism that leads students (and for that matter most social scientists) to deny that one can "know" anything about, for example, what is good and bad for human beings, since judgments about good and bad are not about facts and, properly speaking, knowledge involves the factual realm. Young people learn very quickly today that arguments can be avoided, or ended, by assertions of the relativity of what they call values. This spares them a great deal of the hard work of thinking, or marshaling evidence to support a claim or an argument. It is easier to decline to defend one's views on the ground that they stem from beliefs which are personal and subjective than to argue rationally in favor of a position one asserts is true or right. Relativism is thus often a coward's refuge; but, more important for the way we study human beings and society, it deprives us of the possibility of rational inquiry into what were once the central questions of the social sciences and especially of political science: How should we live? What is good and bad for human beings? What sort of society is best?

Liberal democracies or, more precisely, liberal commercial republics, are the fruit of a revolution in our understanding of what it means to be human, and of our relation to nature, the great revolution understood originally as the revolt of modernity against the ancients, and closely associated with the rise of modern natural science. The founders of modernity understood the political order to flow from the needs of individual human beings and not as something that existed prior to individuals. They emphasized rights over duties and taught that men and women are not political animals, at least not in the sense the ancients attached to the term. They taught that reason is properly regarded not as some sort of divine element in humans, a link to the gods or God, but as a tool which can serve the only objective, natural human end: survival or comfortable self-preservation. As such, reason can be exploited in conquest of the fundamentally hostile nature in which human beings find themselves. This tool, this "new organon" as Bacon called it, is what we call modern natural science. Its goal is to "subdue and overcome the necessities and miseries of humanity."[1] All the hopes of modernity are connected in one way or another with this enterprise. The light of science was to illuminate the dark recesses of superstition and ignorance, and humanity would flourish as never before thanks to the truths discovered by unfettered reason. The social and political order, morality itself, were to have a new—and rational—ground.

Hopes like these, however, were last expressed by sophisticated people near the close of the nineteenth century, and their expression was already quite rare then. By the beginning of our century it was accepted that the truths of modern science are only more myths, that they are invented not discovered, that there is no universal or transhistorical reason capable of producing transhistorical truth. All beliefs are relative, all values merely cultural or temporal. This philosophical development above all, however remote from the minds of ordinary men and women going about their business, has contributed to the pervasive relativism noted above.[2] What does David Hume have to do with it? To see that requires a look at a second consideration: the isolation of philosophy.

There is nothing original in the observation that philosophy—once the queen of the sciences—has been reduced to a pathetic state of irrelevance in the contemporary academy and indeed in the contemporary world. A review of A. J. Ayer's *Philosophy in the Twentieth Century,* for example, begins with the observation that today "thinking people who are not themselves philosophers—that is to say nearly all intellectuals— pay almost no attention to the subject."[3] The reviewer suggests that this has something to do with the increase of what he calls "technical rigor" in philosophy, caused by philosophers' attempts to be more "professional," and concludes that probably "philosophy can be either professionally competent or socially significant but never both at the same time." The increasingly sterile and technical concerns of academic philosophers today have not been forced upon them, however. Why is it that "the big questions regarding the world of human affairs are simply not being asked, let alone answered, by professional philosophers"?

The same founders of modernity who initiated the challenge to ancient and medieval philosophy understood that a new understanding of philosophy itself must be part of their program. Although this theme will be considered explicitly in chapters 2 and 3, we can sketch the issues briefly here. The ancient political philosophers, beginning with Socrates,

were compelled to confront a certain problem with the original philosophy—natural philosophy—invented by their predecessors. That problem was its blindness to human things which, because they seemed
transitory and even ephemeral by comparison with (for example) celes-
tial things, were of no interest to philosophers seeking eternal truths. But
the inquiries of philosophers were not irrelevant to the very human
beliefs they ignored with contempt; the questions of philosophy placed its
practitioners in direct conflict with political and theological authorities,
because they posed a political (we would say "moral") danger.

The grounds of this conflict can be seen most clearly in Aristophanes'
treatment of Socrates in *The Clouds*. Socrates is portrayed as one who
investigates and teaches without bothering to think about the effects of
his teaching on other people. He loves the truth but has not given any
thought to the possibility that others may love some things more than
truth. And he has no understanding of his own inquiry: philosophy is his
way of life, but Socrates engages in it unself-consciously. Aristophanes
demonstrates the disastrous results of "natural philosophy" so practiced.
Socrates' pupil, Pheidippides—the pride and joy of his doting father,
Strepsiades—begins to apply the lessons of nature to his own life. Since
in nature "the strongest rules" (a point he illustrates by way of the
pecking order among chickens), he decides it is not against nature for
him to horsewhip his father, if he can get away with it. He threatens even
his mother. The destruction of his family, which Strepsiades loves even
more than life, drives the old man to attack Socrates and destroy his
"research institute."

Of course the Platonic and Xenophontic Socrates was not a natural
philosopher but rather the founder of political philosophy (though he
may have been a natural philosopher in his younger days).[4] Political
philosophy can be understood as the attempt to understand "the human
things" in the light of reason or rational inquiry. Socrates' redirection of
philosophy to the human things may have resulted from his realization
that our access to "the whole"—that is, to all things—must begin with
thinking about the human capacity to know, the love of wisdom or the
desire to know, and the place these occupy in human life. The attempt to

understand love, knowledge, virtue—and the role these play against the background of the different types of human souls—is the key to any hope we have of understanding the whole. Whether Aristophanes had anything to do with Socrates' redirection of philosophy we can never know, though it is interesting that when Plato's Socrates defends his way of life to the Athenians in his *Apology*, Aristophanes is mentioned by name in connection with what Socrates calls his "old accusers."

In any case we must admit that the Socratic transformation of natural philosophy into political philosophy did not eliminate the tension between philosophy and the city. And the execution of Socrates serves as a permanent warning that philosophic inquiry may be politically dangerous. But a philosophy concerned first of all with human things—what it is to know or to love, for example—will at least consider what effect it has on nonphilosophers, and its practitioners will remain sensitive to the danger they pose. It will, in short, be self-conscious or "political" philosophy. In view of what Socrates' successors regarded as a permanent and inescapable tension between political life and a life devoted to rational inquiry, they took care to philosophize with circumspection. They wrote carefully if they wrote at all, and their discretion was manifested in the elusive, allegorical form of philosophical writing. The Platonic dialogues are only the most famous ancient example. Not coincidentally Plato called on poets to become politically responsible, even as he produced a kind of philosophic poetry.

The first moderns to challenge the long tradition of circumspect philosophic writing believed that a new kind of rationality, and a new social order, could reduce or even eliminate the need for such caution concerning the pernicious effects of philosophic reasoning. After all, they asked, how could reason or philosophy be dangerous to morality if the latter were separated from superstition and placed on a solid rational foundation? The only trick was finding a sufficiently solid base on which to build the foundation, since if it was to be scientific and certain it must not be disputable in any way. "To reduce this doctrine to the rules and infallibility of reason," as Hobbes put it, "there is no way, but first to put such principles down for a foundation, as passion not mistrusting, may not seek not to displace."[5] The founders of modernity had recourse to a new model for knowledge, suggested to them by the great advances in mathematics and the fledgling natural sciences. They were quite explicit about the basis of its attraction for them. It produced certain and clear truths which were immune to the "cavils of the skeptics," because the construction of its truths was preceded by a fog-clearing application of doubt.

Old fashioned thinkers objected to this of course; listen to Shaftesbury writing about the new philosophers' impatience with uncertainty, their attachment to systematic philosophy. The "Academick Philosophy," he writes,

> no-way sutes the Genius of our Age. Men . . . can't bear being kept in suspence. The Examination torments 'em. They want to be rid of it, upon the easiest terms. 'Tis as if men fancy'd themselves drowning, whenever they dare trust to the Current of Reason. They seem hurrying away, they know not whither; and are ready to catch at the first Twig. There they chuse afterwards to hang, tho' ever so insecurely, rather than trust their Strength to bear 'em above Water. He who has got hold of an *Hypothesis*, how slight soever, is satisfy'd. He can presently answer every Objection, and, with a few Terms of Art, give an account of every Thing without trouble.[6]

The proponents of the new sort of philosophy modeled on geometry, mathematics, and natural science were necessarily critical of the old cautious or reticent philosophy and its style. According to this view, what cannot be known with certainty cannot properly be described as knowledge at all, and so the old philosophical writings are to be superseded.[7] As Shaftesbury puts it, "Of all philosophy, therefore, how absolutely the most disagreeable must *that* appear, which goes upon no establish'd Hypothesis, nor presents us with any flattering scheme, talks only of Probabilitys, Suspence of Judgment, Inquiry, Search, and Caution not to be impos'd on, or deceiv'd?"[8]

It is not farfetched to suggest that the view to which Shaftesbury objected is the source of the insistence on "technical rigor" which was mentioned above as characteristic of contemporary Anglo-American philosophy. The last two centuries have witnessed the gradual jettisoning, from serious philosophy, of more and more of the concerns which were once central to it but which proved intractable when approached with technical rigor. "Rigorous Philosophy" is a kind of euphemism for the bits left after this jettisoning—that is, for the *arcana* on which professional or academic philosophers focus today. Philosophy which models its conception of knowledge on the natural sciences or mathematics has developed into philosophy only for philosophers; these can converse intelligibly only with one another because all connection with ordinary human concerns, or common life, has been lost. Anyone who bothers to apologize for such a state of affairs is likely to concede the isolation of philosophy but claim that that is the price which must be paid for coherence and rigor. The older sort of "literary philosophy," what Shaftesbury calls "The way of *Dialogue,* and patience of Debate and Reasoning," is considered hopelessly outdated today. Those with an interest in such things—even if they would once have been considered philosophers—today are found in other academic departments working in such areas as political theory or literary criticism.[9]

The isolation of philosophy from common life, then, may have been implicit from the very beginning of modernity, the unavoidable, if unintended, consequence of the attempt to put philosophy on a new footing. That transformation of philosophy, as I have already suggested, required both a relentless critique of ancient philosophy as a sort of useless, uncertain woolgathering, and a demonstration that the fears associated with the old philosophy about the dangers of philosophic reason were groundless. There is no need for philosophic circumspection, for dialogues and allegories, if reason poses no threat. But the bold assertion that philosophic reason is not in tension with common life seems now to have been contradicted by events. The crisis of Western rationalism has been described as the undermining of reason by reason itself, the discovery that there is no truth but what is temporarily expedient, that nothing can be known about the things which matter most. And seen in this way, the isolation of philosophy from "the important questions"—another phrase which sounds quaint today—is simply the unavoidable by-product of the liberation of reason.

Now, when the two phenomena discussed here are understood to be merely two sides of the same coin, Hume's importance for us emerges. For as I will attempt to show in this study, the central concern of Hume's philosophical career, amounting at times almost to a preoccupation, is the status of reason and specifically the tension between reason and "common life," as Hume calls the concerns of prephilosophic human existence. All his (well-known) attention to the nature of causation and the foundations of science were in the service of this concern; his investigation of the nature of various forms of skepticism, his consideration of the nature of religious faith, and his inquiry into the foundations of morals, center around his rediscovery of the tension between philosophic reason and common life. More than that, I will argue that the very manner of his philosophic writing, and in particular his concern with history, were the fruits of his sustained reflections on this fundamental problem.

Anyone familiar with scholarship on Hume in the past fifty years will know immediately that his work is not generally understood this way. Students of what may loosely be called political theory are likely to think of David Hume—to the extent that they think of him at all—as a "philosopher's philosopher." His chief work is almost universally considered to have been the *Treatise of Human Nature,* excerpts from which are often used as introductions to "philosophical thinking" in introductory philosophy courses. Hume is known for his arcane investigation of the nature of causation and probability, for example, or for his comment on the distinction between "is" and "ought," or for having exposed the inadequacy of the common sense assumption that the future will be like the past. This is the Hume of "Philosophy 1."

If Hume is mentioned in connection with political theory, it is generally to point out his close connection with Adam Smith, in relation to whom Hume is regarded as a brilliant but rather unsystematic precursor, in consequence of Hume's incidental essays on commerce and the rudiments of political economy and demography.[10] In recent years some attention has been paid to Hume's influence on the American founders, again primarily with respect to the political essays.[11] But on the whole Hume's essays are regarded as, well, essays—that is to say, as incidental pieces that occupy an ancillary place in his overall body of work, which was chiefly in "pure" philosophy. The *Treatise of Human Nature* and the *Enquiries* continue to be looked on as the core of Hume's writings.

There are two things wrong with this conventional view. First and most important, such an approach focuses on a very small portion of Hume's writings, and mainly on the one published work which he more or less repudiated. The *Treatise* was not only his first work but was composed, as Hume says with regret, before he was twenty-five. Neither it nor the *Enquiries* constructed out of it were looked on, at least in Hume's own lifetime, as his most important writings.[12] It was the *Essays* which brought him fame, and the *History of England* was his crowning achievement; Hume was most famous in his lifetime and for at least a century thereafter as a historian. The best testimony to this is the entry for Hume in the Catalogue of the Library of the British Museum, which to this day classifies him as a historian.

The second objection to the conventional view of Hume as philosopher's philosopher is that the view of philosophy implicit in it is not Hume's, nor indeed is it characteristic of any thinker of the eighteenth century, or earlier. It is, in fact, the self-understanding of twentieth century academic or professional philosophers, who have claimed Hume as one of their own. That there is some warrant for this is beyond dispute, for Hume's early writing shares with twentieth-century philosophy a conviction of the primacy of epistemology. But—and this study will contend it is a large but—Hume somehow overcame his preoccupation with epistemology. It would be more accurate to say he passed beyond epistemology than that he rejected or turned away from it. I shall argue that Hume's career as a writer and thinker was all of a piece and that the writings for which he was most renowned in his own lifetime are neither less important nor, with some qualifications, less philosophical than the works which are studied in philosophy courses.

According to a once common and still persistent view, Hume began as a philosopher and then, dashed by the reception (or lack of it) accorded his *Treatise* but with his ambition for literary fame unquenched, gave up philosophy to pursue a career as belletrist, essayist, and man of letters.[13] On this account, anyone interested in Hume as a philosopher need concern himself only, or primarily, with the *Treatise*.[14] Now, it is true that in his first work Hume confronted epistemological conundrums of the deepest and most intractable sort, and it must be admitted—he himself admitted—that he could not solve them satisfactorily. It is tempting to say that Hume had merely uncovered, a bit early, the grounds of what is called in the twentieth century the "crisis of reason."[15] The intractable problems Hume confronted continue to be confronted, and are equally intractable, today. But somehow Hume passed beyond them, and his later writings show almost no trace of their existence.

It seems to me that a proper understanding of Hume depends on seeing not only how and why the problem of reason was central to him as a philosopher but how he managed to work through the problem in a way that allowed him to get on with philosophy, rather than abandon it. On this view the *Essays* and the *History,* together with the *Dialogues concerning Natural Religion,* are the flower of Hume's philosophic career and not merely a testimony to his literary vanity. In the chapters which follow I present the grounds for this view. I will suggest that the amused detachment about philosophy which marks Hume's later writings was the hard-won product of his reflections on what he came to call the "strange infirmities" of human understanding.

The general plan of the book can be sketched as follows. The eight chapters which precede the conclusion fall roughly into two groups. The first group, chapters 2 through 5, is concerned mostly with the "problem of reason," both what it means and how Hume confronted it. Chapters 6 through 9 are concerned with Hume's political writings (using political in the broadest philosophical sense), or with what I take to be the mature philosophy of Hume.

In the next chapter I consider the problem of reason as manifested in our century, especially in social science, and suggest that it has its roots not in philosophy simply but in the particularly modern formulation of the goal of philosophy. In chapter 3 I turn to Hume, specifically to his initial confrontation with the problem of reason in the *Treatise*. This consideration leads me to a brief reconstruction, in chapter 4, of the new foundation of philosophy which was attempted by Hume's great modern predecessors and which set the stage for Hume's grappling with the problem of reason. Starting from what Hume calls the "fundamental principle" of modern science, which is its claim about the epiphenomenality of the senses, I suggest that Hume confronted the separation of science from experience implicit in the writings of his modern predecessors, the founders of modern science. The skepticism about the senses which is found in Bacon, Hobbes, Descartes, and others led Hume to his famous investigation of the nature of causation, and this in turn taught him the necessity for rejoining science and experience. This joining, I suggest, was the result of Hume's discovery of what he called the "strange infirmities" of the human understanding, and it pointed the way to a corrected philosophical stance. Such a stance overcomes debilitating philosophical skepticism by returning to "common life" or what would today be called prephilosophical consciousness, as a kind of ballast or "gross earthy mixture" which forestalls the philosophic tendency to rise into the ether.

In chapter 6, I consider Hume's explicit suggestion that *history* "keeps a just medium" between the philosopher "in his closet"—who cannot get an adequate grasp on human affairs—and the overly interested and thus prejudiced viewpoint of the "man of business." I suggest that Hume's *History of England*—along with his *Essays*—constitute the heart of Hume's political philosophy, a suggestion which needs to be justified by some attention to the problem of historicism and the alleged incompatibility of historical with philosophical (timeless or transhistorical) truth. In chapters 7 and 8 I take up the question of what the *History* teaches, in a very general way, about moral and political affairs. Finally, in chapter 9 I consider Hume's *Dialogues concerning Natural Religion*. Here the theme is the relationship of religion to philosophy, and of both to morals. I argue that this final testament, which Hume was so concerned to have published, even posthumously, offers us his most mature reflections on the problem of reason and skeptical philosophy and gives us a final glimpse of Hume at his most "classical."

Some books seem to write themselves or at least to outline themselves; others are the result of conscious decisions among alternatives which sometimes seem equally attractive. This book belongs to the latter class. I will make no attempt to defend every such decision, but the reader should know that I am keenly aware of roads not taken. Much as been ignored or given short shrift that another might think useful or even indispensable. Hume is too vast and deep, and I can only hope that those who know him well will be sympathetic. In my reading of the *History*, for example, an early ambition to treat all six volumes systematically had to give way to necessity; almost all my references, as the reader will discover, are to the first three volumes (the first and second were the last Hume composed). I believe there is justification for this emphasis in that the first volumes are the most general, least specific to England, and so the most appropriate to my purposes here. The later volumes are at least as rich and complex, however: I hope to write on them in the future, but the plans for doing so in this study came to seem overly ambitious. Volumes five and six of the *History*, in particular (on the Stuarts, the Civil War, and Commonwealth) present Hume's mature teaching about the power of religious enthusiasm, superstition, and prejudice in political life; that this is a timely theme, in view of recent resurgence of religious fundamentalism in various parts of the globe, is obvious.

Another sin of omission, which will be more bothersome to some than to others, is that the historical and biographical circumstances of Hume's career are largely passed over in this study in favor of a focus which is both more inward and more outward: I try, on the one hand, to concentrate on the content of Hume's philosophy by attention to texts and, on the other, to trace some relationships between this content and a philosophic tradition the existence of which I largely take for granted here. That Hume and his great contemporaries, whether D'Alembert, Montesquieu, Rousseau, or Adam Smith, saw themselves as part of a philosophic tradition stretching back to Cicero and the Greeks seems to me indisputable from their writings, in any case. All of this is only to admit at the outset what every author knows but every reader needs to be reminded of: that this book is not comprehensive or definitive, that it leaves out much that could have been included, that it could have been different in various ways. I hope only that it is sensible in what it tries to do, and I believe that the road it follows, while not the only, the widest, or the best paved of roads, follows the contours of the terrain, keeps out of bogs, and conveys the reader to a better understanding of both a philosophical problem and of the writings of David Hume.

2 Science and Truth

It is a curious fact that in contemporary social science the most formal and abstract treatments of social phenomena (at the extreme this means analyses couched in purely mathematical terms) are considered most empirical. The book review section of the major American political science journal, for example, distinguishes normative theory from empirical theory and methodology. In the latter category are found studies which raise the most arcane methodological and statistical issues without so much as a mention of anything the ordinary citizen would recognize as part of the political world. How has this peculiar state of affairs developed?

To an unsophisticated observer it seems obvious that we can have genuine knowledge only of what *is*— that is, of what is permanent or unchanging, such as the structure of hydrocarbon molecules or the physical properties of nitrogen. Knowledge is the province of scientists. Human affairs, by contrast, are neither permanent nor even intelligible outside of a context; the social sciences are merely accustomed to taking this context for granted. The social sciences belong to a different realm, a realm whose foundations are somehow not solid like those of natural science. Views or beliefs, or opinions about what is good and bad, are, as we say, normative, and while there may be a temporary consensus about such issues, the consensus is grounded in nothing deeper or more solid than our practices themselves. All this is part of conventional wisdom; any sophisticated tenth grader can confirm it. Those who reflected most deeply on these things during the late eighteenth and the nineteenth century used a particular word for the context which is necessary to understand human affairs: history. The relocation of human affairs to the realm of history resulted, one could say, from the separation of human beings from nature. According to this understanding, nature is the proper object of the true sciences, the natural sciences, which uncover the laws or regularities guaranteed by causal necessity, by which we explain the physical universe. But men and women are self-conscious free beings, and human freedom—our capacity to overcome the mere causal necessity of nature—sets the human realm apart.[1]

At the end of the eighteenth century many thoughtful men and women believed that history was a story of human progress, that history operates by its own laws which it is the purpose of the human sciences to discover. By studying the objective forces of history, then, human beings could recover the guidance once thought to come from nature as to what is right or wrong, good and bad: by aligning themselves with historical progress they could discern standards by which to conduct themselves in politics. In the words of Condorcet,

> What happens at any particular moment is the result of what has happened at all previous moments, and itself has an influence on what will happen in the future.
>
> So such a picture is historical, since it is a record of change and is based on the observation of human societies throughout the different stages of their development, and so ought also to show, in the modifications that the human species has undergone, ceaselessly renewing itself through the immensity of the centuries, the path that it has followed, the steps that it has made toward truth or happiness.
>
> Such observations upon what man has been and what he is today, will instruct us about the means we should employ to make certain and rapid the further progress that his nature allows him still to hope for.[2]

By the end of the nineteenth century, however, the grounds for Condorcet's optimism had largely disappeared, and the events of the first half of our century obliterated whatever optimism was left, except in countries living under a rigid Marxist orthodoxy. Even there the optimism was probably only official.

But the story is much more complicated, as the high school student learns when he gets to college. Unless shielded completely from courses in what are loosely called the humanities, the student will confront the nearly complete disintegration of the traditional perspective once known as liberal studies. Whether in philosophy or literature courses—and these are occasionally indistinguishable—the student will encounter approaches to the human world which trace their lineage to Nietzsche or to Heidegger and their followers and which teach that the two-thousand-year-old philosophic tradition of the Western world is bankrupt. That this tradition produced the apparently successful enterprise called modern natural science is no obstacle to claims that Western philosophy rests on a delusion.

Modern science, both natural and social, was conceived by its earliest founders as a tool of mastery to help mankind overcome a hostile nature, enabling us to escape the situation of scarcity and insecurity in which we "by nature" find ourselves. This science is dedicated to the securing of knowledge of the causes of things, "to the end to be able to produce, as far as matter, and human force permit, such ends as human life requireth."[3] To accomplish this, the new science was to begin by recognizing openly the confusion and obscurity which is everywhere characteristic of the surface of things, the "face" presented by nature to the human observer. Since appearances deceive, clear knowledge can be secured only in one of two ways: by imposing it on, or by discovering it underneath, the confusing surface. (The latter view was implicit in Galileo's announcement that mathematics is the language which must be mastered in order to read the book of nature.) But this is exactly the question which is decisive for coming to an understanding of the peculiar usage today of the word empirical. Is scientific clarity imposed or discovered? Is nature or the universe a chaos, with respect to which human beings as knowers stand outside, so that the only source of order or clarity is the human mind itself? Or is nature orderly in some sense, operating by regular principles which can be grasped by the human mind, itself a part of that nature and so in tune or in touch with it?

The etymology of *empirical* suggests it has something to do with experience. But there is considerable disagreement about what precisely constitutes experience and what its connection to scientific knowledge is. One of the more extreme claims is that empiricism and natural science have nothing to do with each other and are, in fact, opposites. According to Alasdair MacIntyre, "there is . . . something extraordinary in the coexistence of empiricism and natural science in the same culture, for they represent radically different and incompatible ways of approaching the world."[4] He identifies the opposition between empiricism and natural science by suggesting that the "empiricist concept of experience" was "intended as a device to close the gap between *Seems* and *Is*, between appearance and reality," whereas "the natural scientific concepts of observation and experiment were intended to enlarge the distance between *Seems* and *Is*."[5]

The opposition noted by MacIntyre, many would say, is too strong; surely modern natural science is itself empirical or empiricist in some important sense.[6] While no doubt we must be cautious about insisting on only one characterization of science and its procedures, there is no denying that scientific knowledge today claims, at least implicitly, to be the only genuine knowledge. It does not, for example, recognize any rival claims from revelation or from inspiration (such as poetry); these may at most supply us with hypotheses to be tested.[7] What distinguishes astronomy from astrology is precisely the adherence of astronomers to the canons of scientific procedure: astronomy is committed to a body of principles and theories which are accepted, at least provisionally, only to the extent that they are verified by their predictive power—that is, tested by experience. This aspect of science, its testability, according to its founders distinguished it from various theological and scholastic predecessors, as well as from such other forms of rationalism as pure mathematics. Rationalism of the sort which disdained getting its hands dirty was attacked by Francis Bacon as a serious obstacle to the generation of useful knowledge.[8] All of this is well known and is repeated here only to emphasize the close connection between scientific knowledge and actual experience.

Bacon's conception of empirical science is, however, dismissed by most contemporary scholars.[9] Bacon's notion that the scientist begins by collecting facts—by observation of the world—is rejected as naive; it is an error "to suppose that the observer can confront a fact face-to-face without any theoretical interpretation interposing itself."[10] According to what is called the post-empiricist view, before we can even speak of facts there must be some theoretical construct, because what counts as fact, or the meaning of a theoretical term, "is partly determined by its relations with other terms in its theory." It follows, in consequence of what Thomas calls holism, that "there is no absolutely pretheoretical observation language relevant to the conduct of science."[11] This point is of considerable importance for understanding the connection between social science knowledge and actual (common sense or common language) experience, since it opens the way for the claim that mathematical notation may be a valid, or even the most valid, language for an empirical social science.

The claims of postempiricism are not original, of course. They are anticipated in the epistemological writings of the founders of modern science and most notably in the writings of Thomas Hobbes. That postempiricism shares with its Hobbesian ancestor several features which are highly problematic is not surprising. Most notably, both approaches cast serious doubt on the very notion of truth and hence raise questions about whether it is possible to have genuine knowledge about the world, to have an empirical science at all. This requires some explanation.

To understand a phenomenon means to be able to give an account of it, to attend to "the end or the ends without which no phenomenon can be understood."[12] For classical or ancient science, to understand something meant to discover the *telos*, the purpose or end according to nature, appropriate to what was under scrutiny. The end was thus thought to be supplied by nature, and discovered by observation, beginning from ordinary or prescientific consciousness. The point of contact between the world and an empirical science, which must be "in touch" with the world at some point, is then found in its beginnings, its starting point in prescientific consciousness; what orients the scientist is ordinary life. He asks what nature is doing in this or that process and uses principles of reasoning to abstract from the confusion implicit in the phenomenal world. The end is discovered, not invented.

The alternative understanding rejects a beginning in ordinary consciousness. According to the postempiricist view, scientific theories are not ways of accounting for prescientific or pretheoretical facts, because facts themselves are only capable of being understood (they only become facts) in the context of a theory. Scientists, in their shared work, thus develop a way of seeing the world, together with a language in which to express themselves, and the entire enterprise must be understood holistically. When a way of seeing the world changes (when scientists begin to operate with a new paradigm, to use Thomas Kuhn's term), new facts, or a different set of facts and observations, matter.[13] Science produces different interpretations of what can in principle only be interpreted, never known in the sense reserved for truth. Scientific theories are thus capable of being judged on the basis of predictive power, but not as accurate accounts of what *is,* of the beings which altogether constitute the universe. What was once called scientific truth is in this view only interpretation, the suitability of which is to be judged according to the purpose for which we interpret ("What's true is what works").

But this end posited from outside by the scientist, or in contemporary terms by the scientific paradigm or the shared view of a scientific community, has no foundation beyond the shared commitment to it. Such a science is purely instrumental, and as a consequence can only make sense when an end is shared. For Hobbes this was no problem because he believed in the existence of a universal though not self-evident human need, namely peaceful self-preservation. His civil philosophy or political science was conceived as an instrument to attain this end, to master nature in order to satisfy a natural and universal human desire, though not one which was evident to prescientific consciousness. But in our century we are told there is no natural ground for such ends, which are merely preferences or values. Hence our social science seems to have lost its purpose and, with it, its point of contact with the world outside its own terminology. The slogan "what's true is what works" only serves as an epistemological foundation when one is trying to *do* something. It no longer makes sense to inquire how politics works if the ends implicit in the activity are rejected or ignored, and the end posited from outside in order to make knowledge intelligible has disappeared. At least in social science, we seem to be confronted today with a plethora of terminologies and paradigms, each apparently intelligible to its group of practitioners but offering no criteria by which an intelligent outsider can judge among them, nor any account of why they should interest him.

If scientific theories are only creations of the human mind, more or less acceptable, decorative, or powerful according to our particular goals at any given time, truth is a delusion. The delusion of modern science is now seen at least by some to be not merely modern. It is said to inhere in the very idea of the possibility of truth which has, since about the time of Plato, been a part of Western metaphysics. The notion that when we seek the truth we are trying to find out how things really are, or what reality is, is fundamentally mistaken. Where poets and philosophers once competed in their claims to teach or reveal the truth, or how things are, they have now come to see this as misguided, as the result not merely of wrong metaphysics but of metaphysics simply. That is why philosophers who have come to accept this view are indistinguishable from literary critics: each enterprise is essentially a matter of showing how one can—or cannot—make sense of what ultimately is only a text to be interpreted hermeneutically, that is, from within. This is the case whether what is under scrutiny is a book or the universe.

The clearest and most important exponent of this view in the 1980s is probably Richard Rorty, whose own migration in the academy from philosophy professor to professor of humanities and literary criticism is a nice example of what might be called the transformation of the notion of truth itself. Rorty's lucid accounts of the philosophical currents of recent decades should be consulted by anyone curious about the intellectual scene today.[14] He identifies a number of modern thinkers, including not only Jacques Derrida and Michel Foucault but also Yale literary critics Harold Bloom, Paul De Man, Geoffrey Hartmann, and J. Hillis Miller, as "textualists" and suggests that textualism is best understood as a contemporary manifestation of some core ideas of nineteenth century idealism. "Both suggest that the natural scientist should not be the dominant cultural figure, that scientific knowledge is not what really matters. Both insist that there is a point of view other than, and somehow higher than, that of science."[15] Textualists, as Rorty says, "start off from the claim that all problems, topics, and distinctions are language-rela-tive—the results of our having chosen to use a certain vocabulary, to play a certain language-game." This seems to entail the claim that "the vocabulary of science is merely one among others—merely the vocabu-lary which happens to be handy in predicting and controlling nature. It is not, as physicalism would have us think, Nature's Own Vocabulary." Science, then, is just as creative as the creative arts, for it consists of inventing rather than discovering. According to Rorty's textualists, "the literary artist's awareness that he is making rather than finding . . . puts him one up on the scientist." In fact, textualists regard the scientist "as naive in thinking he is doing something *more* than putting together ideas, or constructing new texts."[16] Even science, on this account, is essentially the creation of new myths.

The most sophisticated among our college students learn that tradi-tional education is based on delusions, that it is impossible to make sense of history from anything but a strictly subjective viewpoint, that not just art—including that of the greatest poets of the past who claimed to hold up the mirror to nature—but all intellectual endeavor, including sci-ence, is merely imaginative construction. The methodological program of modern science, notwithstanding that for three centuries it has been a wonderfully successful tool in our efforts to master nature for the better-ment of human life, has in our century managed to undermine all claims to genuine truth. If what's true is what works, then power is our only standard for determining if something is provisionally true. Power may mean political power, whether the power of liberal commercial republics or of Nazi empires, for whoever controls or develops the tools that work must ipso facto possess the truth. Many would prefer not to confront this conclusion, and even those willing to confront it might hope that it is false. Anyone who has not simply given up in cynicism must feel the need to retrace the steps of the intellectual or philosophical path which brought us to this point.

It seems likely that the path begins in the early modern formulations of the epistemological standards of modernity, but to what precisely can the problem be traced? Modern natural science itself does not seem to be the culprit. Efforts to unlock the secrets of nature, even to duplicate the natural workings of our biological and physical universe, do not in themselves appear to be connected to the spiritual difficulties in which we find ourselves. Perhaps the attempt to extend the methods of inquiry of modern natural science to other realms (such as human activity) is to blame, but the approach itself is scarcely accountable for that. It seems more likely that our ills are linked only indirectly, if at all, with modern natural science.

One striking characteristic of the early enthusiasts of the new science was their optimism, their nearly limitless hopes for what science could accomplish. These hopes are especially striking in the cases of Descartes and Hobbes, and for the same reason: both focused on the method of the new science. Both sought to apply a new epistemological standard, and their strictness, their radicalization of what it means to know, not only separated scientific knowing from all prudential or experiential knowledge but also gave them reason to think the new science opened up new possibilities to humanity because it would not be limited by the uncertainties of prudential knowledge, which infected all previous science. In fact, to Hobbes the phrase "prudential knowledge" was an oxymoron. Both Hobbes and Descartes claim that genuine knowledge is achieved by assembling chains of propositions, leading back to (or formulated in terms of) carefully defined simple terms. The certainty of conclusions is only as strong as—but is guaranteed to be as strong as—the clarity of elementary definitions, so long as the propositions are constructed systematically. The key to clarity in the initial stages—here Descartes is justly famous—is in *doubting,* extensively and radically, in order to eliminate anything heretofore accepted merely from hearsay, habit, or unexamined common sense.[17]

I wish to focus on two aspects of this Cartesian and Hobbesian account of science. One is the fundamental separation it entails between science and common sense—a subject taken up in the next chapters. The other, which concerns us here, is the lack of moderation, the almost unlimited hopefulness implicit in this radicalization of what it means to know. As long as knowledge was a possibility merely continuous with wise judgment or careful investigation, and not something different in kind, the process of coming to know was understood to be liable to the same weaknesses and fallibility as other human endeavors. But the Hobbesian and Cartesian account of scientific method implied the possibility of something different and better. To Hobbes, knowing scientifically seemed a new kind of thing:

> the most part of men, though they have the use of Reasoning a little way, as in numbring to some degree; yet it serves them to little use in common life; in which they govern themselves, some better, some worse, according to their differences of experience, quicknesse of memory, and inclinations to severall ends; but specially according to good or evill fortune and the errors of one another. For as for *Science*, or certain rules of their actions, they are so farre from it, that they know not what it is. (*Leviathan*, 5.116)

This new way of attaining truth—or, as Hobbes tells us, the first genuine method for generating truth, as opposed to discovering it haphazardly—promises to open for men a new opportunity, one not constrained by previously inescapable weaknesses: fallible judgment, inadequate experience, defective prudence. Henceforth only what is generated and tested by the standards of scientific method, namely clarity and certainty (and notwithstanding the hypothetical character of scientific knowledge—about which more later), is to be called knowledge. Everything else is relegated to a lower order, the order of prudence or experience, which is shared by man and beasts. This prelinguistic kind of thought, based only on experience, "is called *foresight*, or *prudence* or *providence*, and sometimes *wisdom*, though such conjecture, through the difficulty of observing all circumstances, be very fallacious."[18]

It is not difficult to understand the very high hopes which were initially attached to the project of generalizing this kind of knowledge. The method for securing such knowledge, a method involving the careful manipulation of rigorously defined symbols (called words and, later, variables), was not new: Hobbes and Descartes both explicitly acknowledge their debt to geometry and mathematics.[19] The generalization of it for use in what we call physics promised great things, and that promise has been justified in practice. But perhaps Hobbes overstated the degree to which the new method escapes the defects of prudence and experience. In any case the high hopes, the immoderate expectations, were not justified in the case of the moral sciences, as they were then called, despite Locke's later hope of a moral science which might be placed "amongst the *sciences capable of demonstration.*"[20]

I believe the disappearance of the notion of truth in our times is traceable precisely to these immoderate expectations. By setting the standard for truth so high, Hobbes and others doomed those who followed them to disappointment and made inevitable, in later centuries, the reluctant abandonment of truth as a possibility. We have already glanced at the ramifications of this disappearance of truth. The loss of courage or commitment, so characteristic of our crisis, has its roots in the forgetting of moderation at the time our modern situation was beginning to take shape. For those familiar with the indictment of the West by Solzhenitsyn and others this is no surprise, for he too locates what he calls the "mistake" of modernity in a kind of loss of moderation: "the proclaimed and enforced autonomy of man from any higher force above him," as he puts it, or "anthropocentricity, with man seen as the center of everything that exists."[21] This in fact sounds a bit like the classical understanding of hubris, a forgetting of limits by one who overreaches, overlooking the difference between human beings and divinity.

Not everyone, however, accepts the arguments or the stance of Solzhenitsyn, a committed Christian who has faith in a living God. At least to many people in our century, God is dead. Here David Hume's importance in respect to these issues can be seen. For Hume offered what amounts to a secular anticipation of Solzhenitsyn's quarrel with modernity. If the decline in courage among the political elite, so striking today, is the delayed effect of a loss of moderation hundreds of years earlier, Hume's reaction to the earlier developments should be of great importance to us. Though himself a "modern" in all important respects, Hume is an "ancient" insofar as he reminded modernity of human limits, of what he called the "strange infirmities" of our understanding. He undercut the high hopes of Hobbes by denying the disjunction between "scientific" and "experiential" knowing.

Hume's significance here can be seen in a general way by contrasting his contribution with that of others who reacted to the limitless optimism of modernity and its new conception of knowledge. Descartes and Hobbes attempted to use the paradigm of mathematics to set a new standard for knowledge, and in doing so they could be said to have attempted to drive a wedge between prudence or experience, on the one hand, and genuine scientific knowledge, on the other. In one way or another subsequent thinkers have tried to adjust the position of the wedge. Whereas Locke believed morality might be placed "amongst the sciences capable of demonstration," for example, Kant sought to circumscribe the realm of scientific knowledge more narrowly, by dividing the universe into noumenal and phenomenal realms and declaring that science can tell us nothing about the former. We have witnessed ceaseless arguments over the last eighty years as to whether the human sciences belong with physics (above the wedge) or with history (below it). In fact many argue that historical science belongs with the hard sciences, but in this view history cannot be normative.

Hume denied the existence of the wedge itself. The grounds on which he did so are the subject of the next chapters. They explain why Hume himself was both a great social scientist and a great historian, indeed a normative historian who believed history has lessons for us.

3   *Hume's First Formulation of the Problem of Reason*

David Hume is often thought of as the preeminent epistemologist, a philosopher in precisely the twentieth century sense of the term. Students encounter Hume today almost exclusively in introductory philosophy courses or in courses in the philosophy of religion. What of the fact that his writings encompassed politics, epistemology, psychology, economics, history, rhetoric, religion, and virtually every other subject on which an educated mind can touch? The explanation for this breadth was at one time given in biographical terms: Hume's mortification at the learned world's reception of his great philosophical work, the *Treatise of Human Nature*, was once thought to have prompted a turn to essay writing, to a sort of abandoning of pure philosophy for the sake of a career as belletrist.[1] Hume himself seems almost to have admitted as much in his celebrated autobiography, where he writes that literature, not philosophy, was the "ruling passion" of his life. He goes further, in fact, and identifies his ruling passion as a "love of literary fame" (*E*, xxxiii, xl).

Although this view has been modified, a casual consensus has emerged among philosophers of the past half century that in studying the *Treatise* they are resurrecting a work whose depth and importance were insufficiently recognized by Hume's contemporaries. The judgment of John B. Stewart in his well-known study of Hume from two decades ago expresses this view accurately: The *Treatise* "is the greatest of Hume's works. . . . His later philosophical works are lesser, not because his genius declined, but, because, although presented as separate edifices, they are structures anticipated or implied in the *Treatise*."[2] The philosophical Hume, according to this view, is found in the clearest, most original and striking form in the *Treatise*, the claims and insights of which were blunted as they were polished for more literary audiences in the *Enquiries* and *Essays*.[3] Despite repeated claims that the nineteenth century view (according to which Hume abandoned philosophy for the sake of fame) is wrong, traces of the older perspective remain. Its tenacious hold is manifested in the view—almost unchallenged today—stated clearly by David Miller in a very recent study: "The *Treatise* is correctly regarded as Hume's greatest work, and it is also the key to everything else that he wrote. It contains a system of philosophy which underlies his more practical studies in economics, politics, and history. The *Enquiries* do not present an alternative system of thought, but merely less well-integrated fragments of the original system."[4] The chief differences then, revolve around the question of tone and style, and above all the loss of the systematic character of his first writing.

The *Treatise* is Not the Center

I believe that this reading of Hume has serious defects and that its general truth obscures a very important aspect of his work, which might be described as his understanding of the meaning of philosophy. By reading him through twentieth-century lenses we risk unwittingly supplanting Hume's understanding of his endeavor with our own more narrow view of what constitutes philosophy. He, at least, continued to regard himself as a philosopher, and the most important of his philosophical contemporaries—Montesquieu and Rousseau, for example—agreed in that judgment.[5] In equating Hume's conception of philosophy and the predominant twentieth-century understanding we deprive ourselves of the possibility of understanding Hume's thought as a coherent whole.[6]

I believe that Hume's understanding of philosophy at the time he composed the *Treatise,* when he was still in his twenties, differs in a subtle way from the understanding which underlies his later writings, above all the *Dialogues concerning Natural Religion.*[7] Since the *Dialogues* were composed in 1751 (Hume was forty) and subjected to revision intermittently until his death twenty-five years later, the shift seems to have occurred in the first decade after the publication of the *Treatise* in 1739. We may date the shift before 1748, and if Mossner is correct, it must have occurred in the first years after the publication of the *Treatise.*[8] It reflects Hume's gradual realization of the inadequacy of a certain notion of philosophy, or the potential danger of a certain sort of philosophic writing. That his initial effort, in the form of the *Treatise,* is more readily recognizable today as philosophy says more about our preoccupations than it does about Hume.

The transformation in Hume's philosophic stance could be described merely as a change in his expectations of what philosophy can accomplish. The consequence of the change in expectations, however, was a different estimate of the place of philosophy in human life and a different manner of writing philosophy. Hume's concern with the relationship of philosophy to the rest of life was a constant theme in his works. Anyone in the least acquainted with his writings will be familiar with Hume's frequent wrestling bouts with the effects of philosophy, in particular skeptical philosophy, on ordinary beliefs. It is not too much to say that the central preoccupation of his career was the place of reason in human life.[9]

If what remains constant in Hume's thought is the theme of the problematic nature of reason and philosophy, what changes is his manner of dealing with the problem. A first indication of this change can be seen by looking at Hume's later assessment of the *Treatise of Human Nature.* Although it would be tendentious to suggest that Hume ever repudiated the central arguments of the early work, the mature Hume was undeniably critical of at least the manner or tone of the *Treatise.* Norman Kemp Smith goes so far as to suggest that "could Hume have obtained possession of every published copy of the *Treatise,* there can be no question that—such was his attitude to it in these later years!—he would have rejoiced to commit them to the flames."[10] Hume's own remarks on the *Treatise* are well known. He acknowledged it a "great mistake in conduct" to have published "a Book, which pretended to innovate in all the sublimest parts of philosophy, and which I compos'd before I was five and twenty." What he objected to was "the positive Air, which prevails in that Book" (*Letters* 1.187).[11]

His youthful hopes led him, in the introduction to the *Treatise,* to insist that philosophers abandon "the tedious *inquiring* method, which we have hitherto followed," in the sciences. "The only expedient, from which we can hope for success in our philosophical researches," he wrote, is "instead of taking now and then a castle or village on the frontier, to march directly up to the capital or center of these sciences, to human nature itself; which being once masters of, we may everywhere else hope for an easy victory" (*T,* xvi). The enthusiastic hopes implied in this martial metaphor disappear completely from his later writings, where philosophy is handled chiefly in terms of two other metaphors. Hume later speaks of the philosopher as a "moral astronomer" and as an anatomist; in the latter case he seems to mean the anatomical researches which are preliminary to painting, not medicine. It appears Hume found himself increasingly doubting the efficacy of what he came to call "abstruse philosophy," and there are passages—especially in the *Dialogues*—which seem to go further and suggest that philosophy can be dangerous to healthy civil or political life. As I suggest in the next section, the currents of philosophical doubt which surface more clearly in later writings are not entirely absent even from the *Treatise.*

A part of the excitement of the *Treatise* comes from the nakedness, as it were, of Hume's thoughts and emotions in that work. He begins with a call to arms, a plan for a new philosophy which will remedy the "present imperfect condition of the sciences," a condition which disgraces the temple of the sciences, so that "even the rabble without doors may judge from the noise and clamour which they hear, that all goes not well within" (*T,* xii, xiv). In a passage strongly reminiscent of Hobbes's similar complaints[12] and with much the same spirit of dogmatic optimism about a remedy, Hume complains that

> there is nothing which is not the subject of debate, and in which men of learning are not of contrary opinions. The most trivial question escapes not our controversy, and in the most momentous we are not able to give any certain decision. Disputes are multiplied, as if everything was uncertain; and these disputes are managed with the greatest warmth, as if everything was certain. Amidst all this bustle 'tis not reason, which carries the prize, but eloquence; and no man needs ever despair of gaining proselytes to the most extravagant hypothesis, who has art enough to represent it in any favourable colours. The victory is not gained by the men at arms, who manage the pike and the sword; but by the trumpeters, drummers, and musicians of the army. (*T*, xiv)

Hume launches into the *Treatise* in search of the truth, which must "lie very deep and abstruse," but which it is necessary to locate before "any question of importance . . . can be decided with certainty." "In pretending therefore to explain the principles of human nature, we in effect propose a compleat new system of the sciences, built on a foundation almost entirely new, and the only one upon which they can stand with any security" (*T*, xvi). With such breathless optimism Hume's campaign is launched.

In the *Abstract* written by Hume as an advertisement for the *Treatise* in 1740, a year after publication of the first two books of the *Treatise*, the same spirit of novelty is evident. Despite the detached tone which results from Hume's pretending to describe the work of someone else, the same enthusiastic hopes are here. The *Treatise* is introduced as an exemplar of the new "philosophical spirit" which "improved all over Europe in the last fourscore years," and Hume contrasts this with the moral philosophy of the ancients. "Our writers seem even to have started a new kind of philosophy, which promises more both to the entertainment and advantage of mankind, than any other with which the world has been yet acquainted" (*Abstract*, 5). Of particular interest here is Hume's characterization of the ancient style of moral philosophy, since I suggest below that his later view is in fact much closer to this classical approach than to the spirit of Newtonian science, about whose prospects he was at this point so sanguine.

> Most of the philosophers of antiquity, who treated of human nature, have shewn more of a delicacy of sentiment, a just sense of morals, or a greatness of soul, than a depth of reasoning and reflection. They content themselves with representing the common sense of mankind in the strongest lights, and with the best turn of thought and expression, without following out steadily a chain of propositions, or forming the several truths into a regular science. But 'tis at least worth while to try if the science of *man* will not admit of the same accuracy which several parts of natural philosophy are found susceptible of. (*Abstract*, 5–6)

In 1748 Hume published the *Philosophical Essays concerning Human Understanding*, known to us as the *Enquiry concerning Human Understanding*.[13] The tone in the *Enquiry* can be described as rather more defensive: in the first section Hume self-consciously considers "what can reasonably be pleaded" on behalf of what he calls "the accurate and abstruse" or "abstract and profound" philosophy as contrasted with the "easy and obvious" sort. The *Treatise* clearly belongs to the former species. By the time he wrote section 1 of the first *Enquiry*, Hume had clearly begun to reconsider his initial enthusiasm. In the essay "Of Essay Writing," written after publication of the *Treatise* but before 1742,[14] Hume pictures himself as an ambassador from the learned world to the world of belles lettres, both of which have suffered by being cut off from one another during "the last age." He might almost be describing his own *Treatise* when he says: "Even Philosophy went to Wrack by this moaping recluse Method of Study, and became as chimerical in her Conclusions, as she was unintelligible in her Stile and Manner of Delivery. And indeed, what cou'd be expected from Men who never consulted Experience in any of their Reasonings, or who never search'd for that Experience, where alone it is to be found, in common Life and Conversation?" (*E*, 534–35).[15]

In the essay on history written at about the same time, in the early 1740s among the earliest of his essays, we find other evidence of Hume's having begun to entertain some doubts about the adequacy of a certain kind of philosophy: in making an argument for the superiority of historical writing he tells us that "even philosophers are apt to bewilder themselves in the subtility of their speculations; and we have seen some go as far as to deny the reality of all moral distinctions" (*E*, 567). The inadequacy of this sort of philosophy—which may or may not include Hume's *Treatise,* though we will see some reason below to think his doubts included even that work—stems from its loss of contact with ordinary human life: "When a philosopher contemplates characters and manners in his closet, the general abstract view of the objects leaves the mind so cold and unmoved, that the sentiments of nature have no room to play, and he scarce feels the difference between vice and virtue" (*E*, 568). Notwithstanding these reservations Hume is still prepared in section I of the first *Enquiry* to defend "accurate and abstruse" philosophy; without it the "easy and humane" philosophy "can never attain a sufficient degree of exactness in its sentiments, precepts or reasonings" (*EHU*, 9). He makes use of the metaphor of the anatomist:

An artist must be better qualified to succeed . . . who . . . possesses an accurate knowledge of the internal fabric. . . . How painful soever this inward search or inquiry may appear, it becomes, in some measure, requisite to those, who would describe with success the obvious and outward appearances of life and manners. The anatomist presents to the eye the most hideous and disagreeable objects; but his science is useful to the painter in delineating even a Venus or an Helen. While the latter employs all the richest colours of his art, and gives his figures the most graceful and engaging airs; he must still carry his attention to the inward structure of the human body, the position of the muscles, the fabric of the bones, and the use and figures of every part or organ. Accuracy is, in every case, advantageous to beauty, and just reasoning to delicate sentiment. In vain would we exalt the one by depreciating the other. (*EHU*, 9–10)

Other evidence points to yet another stage in the development of Hume's conception of philosophy. This appears primarily in his most literary writings, and of these chiefly in two of his three dialogues, the first of which appeared as chapter 11 in the first *Enquiry* itself: "Of a Particular Providence and of a Future State." Here we find hints of the attitude which became, I believe, Hume's final position on philosophy. The view reaches its full development only in the *Dialogues concerning Natural Religion* and sub rosa in the *History* and some of the *Essays*. It may be understood as a correction of Hume's earlier assertion that "generally speaking, the errors in religion are dangerous; those in philosophy only ridiculous" (*T*, 272). He appears to have come gradually to the view that a certain species of philosophy (and one, I would add, to which modernity is peculiarly vulnerable) is also dangerous. Why modernity is particularly susceptible to this corrosive philosophy I will discuss further below. It suffices here to say that in the chapter "Of Particular Providence" Hume considers the relationship between philosophy and society, and the relation of both to religion, and expresses (in his own name) the view that certain philosophies have political consequences. He maintains this against an unnamed interlocutor who insists on the political and moral irrelevance of philosophic inquiry. The details of the dialogue raise, not by coincidence, all the questions and issues explored at greater length in the *Dialogues concerning Natural Religion*. If the view sketched here is correct, and given what has transpired since 1748, the development of Hume's thinking on the nature of philosophy is of considerably more than biographical or historical interest.

Hume's recognition that the political consequences of philosophy are problematic is reminiscent of Socrates' similar discovery, which I discuss in chapter 1. Indeed Hume draws an explicit comparison. In a paragraph which opens with the observation that "the science of man is the only solid foundation for the other sciences," Hume points out that the origin of the "moral sciences" followed that of the "natural sciences" by the space of about a century. He continues, "reckoning from *THALES* to *SOCRATES*, the space of time is nearly equal to that betwixt my Lord Bacon and some late philosophers in *England*, who have begun to put the science of man on a new footing" (*T*, xvi–xvii)—a description which reminds us that this is the task which Hume understands himself to be completing.[16]

"Philosophical Melancholy and Delirium"

Hume's devotion to philosophy was a turbulent affair from the beginning, when he resolved to abandon the career in law sought for him by his family because he "found an unsurmountable Aversion to everything but the pursuit of Philosophy and general Learning" ("My Own Life" in *E*, xxxiii). Perhaps the turbulence is expressed most vividly in the concluding section of book 1 of the *Treatise*. This section has long puzzled commentators and supplied ammunition to Hume's critics. It is a deeply personal reflection on the relation of the philosopher to common life, full of Hume's doubts about his ambitious plan for a science of human nature. Here he writes, movingly, of the "philosophical melancholy and delirium" to which he is driven by his investigations.

For a philosopher to conclude his work with such a complaint is at least uncommon, and it behooves us to pay close attention to the nature of his plight. We find in this section some of Hume's most profound reflections on the nature of the philosophic life, and while I believe he adjusted his views somewhat in later writings, the core of his understanding of the tension between ordinary life and philosophy is found here in all essentials.

Book 1 is primarily epistemological and is undoubtedly Hume's most famous writing today. By the end he has examined the structure of our understanding of causation, as the most important part of an inquiry into the nature of beliefs in general and of belief in the continued existence of external objects, in particular. But all this is only the foundation of the "science of human nature" projected by Hume in the introduction. Yet the spirit of reveille, the call to arms so evident in the introduction to the *Treatise,* is wholly absent from this section. Here Hume himself makes use of the metaphor so beloved by some commentators on the *Treatise,* the voyage of discovery.[17]

> But before I launch out into those immense depths of philosophy, which lie before me, I find myself inclin'd to stop a moment in my present station, and to ponder that voyage, which I have undertaken, and which undoubtedly requires the utmost art and industry to be brought to a happy conclusion. Methinks I am like a man, who having struck on many shoals, and having narrowly escap'd ship-wreck in passing a small frith, has yet the temerity to put out to sea in the same leaky weather-beaten vessel, and even carries his ambition so far as to think of compassing the globe under these disadvantageous circumstances. My memory of past errors and perplexities, makes me diffident for the future. The wretched condition, weakness, and disorder of the faculties, I must employ in my enquiries, encrease my apprehensions. And the impossibility of amending or correcting these faculties, reduces me almost to despair, and makes me resolve to perish on the barren rock, on which I am at present, rather then venture myself upon that boundless ocean, which runs out into immensity. (*T,* 263–64)

Is this mere rhetorical flourish? In view of Hume's later position on the relation of philosophy to ordinary life, the answer must be negative. What we find here rather is an articulation of Hume's first impressions, as it were, of the problem philosophy poses. He is still sanguine enough to think that, "generally speaking, the errors . . . in philosophy [are] only ridiculous" (*T,* 272), a position I have suggested he no longer advances in some of his later writings. But he is aware of at least a personal problem in living philosophically: "I am first affrighted and confounded with that forelorn solitude, in which I am plac'd in my philosophy, and fancy myself some strange uncouth monster, who not being able to mingle and unite in society, has been expell'd all human commerce, and left utterly abandon'd and disconsolate" (*T*, 264). What is the source of this isolation? What is the character of Hume's doubts?

He recognizes first that some part of the problem may be of his own making, or the result of his own deficiencies. When he anticipates the likely public reception of his critical philosophy, he foresees "on every side, dispute, contradiction, anger, calumny, and detraction." That is, of course, not an uncommon fate of radical philosophizing, as Hume well knows, and it may at first seem he is only confessing personal inadequacy: "When I turn my eye inward, I find nothing but doubt and ignorance. All the world conspires to oppose and contradict me; tho' such is my weakness, that I feel all my opinions loosen and fall of themselves, when unsupported by the approbation of others" (*T*, 264–65). But a dearth of self confidence, Hume knows, is not the real problem, if Hume suffered from such a dearth. The source of the difficulties lies in philosophy itself.

As we shall see in chapter 4, his teaching about the nature of belief has suggested, or, better, established, that philosophical truths are not demonstrable; they rest ultimately on the same ground as all other beliefs. The philosopher as a result of his reasonings holds "certain ideas in a more intense and lively manner, than others, which are not attended with the same advantages" (*T*, 265). "After the most accurate and exact of my reasonings," he confesses, "I can give no reason why I shou'd assent to it; and feel nothing but a *strong* propensity to consider objects *strongly* in that view, under which they appear to me" (ibid.). This problem is not peculiar to Hume, for it belongs to the nature of human reasoning, which in the end rests on what Hume calls "imagination": "The memory, senses, and understanding are, therefore, all of them founded on the imagination, or the vivacity of our ideas" (ibid.).[18]

If philosophy shows that there is no discontinuity between philosophic reasoning and the sort of reasoning we employ everyday in "common life," why should there be any tension between the two? This question lies at the core of the concluding section of book 1, and it leads to what Hume calls "a very dangerous dilemma." Philosophic inquiry into the principles of human understanding exposes the deficiency of human understanding. "This deficiency in our ideas is not, indeed, preceiv'd in common life, nor are we sensible, that in the most usual conjunctions of cause and effect we are as ignorant of the ultimate principle, which binds them together, as in the most unusual and extraordinary" (*T*, 267).

The conjunction of cause and effect is only Hume's favorite example of the deficiency of human reasoning. That we act and reason in common life without being aware of the deficiency of our understanding, Hume writes, "proceeds merely from an illusion of the imagination; and the question is, how far we ought to yield to these illusions. The question is very difficult, and reduces us to a very dangerous dilemma, whichever way we answer it" (ibid.).

Hume's "Dangerous Dilemma": Philosophic Aporia

The dilemma arises from the fact that if, on the one hand, "we assent to every trivial suggestion of fancy," we not only involve ourselves in manifest contradictions because the illusions are "often contrary to each other"—for example, the belief in the continued existence of external objects contradicts the reasoning from cause and effect to which we are equally prone, and which is easily shown to imply solipsism (*T*, 231)—but we are led "into such errors, absurdities, and obscurities, that we must at last become asham'd of our credulity" (*T*, 267). "But on the other hand," Hume continues,

> if the consideration of these instances makes us take a resolution to reject all the trivial suggestions of the fancy, and adhere to the understanding, that is, to the general and more establish'd properties of the imagination; even this resolution, if steadily executed, wou'd be dangerous, and attended with the most fatal consequences. For I have already shewn that the understanding, when it acts alone, and according to its most general principles, entirely subverts itself, and leaves not the lowest degree of evidence in any proposition, either in philosophy or common life. (*T*, 267–68)

If we decide to reject "refin'd or elaborate reasoning" because it undermines itself, Hume invites us to "consider well the consequences of such a principle."

> By this means you cut off entirely all science and philosophy: You proceed upon one singular quality of the imagination, and by a parity of reason must embrace all of them: And you expressly contradict yourself; since this maxim must be built on the preceding reasoning, which will be allow'd to be sufficiently refin'd and metaphysical. What party, then, shall we choose among these difficulties? If we embrace this principle, and condemn all refin'd reasonings, we subvert entirely the human understanding. We have, therefore, no choice left but betwixt a false reason and none at all. (*T,* 268)

For my part, Hume adds, "I know not what ought to be done in the present case." This condition is philosophic *aporia,* a state of perplexity which is exactly described by Hume's words. He begins to add that the problem is usually ignored, since such "very refin'd reflections" as he has here presented "have little or no influence upon us." But he catches himself, and what follows is a notorious paragraph describing the debased condition to which he is reduced by philosophizing.

> But what have I here said, that reflections very refin'd and metaphysical have little or no influence upon us? This opinion I can scarce forbear retracting, and condemning from my present feeling and experience. The *intense* view of these manifold contradictions and imperfections in human reason has so wrought upon me, and heated my brain, that I am ready to reject all belief and reasoning, and can look upon no opinion even as more probable or likely than another. Where am I, or what? From what causes do I derive my existence, and to what condition shall I return? Whose favour shall I court, and whose anger must I dread? What beings surround me? and on whom have I any influence, or who have any influence on me? I am confounded with all these questions, and

begin to fancy myself in the most deplorable condition imaginable, inviron'd with the deepest darkness, and utterly depriv'd of the use of every member and faculty. (*T*, 268–69)

Is there any remedy for this desperate condition? Hume allows that, "most fortunately," there is. The remedy has nothing to do with reason, however: Philosophy cannot supply its own ground. "Nature herself" is required to cure Hume of this "philosophical melancholy and delirium," to "obliterate all these chimeras" (*T*, 269). One of the most quoted sentences in all Hume's writings describes his cure for philosophy: "I dine, I play a game of back-gammon, I converse, and am merry with my friends; and when after three or four hours amusement, I wou'd return to these speculations, they appear so cold, and strain'd and ridiculous, that I cannot find in my heart to enter them any farther" (ibid.). Hume goes on to relate the effects of the "natural propensity," which together with his "animal spirits and passions" reduce him to an "indolent belief in the general maxims of the world." Much earlier in the *Treatise* he stated this in somewhat different terms: "As long as our attention is bent upon the subject, the philosophical and study'd principle may prevail; but the moment we relax our thought, nature will display herself, and draw us back to our former opinion," that is, to opinions "such as we embrace by a kind of instinct or natural impulse, on account of their suitableness and conformity to the mind" (*T*, 214). In the next chapters we come back to this theme of instinct or natural impulse when discussing the "natural workings of the mind." For the present it is enough to have indicated Hume's initial formulation of what seems to be an insuperable tension between philosophic reason and common life, the source of his aporia.

4 Hume's Predecessors and the Separation of Science and Experience

The claim that Western metaphysics since Plato has reached a dead end because it is based on a delusion may be, like reports of Mark Twain's death, exaggerated. We have suggested that the abandonment of truth, or "the crisis of reason," as it is sometimes known, may rather be the result of the disappointment of immoderate hopes, hopes engendered by the prospect of a new kind of knowledge which was to be secured by a new scientific method. Among the thinkers who presented the case for this new epistemological project, Thomas Hobbes ranks as one of the most accessible because of the clarity and forthrightness of his prose.

But the clarity of expression in Hobbes' writings can be revealing in unexpected ways. I believe it is possible to glimpse, beneath the clear surface of his account of modern scientific method, the shadow of the ambiguity which was mentioned in the last chapter, namely the problematic relation between mind and world which has led to our current paradoxical notion of what is empirical. A consideration of this issue will lead to closer scrutiny of what Hume was later to call the "fundamental principle" of modern philosophy—"the opinion concerning colours, sounds, tastes, smells, heat and cold; which it asserts to be nothing but impressions in the mind, deriv'd from the operation of external objects and without any resemblance to the qualities of the objects" (*T*, 226).

40

According to Hobbes we are acquainted with the world, and our minds receive the "materials" in which consists consciousness, only from the senses, "for there is no conception in mans mind, which hath not at first, totally, or by parts, been begotten by the organs of Sense" (*Leviathan*, 1.85). Yet according to both Descartes and Hobbes the senses are unreliable and thus cannot serve as the basis for genuine knowledge. Nevertheless the common sense of humankind exerts a strong pull on us, which the sciences must overcome. As Hobbes puts it, "because the image in vision consisting in colour and shape is the knowledge we have of the qualities of the object of that sense; it is no hard matter for a man to fall into this opinion, that the same colour and shape are the very qualities themselves."[1] Hobbes is thus concerned to overcome a prejudice with very deep roots: "this opinion hath been so long received, that the contrary must needs appear a great paradox" (*EL*, 1.2.4). Now, the cause of Sense is "the Externall Body, or Object, which presseth the organ proper to each Sense" (*Leviathan*, 1.85), and more than this we cannot know. The "qualities called *Sensible*, are in the objects that causeth them, but so many motions of the matter, by which it presseth our organs diversly" (ibid., 86). What Hobbes calls "decaying sense" is the source both of imagination and memory, which are "but one thing, which for divers considerations hath divers names." And "much memory, or memory of many things, is called *Experience*" (ibid., 89).

None of this is restricted to human beings; the faculties of sense, imagination, and memory, and the capacity for experience, are common to all animals. Thus Hobbes is compelled to identify prudence as only a kind of "savvy," an ability to predict the likely consequences of various events or actions, as when even a dog expects a reward for fetching the newspaper. It is worth quoting Hobbes' account of prudence (or wisdom) at some length, because it illuminates the radical separation between science and experience:

> Sometime a man desires to know the event of an action; and then he thinketh of some like action past, and the events thereof one

after another; supposing like events will follow like actions. As he that foresees what will become of a Criminal, re-cons what he has seen follow on the like Crime before; having this order of thoughts, The Crime, the Officer, the Prison, the Judge, and the Gallowes. Which kind of thoughts, is called *Foresight,* and *Prudence,* or *Providence;* and sometimes *Wisdome;* though such conjecture, through the difficulty of observing all circumstances, be very fallacious. But this is certain; by how much one man has more experience of things past, then another; by so much also he is more Prudent, and his expectations the seldomer faile him. The *Present* onely has a being in *Nature;* things *Past* have a being in the Memory onely, but things *to come* have no being at all; the *Future* being but a fiction of the mind, applying the sequels of actions Past, to the actions that are Present; which with most certainty is done by him that has most Experience; but not with certainty enough. And though it be called Prudence, when the Event answereth our Expectation; yet in its own nature, it is but Presumption. (*Leviathan,* 3.97)

Two features of this account need to be stressed. First, "it is not prudence that distinguisheth man from beast. There be beasts, that at a year old observe more, and pursue that which is for their good, more prudently, than a child can do at ten" (*Leviathan,* 3.98). Second, in the account of consciousness Hobbes has given thus far, every thing is *natural,* and in fact the natural workings of the mind are restricted to these capacities. "There is no other act of mans mind, that I can remember, naturally planted in him, so, as to need no other thing, to the exercise of it, but to be born a man, and live with the use of his five Senses" (ibid.). We have as yet seen no glimpse of either knowledge or science. Hobbes is careful to emphasize this, because what truly distinguishes man from beast is something artificial or conventional, not grounded in nature.

Those other Faculties, of which I shall speak by and by, and which seem proper to man onely, are acquired, and encreased by study and industry; and of most men learned by instruction, and discipline; and proceed all from the invention of Words, and Speech. For besides Sense, and Thoughts, and the Trayne of thoughts, the mind of man has no other motion; though by the help of Speech, and Method, the same Facultyes may be improved to such a height, as to distinguish men from all other living Creatures. (Ibid., 98–99)

This seems to have been behind Leo Strauss' observation that according to Hobbes "there is no natural harmony between the human mind and the universe."[2] Precisely on this point, I will suggest, Hume's account tells against his predecessors' account of human nature. Hobbes' account teaches us, again according to Strauss, that "since natural things are, as such, mysterious, the knowledge or certainty engendered by nature necessarily lacks evidence. Knowledge based on the natural workings of the human mind is necessarily exposed to doubt."[3] Strauss saw in this a break with premodern nominalism, which "had faith in the natural working of the human mind" and taught that "the 'anticipations' by virtue of which we take our bearings in ordinary life and in science are products of nature."[4] This theme will be important again in the discussion of Hume, below. For the moment it suffices to observe that Hobbes locates the capacity to achieve genuine knowledge *outside* nature, because genuine knowledge cannot be based in experience alone.

An entirely different realm is opened to us by what Hobbes calls an improvement of natural faculties "by the help of Speech, and Method." This is what permits us to have reason and science, the only real knowledge, strictly speaking, to which men can attain. Modern science is needed in order to reconstruct the world for us, on a foundation different from our common sensical but mistaken assumptions about the world around us. We must acknowledge, Hobbes claims, that "whatsoever accidents or qualities our senses make us think there be in the world, they are not there, but are seemings and apparitions only" (*EL*, 1.2.10). We "learn the world" first through senses and experience—most obviously because our rational faculty develops only several years after our formative encounters with the world around us. If we do not succeed in reconstituting the world rationally, we are permanently limited to that imperfect and untrustworthy knowledge which is properly called prudence. Most of us acquire our understanding of things from our own experiences or at most from books, which contain only the opinions of others based on *their* experiences. Descartes expresses the problem with great clarity: "Since book-learning, at least in so far as its reasonings are only probable, not demonstrative, has been made up, and has developed gradually, from the opinions of many different men, it is therefore not so close to truth as the simple reasonings that a man of good sense may perform as regards things that come up."[5] As it turns out Descartes means by "simple reasonings" the chains of propositions constructed by science, the truth of whose conclusions is assured by careful attention to scientific method, including operational definitions. The alternative, prudence, can never attain to genuine truth. Prudence would only be satisfactory if we could use reason from the beginning of our lives to constitute the world we live in.

> We were all children before we were men; we must have been governed a long time by our own appetites on the one hand and our preceptors on the other; these two sides must frequently have been opposed, and very likely there have been times when neither side urged us to the best course. Thus it is practically impossible for our judgments to be so clear or so firm as they would have been if we had had the full use of our reason from the moment of birth, and had never had any other guide.[6]

The core of this understanding is the skepticism about the senses. For both Descartes and Hobbes, scientific knowledge is conceived as a *replacement* for prudence and experience, *not as a means of improving or correcting them*. What this implies about the relation between mind and world will be examined below, when we take up Hume's "decisive objection." First it will be useful to examine more closely the mental geography which is implicit in the approaches of Hobbes, Descartes, Locke, and others who formulated an account of the new epistemological procedure, and the discomfiting fruit of that approach in the reflections of Bishop Berkeley.

Ideas and Things

The untrustworthiness of our senses leads Hobbes to assert, with his usual directness, that the color we see "is not inherent in the object, but an effect thereof upon us, caused by such motion in the object, as hath been described" (*EL*, 1.2.9). Our conceptions of the "accidents or qualities" of things around us are "seemings and apparitions only," and by the time Hobbes wrote his masterpiece *Leviathan* twenty years later, he calls them more plainly "fancies." "The things that really are in the world without us," according to Hobbes, "are those motions by which these seemings are caused" (*EL*, 1.2.10).

By attaching names to these conceptions, as he calls the seemings within us, and (more important for science) by agreeing on definitions of these names, we can begin to assemble the propositions of our rational reconstruction of the world, which is to replace the haphazard cognitive scheme of the world given by the deceitful senses. But there are pitfalls for the unwary in this procedure, and there are difficulties in Hobbes' account of it as well, although they are fairly obscure. We are to keep in mind, Hobbes warns, that names are often "equivocal": In fact, "there is scarce any word that is not made equivocal by divers contextures of speech, or by diversity of pronunciation and gesture" (*EL*, 1.5.7). Notwithstanding that this "equivocation of names maketh it difficult to recover those conceptions for which the name was ordained," it is possible to use terms clearly in science if not in ordinary speech (*EL*, 1.5.8).

Anything to which names can be applied is a potential subject for science, though to speak strictly, we can apply names only to our conceptions and not to things outside us. Reason is the careful manipulation of names, the "*Reckoning* (that is, Adding and Subtracting) of the Consequences of generall names agreed upon, for the *marking* and *signifying* of our thought" (*Leviathan*, 5.111). As Hobbes puts it:

Reason is not as Sense, and Memory, borne with us; nor gotten by
Experience onely; as Prudence is; but attayned by Industry; first in
apt imposing of Names; and secondly by getting a good and orderly
Method in proceeding from the Elements, which are Names, to
Assertions made by Connexion of one of them to another; and so to
Syllogismes, which are the Connexions of one Assertion to another,
till we come to a knowledge of all the Consequences of names
appertaining to the subject in hand; and that is it, men call
SCIENCE. And whereas Sense and Memory are but knowledge of
Fact, which is a thing past, and irrevocable; *Science* is the knowledge of Consequences, and dependance of one fact upon another:
by which, out of that we can presently do, we know how to do
something else when we will, or the like, another time: Because
when we see how any thing comes about, upon what causes, and by
what manner; when the like causes come into our power, wee see
how to make it produce the like effects. (Ibid., 5.115)

This remarkable passage deserves a moment's reflection because it seems
to imply a very strong, even dogmatic conviction concerning the "fit"
between scientific theories and the world. Although Hobbes qualified his
view elsewhere, here he seems to drop all reserve and express his belief
that science thus understood is not an arbitrary imposition on an unknowable or chaotic nature but an accurate reflection of the order of
nature, "the knowledge of consequences, and dependance of one fact
upon another." This passage perhaps more than any other contributes to
the impression that Hobbes teaches no more than that there are two ways
of "knowing" or "operating in" the world: the merely prudential way, on
the one hand, and the clear and certain scientific way, on the other.
Hobbes is contemptuous of anything less than science: anyone who does
not proceed scientifically (from definitions)—even in the most mundane
affairs, such as "when a master of a family, in taking an account, casteth
up the summs of all the bills of expence, into one sum" and does it by
trusting others for the accuracy of the figures—such a one, Hobbes says,
might as well not bother; he "loses his labour; and does not know

anything; but onely believeth" (ibid., 5.112). Mere belief, then, is virtually worthless, compared to scientific knowledge, which seems to be a superior *alternative* way of knowing the world we live in.

But elsewhere Hobbes succeeds in establishing a more radical separation between scientific knowledge and what the senses tell us of the empirical world; pure knowledge in this sense is completely divorced from experience. This divorce does not eliminate Hobbes's earlier denigration of belief (or faith) relative to scientific knowledge. But it suggests a deeper pessimism about our ability to know what the world is like in fact. The most important passage on this subject is the statement in chapter 7 of *Leviathan:*

> No Discourse whatsoever, can End in absolute knowledge of Fact, past, or to come. For, as for the knowledge of Fact, it is originally, Sense; and ever after, Memory. And for the knowledge of Consequence, which I have said before is called Science, it is not Absolute, but Conditionall. No man can know by Discourse, that this, or that, is, has been, or will be; which is to know absolutely: but onely, that if This be, That is; if This has been, That has been; if This shall be, That shall be: which is to know conditionally; and that not the consequence of one thing to another; but of one name of a thing, to another name of the same thing. (Ibid., 7.131)

In this formulation, it appears that the world as such —whatever it is— is unknowable. Yet where we expect to find the greatest pessimism, we find the most extravagant hopes. As Strauss puts it, "man can guarantee the actualization of wisdom, since wisdom is identical with free construction. But wisdom cannot be free construction if the universe is intelligible. Man can guarantee the actualization of wisdom, not in spite of, but because of, the fact that the universe is unintelligible."[7] What might have led to gloom about the possibility of empirical science instead becomes hope, because the notion of empiricism is drained of any relevance to science once we realize genuine knowledge is *always* nothing more than "operational." "Since the universe is unintelligible and since control of nature does not require understanding of nature, there are no knowable limits to [man's] conquest of nature."[8] This view finally came to dominate theoretical physics at the beginning of our century.[9]

We have already noted that an equally clear separation of science from experience is apparent in Descartes' *Discourse on the Method.* Even aside from the striking implication of the title, which turns out to mean that there is only one method for securing truth, Descartes is explicit in his denigration of imagination and the senses. These, he points out, are the basis of literature, which has in itself no connection with truth. Eloquence and rhetoric, Descartes indicates even as he pretends to esteem them, are not involved with philosophy or truth.[10]

Because of the radical dubitability of what the senses tell us, "neither our imagination nor our senses can ever assure us of anything at all, except with the aid of our understanding."[11] And even more transparently: "For, in conclusion, waking or sleeping, we should never let ourselves be convinced except by the evidence of our reason. Note that I say our reason, not our imagination or our senses."[12] Descartes is careful to distinguish the realm of reason and truth from that of common life mental processes, which are concerned only with plausibility. Those who seek only reputation, he says, will achieve it more readily "by being content with plausibility, which is not hard to attain on all kinds of questions, than in seeking for truth."[13]

Hobbes' ambivalent account of the relation between science and the world contains a suggestion that pure scientific knowledge may not be connected to the realm of our senses, that it does not stem from them or organize our experience. Knowledge of the operational sort is *secured* independent of experience; the only role played by testing in this understanding is to assess the comparative utility of the knowledge after it has been secured. Such knowledge does not *begin* from actual experience of the world, or from the categories and concepts of everyday social life, which are relevant only to prudential or experiential wisdom or savvy. Hobbes himself, as noted above, does not commit himself fully to such an account, but he at least constructed a foundation for it.

Abstraction: Locke and Berkeley

According to Hobbes what is or exists is always particular; "there is nothing universal but names" (*EL,* 1.5.6). Yet the "universality of one name to many things, hath been the cause that men think the things themselves are universal" (ibid.). There can be no science of particular things, of course; the generalizability of names, or language, is what allows us to construct propositions about classes of things or qualities. How do we arrive at names which are universal, when the things that exist are only particular? What is the relationship among things, words, and the conceptions or ideas with which the words are linked? In this relationship we find the root of a number of difficulties with Hobbes' account of science, particularly the problematic understanding—mystery might be a better word—of the connection between mind and world.

The word *man* is one of Hobbes' favorite examples of a universal name, and Hobbes proceeds with exemplary caution: some people, he says, deceive themselves by contending that "besides Peter and John, and all the rest of the men that are, have been, or shall be in the world, there is yet somewhat else that we call man" (ibid.). General names might better be described as merely indefinite, according to Hobbes, "because we limit them not ourselves, but leave them to be applied by the hearer." As an example, Hobbes says, "if one should desire the painter to make him the picture of a man, which is as much as to say, of a man in general; he meaneth no more, but that the painter shall choose what man he pleaseth to draw, which must needs be some of them that are, have been, or may be, none of which are universal" (ibid.).

Hobbes does not offer any account of how we generate or discover "appellations that be universal, and common to many things." What is more important, he is not very clear about whether we can have universal *conceptions* or ideas: things are particular, names can be either particular or universal, but names signify or stand for "conceptions in the mind." Hobbes slips back and forth in his account between the suggestion that words stand for things and the notion that they signify conceptions of things. Perhaps the clearest he gets in *Elements of Law* is in the assertion, "seeing there be many conceptions of one and the same thing, and for every several conception we give it a several name; it followeth that for one and the same thing, we have many names or attributes; as to the same man we give the appellations of just, valiant, etc., for divers virtues, and of strong, comely, etc., for divers qualities of the body" (*EL*, 1.5.5).

Embedded in this ambiguity is the problem which led Bishop Berkeley, some sixty years later, to his radical conclusions about existence and perception. Berkeley focuses his analysis, however, on the explanation offered by Locke, whose account of the way we arrive at universal names is much clearer than that of Hobbes. Locke calls the process by which we arrive at universal names "abstraction," and he goes so far as to suggest that abstraction is *the* faculty the possession of which distinguishes men from beasts.[14]

The use of words then being to stand as outward marks of our internal ideas, and those ideas being taken from particular things, if every particular idea that we take in should have a distinct name, names must be endless. To prevent this, the mind makes the particular ideas received from particular objects to become general; which is done by considering them as they are in the mind such appearances,—separate from all other existences, and the circumstances of real existence, as time, place, or any other concomitant ideas. This is called ABSTRACTION, whereby ideas taken from particular beings become general representatives of all of the same kind; and their names general names, applicable to whatever exists conformable to such abstract ideas. Such precise, naked appearances in the mind, without considering how, whence, or with what others they came there, the understanding lays up (with names commonly annexed to them) as the standards to rank real existences into sorts, as they agree with these patterns, and to denominate them accordingly. Thus the same colour being observed to-day in chalk or snow, which the mind yesterday received from milk, it considers that appearance alone, makes it a representative of all of that kind; and having given it the name *whiteness*, it by that sound signifies the same quality wheresoever to be imagined or met with; and thus universals, whether ideas or terms, are made. (*Essay*, 2.11.9)

The important feature of this account, as far as science is concerned, is what it implies about the relation between mind and world. In the prescientific understanding, as we might call our common sense view of the world, we take the qualities we sense to be features of the world. But scientific skepticism about the senses compels us to admit that the whiteness or hardness or cold we perceive is not outside of us but within us. These secondary qualities, as Locke calls them, must inhere in something, call it matter or substance, whose properties ("primary qualities")—motion, extension, etc.—we attempt to "construct" rationally. This is a commonly accepted view of natural science and has a considerable hold on us.

The difficulty resides in the general notions, such as extension, motion, or substance, which are supposed to underlie the secondary qualities we actually perceive. Something in the world must correspond to these abstract general notions, and the task of our science is to constitute or construct what it is (the "structure of matter") in order to replace what prescientific consciousness naively takes to be the world. By doing so, science promises to replace the radically defective way we know the world by common sense.

According to Berkeley, as well as to Hume, this entire project is misconceived. In his *Principles of Human Knowledge* Berkeley locates the mistake in the account of abstraction offered by Locke, or to be more precise in Locke's notion of "abstract general ideas." There can be no such thing, according to Berkeley. He begins his critique in agreement with the position of modern science: "It is agreed on all hands that the qualities or modes of things do never really exist each of them apart by itself and separated from all others, but are mixed, as it were, and blended together, several in the same object."[15] This in itself poses no difficulty to Berkeley. "But we are told the mind, being able to consider each quality singly, or abstracted from those other qualities with which it is united, does by that means frame to itself abstract ideas" (ibid.). Berkeley owns himself capable of this procedure, but he disagrees with Locke's characterization of the result. After offering a number of unexceptionable examples, he works his way to this: "The constituent parts of the abstract idea of animal are body, life, sense, and spontaneous motion. By *body* is meant body without any particular shape or figure, there being no one shape or figure common to all animals, without covering, either of hair, or feathers, or scales, etc., not yet naked: hair, feathers, scales, and nakedness being the distinguishing properties of particular animals, and for that reason left out of the *abstract idea*" (*PHK*, Intro., 9). But how do we actually conceive or frame in our minds an "abstract general idea," from which the particulars must be "left out"? Berkeley doubts that this is possible. The Lockean "doctrine of abstraction" seems "remote from common sense." "To be plain," he says,

> I own myself able to abstract in one sense, as when I consider some particular parts or qualities separated from others, with which, though they are united in some object, yet it is possible they may really exist without them. But I deny that I can abstract one from another, or conceive separately, those qualities which it is impossible should exist so separated; or that I can frame a general notion by abstracting from particulars in the manner aforesaid—which two last are the two proper acceptations of *abstraction*. And there are grounds to think most men will acknowledge themselves to be in my case. (*PHK*, Intro., 10)

In Berkeley's understanding, this mistaken notion of abstraction has led men into a thicket of difficulties.[16] He insists that "anyone who takes a survey of the *objects* of human knowledge" can easily see "that they are either ideas actually imprinted on the senses, or else such as are perceived by attending to the passions and operations of the mind, or lastly, ideas formed by help of memory and imagination—either compounding, dividing, or barely representing those originally perceived in the aforesaid ways" (*PHK*, 1.1). Besides what we can know—the objects of thinking—there must exist something which does the knowing: "This perceiving active being is what I call *mind, spirit, soul,* or *myself"* (*PHK,* 1.2).

Berkeley's Conclusions

To Berkeley it seems obvious that, as objects of thought exist only in the mind, there "is not any other substance than *Spirit,* or that which perceives." In the case of anything other than the perceiving mind, to be is to be perceived: *esse* is *percipi,* in Berkeley's famous formulation. The notion "strangely prevailing amongst men that houses, mountains, rivers, and, in a word, all sensible objects have an existence, natural or real, distinct from their being perceived by the understanding" is false, and Berkeley is concerned to show it has a defective basis. "If we thoroughly examine this tenet it will be found at bottom to depend on the doctrine of *abstract ideas*" (*PHK,* 1.4–5). Why? Because to suggest that the things perceived by sense—which are ideas—have an existence distinct from their being perceived is to abstract existence from other qualities, and is obviously nonsense. "Can there be a nicer strain of abstraction" than this? Berkeley asks. "Now, for an idea to exist in an unperceiving thing is a manifest contradiction, for to have an idea is all one as to perceive; that, therefore, wherein color, figure, and the like qualities exist must perceive them; hence it is clear there can be no unthinking substance or *substratum* of those ideas" (*PHK,* 1.7).

But the notion that things exist even aside from any perception of them has a very powerful hold on us. And so we resort to the view, which Berkeley anticipates, that "though the ideas themselves do not exist without [outside of] the mind, yet there may be things like them, whereof they are copies or resemblances, which things exist without the mind in an unthinking substance" (*PHK,* 1.8). That is, we resort to something like Locke's distinction between primary and secondary qualities. Primary qualities, in Locke's formulation, are extension, motion, figure, and the like, while secondary qualities are the ideas we perceive—what Hobbes called "fancies"—colors, sounds, hardness, and so forth. Our ideas of secondary qualities are acknowledged by all, as Berkeley suggests, "not to be the resemblances of anything existing without the mind, or unperceived, but they will have our ideas of the primary qualities to be patterns or images of things which exist without the mind, in an unthinking substance which they call 'matter'" (*PHK*, 1.9). But this is merely an attempt to circumvent the logic of Berkeley's argument by adding a new layer to "reality," and it ultimately encounters the same difficulty as did the secondary qualities. How would we know anything of this "inert, senseless substance, in which extension, figure, and motion do actually subsist?" We have already shown, says Berkeley, that "extension, figure, and motion are only ideas existing in the mind, and that an idea can be like nothing but another idea, and that consequently neither they nor their archetypes can exist in an unperceiving substance" (ibid.). This is evidently a sequence which could be repeated indefinitely. The gap between mind and world which is at the foundation of the attempt to delineate a new way of knowing is ineluctable so long as we are applying strict reason to the evidence of the senses. Hobbes and Descartes (and following them, Locke) had urged on us a new standard for knowledge, free from the defects and uncertainty of prudence or common sense. But the fundamental principle at work in this endeavor was skepticism about the senses, and Bishop Berkeley does no more than harvest the necessary consequences.

The denial of the existence of the external world is not for Berkeley the last word, nor is it even a part of his aim to demonstrate such a conclusion. As Thomas Reid was to point out in his analysis of Berkeley's skepticism, Berkeley's aim was to supply irrefutable evidence for the existence of God.[17] By denying that we have any ground for supposing the existence of inanimate matter or material substance Berkeley hoped to show that the skeptical principles of modern science, so far from being atheistic, lead us to the necessary conclusion that the existence of things (the external world) is dependent on an all-perceiving divinity, whose omniperception guarantees what we call reality. As Reid put it, "the powers which inanimate matter is supposed to possess, have always been the strong hold of atheists. . . . This fortress of atheism must be most effectually overturned, if there is no such thing as matter in the universe."[18]

The logic of Berkeley's approach can be summarized as follows. Modern science, in its initial hope for a new kind of knowledge free from the defects of prudence, insists on a radical doubt of the senses. We are thus to regard what we see and hear—the qualities of things—as fancies or ideas *in us,* brought about in some way by the things around us. All we can or do know of the external world is that it consists in, as Hobbes puts it, "matter in motion."

> But, though it were possible that solid, figured, movable substances may exist without the mind, corresponding to the ideas we have of bodies, yet how is it possible for us to know this? Either we must know it by sense or by reason. As for our senses, by them we have the knowledge only of our sensations, ideas, or those things that are immediately perceived by sense, call them what you will; but they do not inform us that things exist without the mind, or unperceived, like to those which are perceived. This the materialists themselves acknowledge. It remains therefore that if we have any knowledge at all of external things, it must be by reason, inferring their existence from what is immediately perceived by sense. But what reason can induce us to believe the existence of bodies without the mind, from what we perceive, since the very patrons of matter themselves do not pretend there is any necessary connection betwixt them and our ideas? (*PHK,* 1.18)

As we saw in the previous chapter, this is one-half of the reasoning which led to Hume's philosophic aporia. Berkeley suggests that we are led inescapably to a denial of the external world or, as he himself professes to believe, to the conviction of our utter dependence on the mind or spirit of God. As he writes many pages later, "nothing can be more evident to anyone that is capable of the least reflection than the existence of God, or a spirit who is intimately present to our minds, producing in them all that variety of ideas or sensations which continually affect us, on whom we have absolute and entire dependence, in short 'in whom we live, and move, and have our being'" (*PHK*, 1.149).

Hume on Skepticism concerning the Senses

Hume's treatment of these matters is not in the service of any theological purpose. But the writings of Berkeley were of considerable importance to him.[19] What Bishop Berkeley had done was to draw out the implications of modern skeptical philosophy in a manner no successor could afford to ignore.[20] Hume was forced to confront them. His consideration of this issue might even be described as a key to his philosophical discourse as a whole, for it led him to the position of "mitigated skepticism" for which he is renowned, but which is so little understood.[21] We can distinguish between two ways in which Hume confronted the issue of the disjunction between reason and the senses. The most widely known, though indirect, is his treatment of causation, which I will consider in chapter 5, below. His more explicit consideration has received surprisingly little attention, if this assessment of its importance is correct.[22] Hume's treatment of what might be called the problem of reason occupies pride of place in the *Treatise*, where it is the central issue in the concluding sections of book 1. It is, if anything, more prominently featured in the first *Enquiry*, where it stands as the conclusion of his reasonings, in section 12. And in a sense it is the central theme of his final work, the *Dialogues concerning Natural Religion*, a work not published in Hume's lifetime but of concern to him for nearly twenty-five years.[23]

As a result of his investigation of human understanding Hume is convinced that what he calls the "fundamental principle" of modern philosophy leads to insuperable difficulties. This is not a rejection of modern science but an objection to its understanding of itself, in particular to its claim to be free from the defects which had always been characteristic of all forms of knowing. "The opinions of the antient philosophers," as Hume writes in the *Treatise*, "their fictions of substance and accident, and their reasonings concerning substantial forms and occult qualities, are like the spectres in the dark and are deriv'd from principles, which, however common, are neither universal nor unavoidable in human nature" (*T*, 226). In contrast, he continues, "the modern *philosophy* pretends to be entirely free from this defect, and to arise only from the solid, permanent, and consistent principles of the imagination" (ibid.). During his inquiry into the grounds of "this pretension" Hume identifies the fundamental principle of modern philosophy in the manner already cited (as "the opinion concerning colours, sounds, tastes, smells, heat and cold; which it asserts to be nothing but impressions in the mind"). He accepts Berkeley's conclusions as to the necessary implications of this premise.[24] But the conclusion which for Berkeley constituted clear evidence of the existence of the deity—that otherwise the external world vanishes when our backs are turned—is for Hume evidence that something has gone haywire in our understanding itself. Hume believes that "many objections might be made to this system," but he confines himself to stating one, "which is in my opinion very decisive" (*T*, 227).[25]

Hume's decisive objection to the system of modern philosophy is this: "I assert, that instead of explaining the operations of external objects by its means, we utterly annihilate all these objects, and reduce ourselves to the opinions of the most extravagant scepticism concerning them. If colours, sounds, tastes, and smells be merely perceptions, nothing we can conceive is possessed of a real, continu'd, and independent existence; not even motion, extension and solidity, which are the primary qualities chiefly insisted on" (*T*, 227–28).

This reasoning suggests how important Berkeley's *Principles of Human Knowledge* was to Hume. But Hume refuses to resort to Berkeley's solution. Reason is not consonant with the senses. As Hume explains in the first *Enquiry,* we are "necessitated by reasoning to contradict or depart from the primary instincts of nature, and to embrace a new system with regard to the evidence of our senses. But here philosophy finds herself extremely embarrassed, when she would justify this new system, and obviate the cavils and objections of the skeptics" (*EHU,* 152). The dilemma arises from what Hume earlier called "a direct and total opposition betwixt our reason and our senses; or more properly speaking, betwixt those conclusions we form from cause and effect, and those that persuade us of the continu'd and independent existence of body" (*T*, 231). As we have seen, Hume maintains that reasoning on the principles of modern philosophy forces us to conclude "that neither colour, sound, taste, nor smell have a continu'd and independent existence. When we exclude these sensible qualities there remains nothing in the universe, which has such an existence" (ibid.).

Berkeley had used this skeptical argument in the service of revelation. Hume believes it has no such implication. In a footnote to *An Enquiry concerning Human Understanding,* he writes that Berkeley "professes . . . in his title-page (and undoubtedly with great truth) to have composed his book against the sceptics as well as against the atheists and free-thinkers. But that all his arguments, though otherwise intended, are, in reality, merely sceptical, appears from this, *that they admit of no answer and produce no conviction.* Their only effect is to cause that momentary amazement and irresolution and confusion, which is the result of scepticism" (*EHU,* 106n–7n).

Why is Hume not persuaded by Berkeley's argument, of the existence of the deity? He is quite direct: "To have recourse to the veracity of the Supreme Being in order to prove the veracity of our senses, is surely making a very unexpected circuit. If his veracity were at all concerned in this matter, our senses would be entirely infallible; because it is not possible that he can ever deceive" (*EHU,* 105). But this nod to religious orthodoxy would not be enough for Berkeley, and Hume's more fundamental reason seems to be what follows: "Not to mention, that, if the external world be once called in question, we shall be at a loss to find arguments, by which we may prove the existence of that Being or any of his attributes" (ibid.). That is, Berkeley's claim that his skeptical argument confirms the existence of God is only compelling to someone who already shares Berkeley's conviction or faith in the existence of the deity; in itself it is not convincing. The skeptical argument by itself leaves us with no other beings in the universe; it is simply a form of solipsism. According to Hume, in topics such as this "the profounder and more philosophical sceptics *will always triumph,* when they endeavor to introduce an universal doubt into all subjects of human knowledge and inquiry" (ibid., emphasis added). In fact Hume himself was tortured by such universal perplexity in his first attempts to work this out, as the famous conclusion to the *Treatise* amply attests. The attempt to ground science on a separation of reason from the senses, apparently, cannot succeed. This is another way of saying we cannot reconstruct the world rationally, if we mean by this to replace the less-than-perfect prudence or experience which constitutes our prescientific world.

This is not to say that modern natural science cannot work. It seems, however, that the *understanding* of scientific knowledge promulgated by Hobbes, Descartes, and Locke tried to claim too much. There can be no scientific knowledge of the world based on radical or universal skepticism about the senses. Scientific knowledge of the kind which so excited Hobbes can be had only so long as we confine ourselves to the subjects which are abstract: In Hume's words, "it seems to me, that the only objects of the abstract sciences or of demonstration are quantity and number, and that all attempts to extend this more perfect species of knowledge beyond these bounds are mere sophistry and illusion" (*EHU*, 112). The world around us is not susceptible to approach by demonstrative science. Aside from the sciences of quantity and number, "all other enquiries of man regard only matter of fact and existence; and these are evidently incapable of demonstration. Whatever *is* may *not be*" (*EHU*, 113).

Fortunately for modern natural science, its progress has never been dependent on philosophers' properly understanding its foundations. If Hume is correct this science does not put knowledge of the world on a new plane, superior to prudence or experience of the garden variety. In dealing with the world, we are limited in fact to precisely those ordinary human faculties, although with care and attention they are capable of great refinement. The existence of any being, Hume writes, "can only be proved by arguments from its cause or its effect; and these arguments are founded entirely on experience" (*EHU*, 113). In what seems like a direct rejoinder to Descartes' wish that we "had had the full use of our reason from the moment of birth," so as to constitute the world rationally, Hume notes that "ADAM, though his rational faculties be supposed, at the very first, entirely perfect, could not have inferred from the fluidity, and transparency of water, that it would suffocate him, or from the light and warmth of fire, that it would consume him" (*EHU*, 17). The Cartesian project is thus impossible; it is also unnecessary.

It remains to examine Hume's understanding of the connection between experience and sciences other than mathematics, algebra, and geometry, which means turning our attention to his well-known account of causation, generally considered the key to all of Hume's philosophy. Everyone who has taken Philosophy 1 can recite the conclusion of that account, the formula for which Hume is most famous, namely that custom "is the great guide of human life" (*EHU*, 44). Hume himself gave pride of place to this discovery. In the *Abstract to a Treatise of Human Nature,* in which he supposedly summarized the contents of the very long *Treatise* for the purpose of advertisement, the "one simple argument" which he chose to trace in some detail was the one on the relation of cause and effect. It may seem strange in view of this consensus to claim that the full implications of this momentous discovery, as Hume understood them, are rarely brought out. One reason is the relative obscurity in which the implications are buried in the *Treatise* itself.

Part 4 of book 1 (the section which immediately follows his account of causation), under the title "Of the skeptical and other systems of philosophy," includes Hume's surveys of "antient" and modern philosophy and culminates in the tortured account of Hume's "philosophical melancholy and delirium." By the time Hume recast book 1 as the *Philosophical Essays concerning Human Understanding* he was much clearer, and the conclusions are condensed into a seventeen-page section of striking force but separated from the account of cause and effect itself by two entirely new "essays" which comprise sections 10 and 11 of the *Enquiry*— "Of Miracles" and "Of a particular Providence and of a future State." The connection between these two essays and the account of causation is not so obvious: The first has almost always been read as merely an attack on Christianity (and landed Hume in some difficulties), under the guise of attacking the existence of miracles. The second is even stranger in character: it is an imaginary dialogue between Hume and someone who undertakes to give a speech for Epicurus, and it is generally treated as an entirely independent essay, raising as it does questions about the political implications of atheism. Only after these two does Hume present the brief essay "Of Academic or Skeptical Philosophy," into which the nearly one hundred pages of *Treatise* book 1, part 4 are condensed. If the core of Hume's philosophy is indeed the investigation of the "necessity of cause and effect" a more careful scrutiny of his own understanding of its implications may be expected to shed light on all his writings, and in particular on the relation between his epistemological works and his *Essays,* the *History of England,* and the *Dialogues.*

5   *"One of the Most Sublime Questions"*

The importance of Hume's account of causation has
long been recognized. We have already suggested that
it has important implications for our understanding of
scientific knowledge, in particular of the relation between science and prescientific consciousness. We
have seen Hume's exploration of the question concerning the existence of the world around us and of other
beings besides ourselves, a question he was compelled
to confront both by the "fundamental principle" of
modern philosophy and by Berkeley's skeptical argument drawing out the implications of that principle.[1]
It may be, Hume suggests, "a subject worthy of curiosity to enquire what is the nature of that evidence
which assures us of any real existence and matter of
fact beyond the present testimony of our senses or the
records of our memory" (*EHU*, 26). This is a part of
philosophy "little cultivated, either by the ancients or
moderns" as Hume says. Why was this question not
addressed by the ancients and why is it novel even in
1735? The answer is probably to be found in the fact
that the success of the new physical science was relatively recent. The teleological science of the ancients
was, after all, not based on skepticism about the
senses. But the success of modern natural science is
perhaps less the explanation than is the success of one
powerful *account* of modern natural science, or of
what it means to know scientifically. I believe it is this
account—in which skepticism about appearances or
what the senses tell us is transformed into skepticism

62

about prescientific consciousness in general—which Hume's investigation of causation addresses.

As Hume tells us in the first *Enquiry*, "all reasonings concerning matter of fact seem to be founded on the relation of *Cause* and *Effect*. By means of that relation alone we can go beyond the evidence of our memory and senses." After offering some examples of how we make judgments about matters of fact using or supposing "a connexion between the present fact and that which is inferred from it," Hume observes that "were there nothing to bind them together the inference would be entirely precarious" (*EHU*, 26–27). There follows a passage which anticipates the arguments of the *Dialogues*:

> The hearing of an articulate voice and rational discourse in the dark assures us of the presence of some person: Why? because these are the effects of the human make and fabric, and closely connected with it. If we anatomize all the other reasonings of this nature, we shall find that they are founded on the relation of cause and effect, and that this relation is either near or remote, direct or collateral. Heat and light are collateral effects of fire and the one effect may justly be inferred from the other.
>
> If we would satisfy ourselves, therefore, concerning the nature of that evidence, which assures us of matters of fact, we must enquire how we arrive at the knowledge of cause and effect. (*EHU*, 27)

The secondary literature offers a number of good summaries of what Hume calls this "simple argument," and Hume's own account is not unduly difficult.[2] A brief rehearsal of the argument itself will suffice before we attempt to reconstruct its context and explore its implications more fully. "All kinds of reasoning," Hume tells us, "consist in nothing but a *comparison*, and a discovery of those relations, either constant or inconstant, which two or more objects bear to each other" (*T*, 73). When objects are present to the senses, we "call *this* perception rather than reasoning." Only in the case of causation does the mind go beyond direct perception in assessing the relation between objects; only causation gives the mind "assurance from the existence or action of one object, that 'twas follow'd or preceded by any other existence or action" (*T*, 73–74).

Yet the idea of causation, like any other idea, must be traceable to some "primary impression," according to Hume (*T*, 75). In tracing the roots of some of the ideas ("relations") crucial to scientific reasoning, such as identity or relations of time and place, we neither can nor need to go further than what is immediately present to the senses. But the idea of causation is different. In fact, Hume notes, the other ideas—identity of objects and relations of time and place—themselves depend on causation, since they require us to conclude something beyond the evidence of the senses (for example, that the object in front of us is the same as it was earlier), and this "can be founded only on the connexion of *cause and effect*" (*T*, 74).

The Idea of Causation

What, then, is the source or root of the idea of causation? In particular, where do we get the idea of the *necessary* connection of cause and effect? As Hume elsewhere notes, such a belief in the necessity of causation is by no means universal:

> The vulgar, who take things according to their first appearance, attribute the uncertainty of events to such an uncertainty in the causes, as makes them often fail of their usual influence, tho' they meet with no obstacle nor impediment in their operation. But philosophers observing, that almost in every part of nature there is contain'd a vast variety of springs and principles, which are hid, by reason of their minuteness or remoteness, find that 'tis at least possible the contrariety of events may not proceed from any contingency in the cause, but from the secret operation of contrary causes. This possibility is converted into certainty by farther observation, when they remark, that upon an exact scrutiny, a contrariety of effects always betrays a contrariety of causes, and proceeds from their mutual hindrance and opposition. (*T*, 132)

Yet what is the status of this conviction, which amounts to an article of faith, that all events are causally connected and thus susceptible to scientific explanation? Hume wrestles with this at some length and is forced to conclude that it is impossible to prove, by reason, the necessity of causation. This is because it is "easy for us to conceive any object to be non-existent this moment, and existent the next, without conjoining to it the distinct idea of a cause or productive principle" (*T*, 79).[3] The separation of cause from effect is thus "so far possible, that it implies no contradiction nor absurdity; and is therefore incapable of being refuted by any reasoning from mere ideas; without which 'tis impossible to demonstrate the necessity of a cause" (*T*, 80).

If our idea of necessary causation does not arise from scientific demonstration and is not susceptible to confirmation by it, where does it come from? It is worth noting that, after convincing himself of the impossibility of proving by reason the necessity of the idea of causation, which is so clearly accepted as necessary by philosophers, Hume does not put causation in question or suggest that we could get along without the notion.[4] He merely asks what *is* the source, if not reason. "Since it is not from knowledge or any scientific reasoning, that we derive the opinion of the necessity of a cause to every new production, that opinion must necessarily arise from observation and experience" (*T*, 82). But how does this occur?

The idea of causation, like any other, must be traced to impressions.[5] But there is no *impression* of causation itself: we have no way of even describing what that would mean. The inference from cause to effect "is not deriv'd merely from a survey of these particular objects, and from such a penetration of their essences as may discover the dependence of the one upon the other. There is no object, which implies the existence of any other if we consider these objects in themselves" (*T*, 86). Hence, the idea must arise indirectly, as it were. It must arise somehow from experience, since it does not derive from reason, but not from experience in any immediate sense. There seems to be a kind of experience which might give rise to the idea of causation: experience of what Hume calls constant conjunction. "We remember to have had frequent instances of the existence of one species of objects; and also remember, that the individuals of another species of objects have always attended them, and have existed in a regular order of contiguity and succession with regard to them. . . . Without any farther ceremony, we call the one *cause* and the other *effect*, and infer the existence of the one from that of the other" (*T*, 87). But this gets us nowhere: "to tell the truth, this new discover'd relation of a constant conjunction seems to advance us but very little in our way" (*T*, 88). By way of explanation, Hume presents the now very famous argument concerning the inadequacy of any and all experience (which is of things past) to establish the course of future events. Clearly, he says, "there can be no *demonstrative* arguments to prove, *that those instances, of which we have had no experience, resemble those, of which we have had experience*" (*T*, 89).

We are forced to conclude that our conviction of the necessity of causation arises from some other fact or principle of human nature. Hume has already suggested he will not turn to the explanation that such a conviction is divinely implanted in man, but neither will he rest with explanations that do not stand up to philosophical scrutiny, as we recall from chapter 4.[6] That certain objects have always been conjoined together seems to give rise to our idea of necessary conjunction. "We only observe the thing itself, and always find that from the constant conjunction the objects acquire an union in the imagination" (*T*, 93). The science of nature is thus based on a principle whose certainty we do not doubt but whose truth cannot be established rationally.

If the causal connection between two objects or events is not established by the constant conjunction of the two objects, because cases from past experience can never demonstrate that the future will be like the past, where does our idea of necessary causation come from? If, Hume writes, he turns his attention to "two objects suppos'd to be placed in" the relation of necessary connection, and examines them in

> all the situations of which they are susceptible, I immediately perceive, that they are *contiguous* in time and place, and that the object we call cause *precedes* the other we call effect. In no one

instance can I go any farther, nor is it possible for me to discover any third relation betwixt these objects. I therefore enlarge my view to comprehend several instances; where I find like objects always existing in like relations of contiguity and succession. At first sight this seems to serve but little to my purpose. The reflection on several instances only repeats the same objects; and therefore can never give rise to a new idea. But upon further enquiry I find, that the repetition is not in every particular the same, but produces a new impression, and by that means the idea, which I at present examine. (*T,* 155)

The new impression is very simple. After frequent repetition, says Hume, "I find, that upon the appearance of one of the objects, the mind is *determin'd* by custom to consider its usual attendant, and to consider it in a stronger light upon account of its relation to the first object. 'Tis this impression, then, or *determination,* which affords me the idea of necessity" (*T,* 156).

Custom and Causation

Hume presents this solution with a certain misleading nonchalance, which turns out, however, to be deliberate and rhetorical. Immediately after indicating that the idea of necessary causation is simply a product of a sort of mental custom or habit, and even claiming that he does not doubt the reader will accept this "without difficulty," Hume suddenly changes his tone and announces: "I think it proper to give warning, that I have just now examin'd one of the most sublime questions in philosophy, *viz. that concerning the power and efficacy of causes;* where all the sciences seem so much interested" (*T,* 156). Indeed, the significance of Hume's treatment of this problem can only be seen in the light of a comparison with the treatments and answers offered in other philosophic accounts of causation. Such a comparison occupies the next few pages of the *Treatise.*

Hume begins by noting that "there is no question, which on account of its importance, as well as difficulty, has caus'd more disputes both among antient and modern philosophers, than this concerning the efficacy of causes, or that quality which makes them be follow'd by their effects" (*T*, 156). This may surprise the reader who recalls the passage from Hume's first *Enquiry*, quoted above, in which he suggests that the part of philosophy concerning the evidence for "real existence and matter of fact" is one "which has been little cultivated, either by the ancients or moderns" (*EHU*, 26), especially since Hume believes the two issues are closely connected. But apparently Hume believes this to be the source of the novelty of his discovery: Hume is the first to see that the proper understanding of the relation of cause and effect constitutes a resolution of the otherwise mysterious—to modern science—problem of "real existence." Berkeley had already taken the skepticism of modern science about the senses to its logical conclusion.

Hume first disposes of what he calls "all vulgar definitions" philosophers have given of "power and efficacy," by noting that "the terms of *efficacy, agency, power, force, energy, necessity, connexion,* and *productive quality,* are all nearly synonimous" (*T*, 157). This means we must search for the idea we are seeking not in circular definitions, but in "the impressions, from which it is originally derived" (ibid.). In this, Hume is merely conforming to his own rule in the *Treatise*—that, in tracing the source of ideas, we ought not to have recourse to innate ideas. This principle he shares with Locke, of course, who devoted the entire first book of his *Essay* to a refutation of the notion of innate ideas. Hume's strategy is to go straight to the heart of "the most general and most popular explication of this matter," which he connects, in a footnote, to Locke's *Essay concerning Human Understanding,* and specifically to Locke's "chapter of power" (*Essay,* 2.21). Locke, along with many others, had worked from a commonsensical notion: in Hume's words, "finding from experience, that there are several new productions in matter, such as the motions and variations of body, and concluding that *there must somewhere be a power capable of producing them, we arrive at last by this reasoning* at the idea of power and efficacy" (*T*, 157; emphasis added). To see why this is not satisfactory, Hume writes, we need only reflect on "two very obvious principles." One is that "reason alone can never give rise to any original idea," and, secondly, "that reason, as distinguish'd from experience, can never make us conclude, that a cause or productive quality is absolutely requisite to every beginning of existence" (ibid.). As Hume notes here, "both these considerations have been sufficiently explain'd" at length earlier in the *Treatise;* he does not insist on them further here. He turns his attention rather to the question of what experiences could give rise to the notion of causal efficacy, since such an idea must arise from "particular instances of this efficacy, which make their passage into the mind by the common channels of sensation or reflection" (ibid.). If we cannot come up with any instance "wherein the efficacy is plainly discoverable to the mind," we must be willing to "acknowledge that the idea is impossible and imaginary" (*T*, 157–58). Hume believes this conclusion is avoidable only by recourse to the principle of innate ideas, which "has already been refuted, and is now almost universally rejected in the learned world"—and most importantly was rejected by the thinkers whose accounts of cause and effect Hume's own is intended to supplant (*T*, 158). "Our present business, then, must be to find some natural production, where the operation and efficacy of a cause can be clearly conceiv'd and comprehended by the mind, without any danger of obscurity or mistake" (ibid.).

But "in this research we meet with very little encouragement," Hume continues, as a result of the "prodigious diversity" to be found in the opinions of the various philosophers (Malebranch is cited) who have "pretended to explain the secret force and energy of causes" (*T*, 158). Hume catalogs some of the explanations which comprise this diversity: some say bodies operate by their "substantial form," others by "accidents or qualities," "matter and form," "form and accidents," or "by certain virtues and faculties distinct from all this" (ibid.).

All these sentiments again are mix'd and vary'd in a thousand different ways; and form a strong presumption, that none of them have any solidity or evidence, and that the supposition of an efficacy in any of the known qualities of matter is entirely without foundation. This presumption must encrease upon us, when we consider, that these principles of substantial forms, and accidents, and faculties, are not in reality any of the known properties of bodies, but are perfectly unintelligible and inexplicable. For 'tis evident philosophers wou'd never have had recourse to such obscure and uncertain principles had they met with any satisfaction in such as are clear and intelligible; especially in such an affair as this, which must be an object of the simplest understanding, if not of the senses. Upon the whole, we may conclude, that 'tis impossible in any one instance to shew the principle, in which the force and agency of a cause is plac'd; and that the most refin'd and most vulgar understandings are equally at a loss in this particular. (*T*, 158–59)

Hume challenges anyone who wishes to refute this assertion. Such a one, Hume suggests, "need not put himself to the trouble of inventing any long reasonings; but may at once shew us an instance of a cause, where we discover the power or operating principle" (*T*, 159). He follows this with a kind of apology to the reader: "this defiance we are oblig'd frequently to make use of, as being almost the only means of proving a negative in philosophy" (ibid.).

What Hume seeks to establish, it appears, is only that philosophers should acknowledge failure in their attempts to discover the secret power of causation; "the ultimate force and efficacy of nature is perfectly unknown to us, and that 'tis in vain we search for it in all the known qualities of matter" (ibid.). Indeed Hume acknowledges here that philosophers have admitted as much: "In this opinion they are almost unanimous." So why all the fuss? The crux of the matter is what philosophers resort to when thus confronted by their own ignorance: " 'Tis only in the inference they draw" from this shared opinion that they "discover any difference in their sentiments" (*T*, 159). Two responses in particular engage Hume's attention.

In the case of one group, whom Hume identifies as "the Cartesians in particular," the inference leads to a theological conclusion. Hume is careful to dispute not the conclusion but the logic employed to reach it. Since matter itself—dead matter, as we may say—is "in itself entirely unactive," and cannot be understood to produce or cause anything of itself, the Cartesians concluded that the "effects" of causation which are evident to our senses must be produced by a power from somewhere else. This power, they say, "must be in the deity," who affords us the only explanation of necessary causation. " 'Tis the deity, therefore, who is the prime mover of the universe, and who not only first created matter, and gave it it's original impulse, but likewise by a continu'd exertion of omnipotence, supports its existence, and successively bestows on it all those motions, and configurations, and qualities, with which it is endow'd" (*T*, 159). Hume notes that "this opinion is certainly very curious," but " 'twill appear superfluous to examine it in this place, if we reflect a moment on our present purpose in taking notice of it" (*T*, 160). He reminds us that all ideas are derived from impressions (the cardinal argument of the *Treatise*); the Cartesians, however, "proceeding upon their principle of innate ideas, have had recourse to a supreme spirit or deity, whom they consider as the only active being in the universe" (ibid.). But if we disallow innate ideas, and keep to the principle that ideas derive from impressions, "the idea of a deity proceeds from the same origin." After all, if we accept an innate idea in the one case, why not in the other as well?

> Since these philosophers, therefore, have concluded, that matter cannot be endow'd with any efficacious principle, because 'tis impossible to discover in it such a principle; the same course of reasoning shou'd determine them to exclude it from the supreme being. Or if they estem that opinion absurd and impious, as it really is, I shall tell them how they may avoid it; and that is, by concluding from the very first, that they have no adequate idea of power or efficacy in any object; since neither in body nor spirit, neither in superior nor inferior natures, are they able to discover one single instance of it. (*T*, 160)

The second inference which Hume challenges is not identified with any philosopher by name but seems to be directed against Locke's account of the psychological origin of the notion of power. Hume speaks of those who maintain that we have an idea of power but admit "that this energy lies not in any of the known qualities of matter" (*T,* 191). In the body of the text Hume dismisses this position out of hand. But in an appendix he considers it in more detail. "Some have asserted, that we feel an energy, or power, in our own mind; and that having in this manner acquir'd the idea of power, we transfer that quality to matter, where we are not able immediately to discover it. The motions of our body, and the thoughts and sentiments of our mind, (say they) obey the will; nor do we seek any farther to acquire a just notion of force or power" (*T,* 632; appendix, for insertion at *T,* 161). This seems to be a clear reference to Locke, who maintained in book 2 of the *Essay concerning Human Understanding* that "the idea of the *beginning* of motion we have only from reflection on what passes in ourselves; where we find by experience, that, barely by a thought of the mind, we can move the parts of our bodies, which were before at rest" (*Essay,* 2.21.4). But there is a confusion here, which Hume seizes on. As Locke admits a few lines below the passage quoted, "if anyone thinks he has a clear idea of power" from observation of the "impulse" bodies "make one upon another," that will be satisfactory: "only I thought it worth while to consider here, by the way, whether the mind doth not receive its idea of active power *clearer from reflection on its own operations, than it doth from any external sensation*" (ibid., emphasis added). The confusion lies in Locke's attempt to juxtapose two possible sources of the idea of power, one internal and one external. Hume believes this distinction spurious and would point to Locke's use of the word "experience" (in the first passage quoted) as evidence. Hume suggests that

> to convince us how fallacious this reasoning is, we need only consider, that the will being here consider'd as a cause, has no more a discoverable connexion with its effects, than any material cause has with its proper effect. So far from perceiving the connexion betwixt an act of volition, and a motion of the body; 'tis allow'd that no effect is more inexplicable from the powers and essence of

thought and matter. Nor is the empire of the will over our mind more intelligible. The effect is there distinguishable and separable from the cause, and cou'd not be foreseen without the experience of their constant conjunction. (*T,* 632)

As he expressed this (more felicitously) in the first *Enquiry,* "our idea of power is not copied from any sentiment or consciousness of power within ourselves, when we give rise to animal motion, or apply our limbs to their proper use and office. That their motion follows the command of the will *is a matter of common experience, like other natural events:* But the power or energy by which this is effected, like that in other natural events, is unknown and inconceivable" (*EHU,* 44; emphasis added). Thus we are driven back to the admission of ignorance as to the secret power or efficacy of causes. We make assessments of cause and effect on the basis of experience alone. When we observe "several instances, in which the same objects are always conjoin'd together, we immediately conceive a connexion betwixt them, and begin to draw an inference from one to another. This multiplicity of resembling instances, therefore, constitutes the very essence of power or connexion, and is the source, from which the idea of it arises" (*T,* 163).

If the power of causation is not in the objects themselves, and cannot be known by experience to be located in any divinity, what is the source of our conviction as to its necessity? "Upon the whole, necessity is something that exists in the mind, not in objects" (*T,* 165). In another formulation Hume puts it thus: "The efficacy or energy of causes . . . belongs entirely to the soul, which considers the union of two or more objects in all past instances. 'Tis here that the real power of causes is plac'd, along with their connexion and necessity" (*T,* 166). The undeniable necessity of causation resides in or is an artifact of the human soul itself.

The sort of reasoning we engage in in science consists in reasoning resting on custom. "Now as we call everything CUSTOM which proceeds from a past repetition without any new reasoning or conclusion, we may establish it as a certain truth that all the belief, which follows upon any present impression, is deriv'd solely from that origin" (*T*, 102). Hume draws the following conclusion:

> Thus all probable reasoning is nothing but a species of sensation. 'Tis not solely in poetry and music we must follow our taste and sentiment, but likewise in philosophy. When I am convinc'd of any principle, 'tis only an idea, which strikes more strongly upon me. When I give the preference to one set of arguments above another, I do nothing but decide from my feeling concerning the superiority of their influence. Objects have no discoverable connexion together; nor is it from any other principle but custom operating upon the imagination, that we can draw any inference from the appearance of one to the existence of another. (*T*, 103)

Natural Workings of the Mind

We are now in a position to examine Hume's understanding of the relation between scientific reasoning and what we called above the "natural workings of the human mind"—that is, the prescientific consciousness which Hobbes claims is defective.[7] Hume's teaching emerges most clearly in the course of his critical examination of what he calls "the skeptical system of philosophy," in Part 4 of book 1 of the *Treatise of Human Nature*. He shows here that the claims which are made about certainty and demonstrability in scientific endeavor—even in algebra and pure mathematics—must be qualified because of the dependence of these sciences on practitioners who are human and fallible. "In all demonstrative sciences the rules are certain and infallible; but when we apply them, our fallible and uncertain faculties are very apt to depart from them, and fall into error" (*T*, 180). As a result of this "enlarged view" we realize that "our reason must be considered as a kind of cause, of which truth is the natural effect, but such-a-one as by the irruption of other causes" is not one hundred percent reliable. It follows that no science can claim to transcend the sorts of reasoning characteristic of all human experience: "By this means all knowledge degenerates into probability; and this probability is greater or less, according to our experience of the veracity or deceitfulness of our understanding, and according to the simplicity or intricacy of the question" (*T*, 180).

Nor is this observation confined to the moral and natural sciences:

> There is no Algebraist nor Mathematician so expert in his science, as to place entire confidence in any truth immediately upon his discovery of it, or regard it as any thing, but a mere probability. Every time he runs over his proofs, his confidence encreases; but still more by the approbation of his friends; and is rais'd to its utmost perfection by the universal assent and applauses of the learned world. Now 'tis evident, that this gradual encrease of assurance is nothing but the addition of new probabilities, and is deriv'd from the constant union of causes and effects, according to past experience and observation. (*T*, 180–81)

Oddly enough Hume refers here to an example nearly identical to that cited above from Hobbes, that is, of the man who computes his accounts without benefit of science, and so "onely believeth," as Hobbes puts it. According to Hume, this is only natural and necessary, because there is no other possibility: even the most careful "accomptant" relies on fallible human skills and so his accounts cannot be more than what "skill and experience" allow. The conclusion Hume draws is of the utmost importance for our present inquiry: "Since therefore all knowledge resolves itself into probability, and becomes at last of the same nature with that evidence, which we employ in common life, we must now examine this latter species of reasoning, and see on what foundation it stands" (*T*, 181).[8]

Hume here turns his attention to the sort of skepticism (reminiscent of Hobbes') which casts doubt on the "natural workings of the human mind," discussed in the previous chapter. He shows that any such skepticism tells as heavily against all scientific reason as it does against the way we reason in common life. And he imagines a likely rejoinder:

> Shou'd it here be ask'd me, whether I sincerely assent to this argument, which I seem to take such pains to inculcate, and

whether I be really one of those sceptics, who hold that all is uncertain, and that our judgment is not in *any* thing possest of *any* measures of truth and falshood; I shou'd reply, that this question is entirely superfluous, and that neither I, nor any other person was ever sincerely and constantly of that opinion. Nature, by an absolute and uncontroulable necessity has determin'd us to judge as well as to breathe and feel; nor can we any more forbear viewing certain objects in a stronger and fuller light, upon account of their customary connexion with a present impression, than we can hinder ourselves from thinking as long as we are awake, or seeing the surrounding bodies, when we turn our eyes towards them in broad sunshine. Whoever has taken the pains to refute the cavils of this *total* scepticism, has really disputed without an antagonist, and endeavor'd by arguments to establish a faculty, which nature has antecedently implanted in the mind, and render'd unavoidable. (*T*, 183)

We are thus thrown back on reliance on the "natural workings of the human mind." Not only empirical science, but even the "Algebraist" must rest content with this, because nothing will transport us beyond our dependency on nature.[9]

"Philosophy Finds Herself Extremely Embarrassed"

We have examined Hume's famous account of causation to shed light on the tension between reason and common life, which Hume examines, and to identify the "strange infirmities" of human understanding which philosophical scrutiny exposes. Hume's investigation of the "necessary connexion of cause and effect" was undertaken in response to the account of the new science offered by his predecessors. The "fundamental principle" of that "modern philosophy," which Hume identifies as its opinion concerning the status of the senses, placed reason on a collision course with common life by calling in question the validity of prescientific consciousness. But after the new science—at least one account of it—used reason to undermine prescientific experience or prudence, it offered no satisfactory replacement for the world it demolished. Hume's account of causation serves to redress the balance, in a sense.

I suggested above that the bearing of this account of causation is rarely appreciated because it is frequently seen only as an example, albeit the preeminent example, of what Kemp Smith called Hume's "naturalism," his demonstration of the subordinate rank of reason in relation to the passions.[10] This is no doubt correct as far as it goes. But the account of causation is also the key to understanding the transformation of Hume's philosophy, his development or reinvention of a philosophy grounded on—even embedded in—common life, in contrast to the efforts of his predecessors.[11] It is in this sense that I wish to advance the claim that Hume's "later" philosophy—the full Humean philosophy—is best represented by the *History of England,* along with the *Essays* and the posthumous *Dialogues.*[12] The usual reading of the account of causation is not wrong, it simply does not go far enough, because it does not bring out the connection to a positive side of his philosophic program.[13] This is why Hume's later writings are rarely seen as an integral part of his philosophic project and why he is so often understood as having abandoned philosophy altogether for the sake of a career in belles lettres.

Hume's accomplishment here resembles the classical Socratic transformation of philosophy into political philosophy, which was also connected to the discovery of a fundamental and insuperable tension between reason and the rest of human life.[14] Hume's explicit treatment of this tension (in the first *Enquiry*) and the understanding of philosophy to which it leads him are worth examining in some detail. The clearest formulation is found in the last section or essay, "Of the Academic or Sceptical Philosophy," which is, in part, a distillation of the much longer discussion of skepticism in the *Treatise,* but which introduces Hume's concept of "mitigated scepticism," a philosophy "which may be both durable and useful" (*EHU,* 161).

Hume begins with an observation about our prescientific consciousness, or what he would call the perspective of common life: "It

seems evident, that men are carried, by a natural instinct or preposses-
sion, to repose faith in their senses; and that, without any reasoning, or
even almost before the use of reason, we always suppose an external
universe, which depends not on our perception, but would exist, though
we and every sensible creature were absent or annihilated" (*EHU*, 151).
This is so little open to doubt that Hume scarcely bothers to adduce
evidence, noting only that "even the animal creation are governed by a
like opinion, and preserve this belief of external objects, in all their
thoughts, designs, and actions" (ibid.).[15] Men and even animals proceed
in their activities without any doubts at all about their relation to an
external world. "But," Hume continues, "this universal and primary
opinion of all men is soon destroyed by the slightest philosophy." The
introduction of philosophic reason to common life leads to an impasse:
Philosophy "teaches us, that nothing can ever be present to the mind but
an image or perception, and that the senses are only the inlets, through
which these images are conveyed, without being able to produce any
immediate intercourse between the mind and the object" (*EHU*, 152).
After providing some illustration, Hume sums up the condition of aporia
to which reason or philosophy leads:

> So far, then, we are necessitated by reasoning to contradict or
> depart from the primary instincts of nature, and to embrace a new
> system with regard to the evidence of our senses. But here philoso-
> phy finds herself extremely embarrassed, when she would justify
> this new system, and obviate the cavils and objections of the scep-
> tics. She can no longer plead the infallible and irresistible instinct
> of nature: for that led us to a quite different system, which is
> acknowledged fallible and even erroneous. And to justify this pre-
> tended philosophical system, by a chain of clear and convincing
> argument, or even any appearance of argument, exceeds the
> power of all human capacity. (*EHU*, 152)

This seems to be a reformulation of the philosophic aporia which
Hume described in the conclusion of book 1 of the *Treatise*, where he says
that it led him to a state of "philosophical melancholy and delirium."

The only means of escape from that aporia was to await the return of a disposition suitable for further reflection; philosophy "has nothing to oppose" to the "sentiments of spleen and indolence" which she produces (*T*, 270). But in the concluding essay of the first *Enquiry* Hume expresses himself quite differently, and in such a way as to suggest he has escaped from that aporia. He is confident that "this is a topic . . . in which the profounder and more philosophical sceptics will always triumph, when they endeavor to introduce an universal doubt into all subjects of human knowledge and enquiry" (*EHU*, 153). He is, however, no longer one of them, if indeed he ever was.

> Do you follow the instincts and propensities of human nature, may they say, in assenting to the veracity of sense? But these lead you to believe that the very perception or sensible image is the external object. Do you disclaim this principle, in order to embrace a more rational opinion, that the perceptions are only representations of something external? You depart from your natural propensities and more obvious sentiments; and yet are not able to satisfy your reason, which can never find any convincing argument from experience to prove, that the perceptions are connected with any external objects. (*EHU*, 153–54)

Hume is now able to see from a distance what is accomplished by this "profounder and more philosophical" skepticism: nothing. Or rather, almost nothing, for as he admits in a footnote, with reference to Berkeley, such skeptical arguments "*admit of no answer and produce no conviction.* Their only effect is to cause that momentary amazement and irresolution and confusion, which is the result of scepticism" (*EHU*, 155). Now he observes that "it may seem a very extravagant attempt of the sceptics to destroy *reason* by argument and ratiocination; yet is this the grand scope of all their enquiries and disputes" (ibid.).[16] Hume does not deny that "within his proper sphere"—which is to say, in the rarefied air of "profound researches"—the skeptic "seems to have ample matter for triumph" (*EHU*, 159). In examining the nature of causation and showing that all our reasoning concerning it, including all science, rests only on "custom or a certain instinct of our nature," which may like other instincts be "fallacious and deceitful," the skeptic triumphs. What the skeptic succeeds in showing according to Hume is "his own and our weakness," a weakness Hume is ready to admit (ibid.). In fact the description Hume offers here is really an account of his own philosophical investigations, with an emphasis on the "prodigious discovery" regarding causation.[17] But by the time Hume wrote the first *Enquiry* he sees clearly both the usual effect of this philosophy, which is that it does no good, and the direction in which it points for a superior philosophy.

Diluting the Vigor of Skepticism

After bringing out some of the arguments characteristic of philosophical skepticism, including his own investigation of causation, Hume says that "these arguments might be displayed at greater length, if any durable good or benefit to society could ever be expected to result from them" (*EHU*, 159). He had displayed them at much greater length in the *Treatise* but now declines to do so. "For here is the chief and most confounding objection to *excessive* scepticism, that no durable good can ever result from it; while it remains in its full force and vigour" (ibid.). Apparently something of its full force and vigor must be abated for anything positive to issue from skeptical philosophy. The full-strength skeptic, or "Pyrrhonian," as Hume calls him, "cannot expect, that his philosophy will have constant influence on the mind, or if it had, that its influence would be beneficial to society" (*EHU*, 160).[18] The apparent public spiritedness Hume displays in this passage may come as something of a surprise, but it is worth remembering both the fate of Socrates and Hume's own acute sensibility to the public effect (as well as public reception) of his philosophy.[19] (We return to this in chapters 6 and 9, below).

What does Hume mean by the suggestion that, in order for skeptical philosophy to have any value, its "full force and vigour" must be diluted? With what must it be diluted? With these questions we come to the heart of what I have suggested is Hume's more positive philosophic program. It is not necessary to use any esoteric scholarly techniques to extract Hume's meaning from the text of the first *Enquiry,* for it is laid out clearly and logically. The final essay (section 12) of the *Enquiry* is divided into three parts of roughly equal length, and the discussion of skeptical philosophy as presented so far is found in the first two, with the judgment about the fruits of full-strength skepticism coming at the end of part 2. Part 3 is simply devoted to what we wish to examine next. It opens thus: "There is, indeed, a more *mitigated* skepticism or *academical* philosophy, which may be both durable and useful" (*EHU,* 161).[20] This attractive philosophy may be, Hume admits, "in part" the result of the "Pyrrhonism, or *excessive* scepticism" already discussed, so long as it is diluted, that is, "when its undistinguished doubts are, in some measure, corrected by *common sense and reflection"* (*EHU,* 161; emphasis added). This is reminiscent of a passage from the *Treatise,* in which Hume calls the reader's attention to the sort of "honest gentlemen" who rarely carry their thoughts beyond common life. Hume wishes "we cou'd communicate to our founders of systems, a share of this gross earthy mixture, as an ingredient, which they commonly stand much in need of" (*T,* 272). Philosophical skepticism of the profounder sort must be diluted with some admixture of common sense or common life in order to make it durable or useful. He goes on to suggest two kinds of "mitigated scepticism," or two ways of understanding the "mitigated scepticism" he is proposing: The one involves philosophical style, the other substance.

The argument for the former has already been suggested; it is based on a few observations from common life. The greater part of mankind tend to be "affirmative and dogmatical." They see things from only one point of view and feel their convictions with the greater force because they are ignorant of countervailing principles and arguments. "To hesitate or balance perplexes their understanding, checks their passion, and suspends their action"—exactly, we may note, the effects of an excess of reasoning or philosophy, as Shakespeare suggests in *Hamlet.* Such men are "impatient till they escape from a state, which to them is so uneasy: and they think, that they can never remove themselves far enough from it, by the violence of their affirmations and obstinacy of their belief"

(*EHU*, 161). This condition, as we see in the next chapters, provides Hume with ample matter for reflection in the *History*. "Mitigated scepticism" can act as a counter to dogmatism: "could such dogmatical reasoners become sensible of the strange infirmities of the human understanding, even in its most perfect state, and when most accurate and cautious in its determinations; such a reflection would naturally inspire them with more modesty and reserve, and diminish their fond opinion of themselves, and their prejudice against antagonists" (ibid.). Even the learned are susceptible—perhaps especially susceptible—to this dogmatical disposition and to "haughtiness and obstinacy."[21] For them, too, Hume prescribes "a small tincture of Pyrrhonism." This might "abate their pride, by showing them, that the few advantages, which they may have attained over their fellows, are but inconsiderable, if compared with the universal perplexity and confusion which is inherent in human nature" (ibid.). An awareness of the "strange infirmities" under which human understanding labors can teach moderation, both to ordinary men and to the learned, and help them to recognize that "there is a degree of doubt, and caution, and modesty, which, in all kinds of scrutiny and decision, ought forever to accompany a just reasoner" (*EHU*, 162). In part Hume teaches here that skepticism can itself be a kind of dogma, as anyone who teaches college students today will recognize. There is nothing a freshman is surer of, for example, than that all moral judgments are subjective and do not require rational support or reasoned explanation. The possibility of a dogmatical skepticism was clear to Hume even in the *Treatise:* "The sceptical and dogmatical reasoners are of the same kind, tho' contrary in their operation and tendency" (*T*, 187). The mitigated skepticism Hume recommends in the *Enquiry*, however, is superior precisely because it is not dogmatic.[22]

The second discussion of mitigated skepticism is concerned less with style or tone than with the question, "What are the proper subjects of science and enquiry?" (*EHU*, 163). This "species of mitigated scepticism," which like the first "may be of advantage to mankind, and may be the natural result of the Pyrrhonian doubts and scruples," consists in "the limitation of our enquiries to such subjects as are best adapted to the narrow capacity of human understanding" (*EHU*, 162). This may be most accurately described as the genuine fruit of Hume's entire "science of human nature," which had set out to discover the "extent and force of human understanding" (*T*, xv). At the end of the first *Enquiry* Hume offers the following characterization of two contrary tendencies:

> The "imagination" of man is naturally sublime, delighted with whatever is remote or extraordinary, and running, without control, into the most distant parts of space and time in order to avoid the objects, which custom has rendered too familiar with it. A correct *Judgement* observes a contrary method, and avoiding all distant and high enquiries, confines itself to common life, and to such subjects as fall under daily practice and experience; leaving the more sublime topics to the embellishment of poets and orators, or to the arts of priests and politicians. (*EHU*, 162)

The result of an exposure to "the force of the Pyrrhonian doubt" is a "salutary" determination to confine ourselves to the matters on which judgment, or philosophic reason, is appropriate. That Hume does not intend this to mean any sort of abandoning of philosophy is perfectly evident. "Those who have a propensity to philosophy will still continue their researches," Hume tells us, "because they reflect, that, besides the immediate pleasure attending such an occupation, *philosophical decisions are nothing but the reflections of common life, methodized and corrected"* (*EHU*, 162; emphasis added). Philosophers who have confronted the strange infirmities of the human understanding "will never be tempted to go beyond common life, so long as they consider the imperfection of those faculties which they employ, their narrow reach, and their inaccurate operations" (ibid.).

Before turning to a consideration of what a philosophic enterprise along the lines Hume suggests would look like, a brief summary of the steps of this lengthy argument may be in order. The starting point for Hume's philosophical investigations seems to have been his grappling with the problem of philosophical skepticism, the arguments of which, with all their power and consistency, seemed to lead only to a condition of aporia or "philosophical melancholy and delirium." The skepticism which concerned Hume most particularly was the skepticism he identified as the "fundamental principle" of modern science, skepticism about the senses. This principle brings into doubt, as Hume demonstrated, the very existence of an external world along with other "maxims of common life" (*EHU*, 150) or what might be called beliefs of prescientific consciousness.

So Hume undertook to examine, as part of his investigation of the powers of the mind, the principle of causation or the belief in the "necessary connexion of cause and effect" which forms the basis of scientific reasoning altogether. Here he made what has been called his "prodigious discovery"—that belief in causation itself is simply a habit of mind, an artifact of the way the human soul is constituted, resting on custom and no different in principle from other beliefs which are features of prescientific consciousness. Thus, he exposed what could be described as a vicious circle: "The first philosophical objection to the evidence of sense or to the opinion of external existence consists in this, that such an opinion, if rested on natural instinct, is contrary to reason, and if referred to reason, is contrary to natural instinct, and *at the same time carries no rational evidence with it, to convince an impartial enquirer*" (*EHU*, 155; emphasis added). Since there is no exit from this circle, or the state of aporia it generates, Hume is determined to rest philosophical reasoning, in the end, directly on prescientific experience. "Nature is always too strong for principle," as he says in expressing his determination to reconnect scientific reason with experience, a connection which as we have seen had been severed by Hume's predecessors, among them Hobbes.

The great subverter of Pyrrhonism or the excessive principles of scepticism is action, and employment, and the occupations of common life. These principles may indeed flourish and triumph in the schools; where it is, indeed, difficult, if not impossible, to refute them. But as soon as they leave the shade, and by the presence of real objects, which actuate our passions and sentiments, are put in opposition to the more powerful principles of our nature, they vanish like smoke, and leave the most determined sceptic in the same condition as other mortals. (*EHU*, 158–59)

When reason is cut loose from its moorings in experience, or common life (an operation Hobbes, for example, attempted), it is indeed possible to generate a chain of reasoning which, though plausible in itself, gives rise only to "momentary amazement and irresolution and confusion." The remedy for this is the addition to philosophy of some of the "gross earthy mixture" of everyday experience. Reason is, as Socrates had discovered, in tension with common life. This fact, which is nothing but a recognition of our fundamental ignorance (Socrates) or of the "strange infirmities of human understanding" (Hume), recommends to us a different sort of philosophy, one which is characterized above all by modernation ("modesty" is Hume's word) and which is careful ever after not to lose its grounding in common life and to preserve its beginnings in everyday experience and ordinary discourse.

6 "This Gross Earthy Mixture": History and Relativism

We have got on to slippery ice where there is no friction and so . . . we are unable to walk. We want to walk: so we need *friction*.

—Ludwig Wittgenstein, *Philosophical Investigations*

We are got into fairy land, long ere we have reached the last steps of our theory; and *there* we have no reason to trust our common methods of argument. . . . Our line is too short to fathom such immense abysses.

—Hume, *An Enquiry concerning Human Understanding*

Among the numerous parallels between the philosophical writings of Hume and Wittgenstein perhaps the most striking is their similar discovery of the difficulties and perplexities which philosophy gets into when it is not grounded in common life. Notwithstanding the usual view of Wittgenstein as primarily interested in language, his concern was focused, like Hume's, on the nature of the human activities which underlie language. We learn from Wittgenstein that a great number of philosophical problems arise only or mainly from the tendency of philosophy to get disconnected from those activities. "The confusions which occupy us arise when language is like an engine idling, not when it is doing work."[1] Philosophy must get "back to rough ground," in Wittgenstein's view, in order to see things clearly or perspicuously. The philosopher must look at language in actual use, in ordinary contexts, if he is to make headway.

In just such a manner and for the same reasons Hume recommends the addition to philosophy of some of "this gross earthy mixture," by which he means the disposition of many "honest gentlemen" who "have carried their thoughts very little beyond those objects, which are every day expos'd to their senses" (*T*, 272). The rough ground for Hume means "common life." Accurate philosophy compels us to confront the "strange infirmities of human understanding" and teaches us to see that genuine philosophy is really only "reflections of common life, methodized and corrected" (*EHU*, 162). In commenting on a particular philosophical theory that "everything is full of God," Hume suggests that it is "too bold ever to carry conviction with it to a man, sufficiently apprized of the weakness of human reason and the narrow limits to which it is confined" (*EHU*, 72). In a passage which sounds remarkably like Wittgenstein, he continues:

> Though the chain of arguments which conduct to it were ever so logical, there must arise a strong suspicion, if not an absolute assurance, that it has carried us quite beyond the reach of our faculties, when it leads to conclusions so extraordinary, and so remote from common life and experience. We are got into fairy land, long ere we have reached the last steps of our theory; and *there* we have no reason to trust our common methods of argument, or to think that our usual analogies and probabilities have any authority. Our line is too short to fathom such immense abysses. (*EHU*, 72)

Why History?

The disconnection from common life to which philosophers in their closets are liable is opposite to, but no better than, the overly interested posture of what Hume calls the "man of business," who is too interested to be able to see things clearly. "When a man of business enters into life and action, he is more apt to consider the characters of men, as they have relation to his interest, than as they stand in themselves," according to Hume. The man of business thus "has his judgment warped on every occasion by the violence of his passion" (*E*, 567–68). But Hume contrasts this with the philosopher who "contemplates characters and manners in his closet." In such a case "the general and abstract view of the objects" leaves him unable to judge accurately. "The sentiments of nature have no room to play, and he scarce feels the difference between vice and virtue" (*E*, 568). If the man of business is too interested to judge accurately, the philosopher in his closet is unable to do so for the opposite reason; he loses his bearings when he casts off the prephilosophic understanding of things, since only this enables us to orient ourselves.[2]

Hume's solution to the dilemma of this pair of unsatisfactory alternatives is to recommend a kind of writing which is neither too interested nor too abstract and dispassionate to understand human things accurately: history. "History keeps in a just medium betwixt these extremes, and places the objects in their true point of view. The writers of history, as well as their readers, are sufficiently interested in the characters and events, to have a lively sentiment of blame or praise: and, at the same time, have no particular interest or concern to pervert their judgment" (*E*, 568).[3] It is surely no accident that Hume the philosopher turned—at the point in his career when he wrote the passage just quoted—to the writing of history.[4] It is not implausible to suggest that the political philosophy of the mature Hume is, in fact, to be found in the *History of England*, together with the *Dialogues* and *Essays* (a number of which are historical in character).[5] It has been suggested that in addition to the *History of England*, "any number of Hume's other works are as much historical as philosophical; and there is a significant sense in which even his most 'philosophical' is historical."[6]

The basis of the turn to history is Hume's insight that any generalization about human things—any principles of what Hume calls the moral sciences—must be based on experience. Excepting only the abstract sciences which deal with quantity and number, "all other enquiries of men regard only matters of fact and existence" (*EHU*, 163–64). The existence of any thing whatsoever, as Hume has shown, "can only be proved by arguments from its cause or its effect; and these arguments are founded entirely on experience" (*EHU*, 164). Because history is the record of human experience, it "is not only a valuable part of knowledge, but opens the door to many other parts, and affords materials to most of the sciences" (*E*, 566). "Indeed," Hume continues, "if we consider the shortness of human life, and our limited knowledge, even of what passes in our own time, we must be sensible that we should be for ever children in understanding, were it not for this invention, which extends our experience to all past ages, and to the most distant nations. . . . A man acquainted with history may, in some respect, be said to have lived from the beginning of the world, and to have been making continual additions to his stock of knowledge in every century" (*E*, 566–67). The primacy of prephilosophical experience or common life is thus reflected in the high place given by Hume to history. In studying the phenomena of human life, philosophic historians are superior to philosophers simply, who are "apt to bewilder themselves in the subtility of their speculations" (*E*, 567).

This view of history could be said to follow from Hume's recombination of science with experience or prudence, based on the investigation of causation. That investigation led Hume to see that "all knowledge resolves itself into probability, and becomes at last of the same nature with that evidence, which we employ in common life" (*T*, 181). If all knowledge about human things has this character, then all moral philosophy is essentially history, or the lessons of common life. This explains why Hume's philosophy moves closer to letters; the quality of literary products is dependent on the degree to which they accord with our experience. A character drawn in a novel, who strikes us as unrealistic, does so because the combination of qualities and character, or of qualities and action, is not consistent with our experience of the moral regularities of our world. "If we would explode any forgery in history," Hume tells us, "we cannot make use of a more convincing argument, than to prove, that the actions ascribed to any person are directly contrary to the course of nature, and that no human motives, in such circumstances, could ever induce him to such a conduct" (*EHU,* 84). Thus in writing history, or novels, for that matter, we must be guided by accurate "reflexions on common life." Any claim—such as that of Hobbes, for example—to have developed a new "scientific" philosophy of human nature should be regarded with more than a little suspicion. Moral philosophy or the science of human nature will always be closer to poetry than to mathematics.

Hume and Relativism

The claim that Hume's *History* is properly read as a kind of philosophy requires some justification. I emphasize that I do not mean to restrict this only to the *History,* which would be to grant one work undue emphasis. But taken together with the *History,* the *Essays, Natural History of Religion,* and *Dialogues*—all forms of writing not generally regarded as philosophy pure and simple—constitute, in my view, a genuine Humean political philosophy. According to Constance Noble Stockton, only since about 1960 has it "ceased to be necessary to argue against the previously received opinion that Hume's *History of England* is an aberration of no relevance to his philosophical writings. From one recent perspective, on the contrary, it is viewed as the logical culmination of his life's work."[7] I share this view, but before I turn to a detailed consideration of Hume's teaching in the historical writings it is necessary to confront an obstacle of major proportions.

It is generally accepted in one form or another that sometime in the middle of the eighteenth century the principles of modern natural right, which had been predominant in political philosophy for more than a century, began to be displaced or eroded by a new awareness of the importance of history, and of the historical character of human judgment itself.[8] This historical consciousness culminated in the nineteenth century (some would say it continues its dominance today) in the writings of Hegel, Marx, and others. Eventually it transformed itself into full-fledged "historicism," the doctrine that every man and every mind is the product of a particular historical age and, as such, fundamentally impenetrable or incomprehensible to human beings in other ages.[9] The obstacle to the suggestion that Hume's political philosophy is found in his *History* consists, then, in the alleged incompatibility of philosophy, understood as the pursuit of truths which are true by nature and thus transhistorical, and history, the record of the various opinions, beliefs, and presuppositions of different ages. Because Hume wrote at the beginning of the "historical age" (a phrase Hume himself used),[10] some would say he should not be held to so strict a standard. But surely if his *History* is to be taken seriously we must attempt to confront the obstacle on his behalf. Where does Hume stand on the relation between historical consciousness or historicism and philosophy?

Stockton identifies E. C. Mossner, the great Hume biographer, as the writer chiefly responsible for the view that Hume's historical writings are the culmination of his life's work. I find this ironic in view of what can only be called Mossner's historicism, since historicism devalues any history written in another age. Stockton wrote, "According to this perspective, developed in the writings of E. C. Mossner and others, the central of Hume's intentions was to set forth the roots and branches of a 'science of man,' to do for 'moral philosophy' what Newton had done for 'natural philosophy.'"[11] This is surely not historicism. Yet, listen to Mossner himself, in the chapter on the *History of England* in his biography of Hume: "Certainly the *History of England* could never be mistaken for the product of any age other than that in which it was written. Its merits and its limitations are the merits and limitations of the Enlightenment."[12] Indeed Mossner is even more explicit. After quoting Dewey to the effect that the writing of history is itself an historical event, he informs us that "every age, consequently, requires its own interpretation of the past and no other will quite do. Although Hume's *History* is *not for our times,* it is proper to turn to it for either of two reasons: to enjoy it as literature, or to learn from it how the greatest mind of the Enlightenment interpreted the past for his age."[13] To construct a more purely historicist judgment than this would be difficult. Could Hume have accepted it?

Before turning to this question some other evidence for the thesis of historicism should be added. In today's terminology, Hume's require-ment that moral or human sciences be grounded in common life bears strong resemblance to the various approaches loosely called "phe-nomenological." The varieties of phenomenology share with each other the principle that, to understand the social activities of human beings in a meaningful sense, one must understand and judge by the standards in use by the human actors themselves.[14] The claim that one must under-stand social action from within the actor's perspective entails a shift in the empirical ground of a moral science, because what is empirical, or what simply is, can only be ascertained, according to this view, by what the actors say. Cultural variables are thus decisive in determining not only what a scientist chooses to study but also, for example, what the politics, economics, or morality consists of in a given society.

It is difficult to see how the phenomenological approach can avoid wholesale relativism, a relativism incompatible with what we have seen to be Hume's understanding of philosophy. One can find evidence in Hume to suggest a view similar to this. In the *Essays*, for example, he tells us that "the manners of a people change very considerably from one age to another, either by great alterations in their government, by the mix-ture of new people, or by that inconstancy to which all human affairs are subject" (*E*, 205–6). Or elsewhere: "Man is a very variable being, and susceptible of many different opinions, principles, and rules of conduct. What may be true, while he adheres to one way of thinking, will be found false, when he has embraced an opposite set of manners and opinions" (*E*, 255–56).

Hume confronted the historicist problem directly. His writings con-tain two pieces devoted precisely to the issue of relativism. One is a short work published as an appendix to the posthumous edition of the *Enquir-ies* (1777), entitled only "A Dialogue." In it Hume reports a conversation with one "Palamedes," who attempts to confound Hume by his disguised recital of the bizarre moral customs of a culture Hume purported to admire (that of ancient Greece), only to be confuted in turn by Hume's explanation of the universal principles which he believes guide all judgment of blame and approbation. The second piece, one of his early essays entitled "Of the Standard of Taste," addresses the question what are the requisite conditions for sound judgments of taste, either in morals or in art—in other words, what is the ground under objective judgments about either moral customs or works of art of different ages and peoples?

Is there a natural basis for moral judgments, a natural component in the judgments we make about virtue and vice, or are such judgments purely conventional and thus appropriate only in the cultural or historical situations in which they are made? "The great variety of taste, as well as of opinion, which prevails in the world, is too obvious not to have fallen under every one's observation," Hume begins. The "great inconsistency and contrariety" is still more obvious to "those who can enlarge their view to contemplate distant nations and remote ages." The variety is no illusion, according to Hume, because the variety of taste will be found, "on examination, to be still greater in reality than in appearance"—even though, at least within a given language, men seem to be in complete agreement: "there are certain terms in every language, which import blame, and others praise; and all men, who use the same tongue, must agree in their application of them" (*E,* 227). Close inspection reveals that agreement in the general terms is illusory because when it comes to particulars—that is, to what counts as a case of, for example, affectation or coldness in writing—the "seeming unanimity vanishes."

Hume is careful to preserve a distinction between matters of taste, on the one hand, and matters of "opinion and science," on the other. Whereas in matters of taste the apparent agreement seems to vanish when we turn to particulars, in matters of opinion and science the case is often opposite: "the difference among men is there oftener found to lie in generals than in particulars; and to be less in reality than in appearance. An explanation of the terms commonly ends the controversy; and the disputants are surprized to find, that they had been quarrelling, while at bottom they agreed in their judgment" (*E,* 227).

To which of these kinds of judgment—taste or opinion—do moral judgments belong? Those who regard moral judgments as founded on sentiment are inclined, Hume tells us, to find them more akin to matters of taste—that is, to be marked by differences *greater* in reality than they seem at first in appearance. Those who insist to the contrary that most men agree about the principles according to which blame and praise are distributed, simply because all languages agree that virtue is praiseworthy while vice is odious, should realize that "the merit of delivering true general precepts in ethics is indeed small." "Whoever recommends any moral virtues, really does no more than is implied in the terms themselves" because the terms themselves are only general and by themselves tell us nothing about which human actions they properly apply to (*E*, 229).

Nevertheless, he says, it is "natural for us to seek a *Standard of Taste;* a rule, by which the various sentiments of men may be reconciled; at least, a decision, afforded, confirming one sentiment, and condemning another" (*E*, 229). Even if we have doubts about placing moral judgments among the sentiments, this approach must interest us because, in the case of sentiments, relativism seems *harder* to escape, and thus the location of a standard of taste in these matters (of artistic judgment, for example) a fortiori solves the problem for morals.[15] There is a way, Hume tells us, of approaching these matters, "a species of philosophy, which cuts off all hope of success in such an attempt." What follows is an extraordinarily prescient account of the sort of relativism which dominates contemporary social science of the positivist variety. This species of philosophy, as Hume describes it, divides judgment from sentiment without qualification; it declares sentiment always right, because it has reference to nothing outside the man who feels it. On the other hand are matters of understanding or reason, where all determinations are not right, "because they have a reference to something beyond themselves, to wit, real matters of fact." Thus Hume anticipates exactly the formulations of Ayer or Stevenson, which place moral judgments in the realm of personal preferences (affective judgments) and divide them sharply from factual statements, which are verifiable by reference to the empirical world.[16]

Hume is not satisfied with this extension of the old adage (presumably *de gustibus non est disputandum*), even though it, "by passing into a proverb, seems to have attained the sanction of common sense." The grounds of his dissatisfaction are the central point of my inquiry. Hume offers an account of the ground of judgments of taste which successfully, if not apodictically, overcomes the positivist position, without succumbing to any sort of actor-centered ethnocentrism—by beginning from the common sense fact of unequal human abilities at judging *anything*.[17] Even though the principle of relativism in tastes has attained the sanction of common sense, Hume says,

> there is certainly a species of common sense, which opposes it, or at least serves to modify or restrain it. Whoever would assert an equality of genius and elegance between Ogilby and Milton, or Bunyan and Addison, would be thought to defend no less an extravagance, than if he had maintained a mole-hill to be as high as Teneriffe, or a pond as extensive as the ocean. Though there may be found persons, who give the preference to the former authors; no one pays attention to such a taste; and we pronounce without scruple the sentiment of these pretended critics to be absurd and ridiculous. (*E*, 230–31)

Anyone who consults his own experience will find this to be the case, according to Hume, and this experience in turn cannot be ignored. Although in cases where judgments are difficult because "the objects seem near an equality" we do allow for disagreement, we must not allow this to govern all our thinking about the nature of such judgment. When we consider the kinds of cases adduced in Hume's example, "the principle of natural equality of tastes is then totally forgot." This has striking ramifications, because once we admit there *are* different capacities for judging, we find ourselves in the complicated middle ground of actual human experience (from which philosophers are continuously trying to escape), where we are faced with the task of elucidating the characteristics of good judgment.

Hume introduces the problem by trying to show how subtle the task of judging can sometimes be. He cites a number of examples of critical literary judgment which require exacting attention and perspicacity. We must admit that in hard cases, at least, the "finer emotions of the mind

are of a very tender and delicate nature, and require the concurrence of
many favourable circumstances to make them play with facility and
exactness, according to their general established principles" (*E*, 232).
The task, then, is to elucidate the favorable circumstances required for
establishing some sort of standard of taste. Unfavorable circumstances
can be of two sorts, according to Hume: "the least exterior hindrance to
such small springs, or the least internal disorder, disturbs their motion,
and confounds the operations of the whole machine" (ibid.).

Hume's Appeal to Common Life

Before considering Hume's detailed account of the external and
internal circumstances which are indispensable to sound judgment, I will
reflect briefly on the philosophical foundation of his reasoning. How is
Hume's account different from the mere assertion, by any critic, of the
universality of his or her judgments? Adherents of the view which denies
any natural ground to judgments of taste may simply deny that Hume's
account can be true. But here Hume has the advantage of an appeal to
common life, to the phenomena, to the facts of human experience. That it
requires "a careful eye" to trace the general principles of blame and
approbation is no more a refutation of Hume's point than the fact that it
requires careful training to be a doctor or a physicist means that the
endeavors of medicine or physics are based on principles without any
natural foundation. The standard of taste which Hume seeks is no less a
standard because it is part of the human world. Hume believes, in fact,
that moral judgments are grounded not less but more solidly in nature
than are the judgments which arise in connection with what Hume calls
"speculative systems." The former are, after all, connected more closely
to everyday human experience, and here the empirical evidence cannot
fail to convince anyone who is not already in the grip of a speculative
system. The facts Hume appeals to are similar to facts about health—
judgments about which cause us little difficulty in ordinary experience,
even though we may be wrong about them.

It appears then, that, amidst all the variety and caprice of taste, there are certain general principles of approbation or blame, whose influence a careful eye may trace in all operations of the mind. Some particular forms or qualities, from the original structure of the internal fabric, are calculated to please, and others to displease; and if they fail of their effect in any particular instance, *it is from some apparent defect or imperfection in the organ.* A man in a fever would not insist on his palate as able to decide concerning flavors; nor would one, affected with jaundice, pretend to give a verdict with regard to colours. (*E*, 233; emphasis added)

But can we say what constitutes the healthy state of the judgmental faculties? Has Hume not simply pushed the original problem of relativism back one step, where he must confront it again? He would answer that the question to which he has shown it to be connected—the question of healthy organs of judgment—is much less susceptible to the objections of skeptical philosophy which initiated the search for a standard of taste. This is the case because of the strength of the appeal to the notion of health itself, which has such solid grounding in ordinary human experience, in the phenomena of everyday life and thought. "If, in the sound state of the organ, there be an entire or a considerable uniformity of sentiment among men, we may thence derive an idea of the perfect beauty; in like manner as the appearance of objects in day-light, to the eye of a man in health, is denominated their true and real colour, even while colour is allowed to be merely a phantasm of the senses." This brings out more clearly what was asserted above: the standard is no less a standard because it is allowed to be a part of the human world, constituted by human nature, rather than a part of the natural world in the strict, nonhuman sense.

One might object that the analogy with sight is misleading because vision is a physical phenomenon. The near uniformity of human judgments about color may be quite different from judgments about morals or other matters of sentiment (or partly of sentiment). After all, the relativist bases his position on the apparent differences in the judgments of taste among different cultures, if not different individuals. Moreover, might not the standards of healthy judgment be entirely culturally determined and hence bring us no nearer to a qualified standard of taste? Can Hume respond to this objection? Here the "Dialogue" appended to the *Enquiry concerning the Principles of Morals* is helpful.

In this brief work Hume presents a conversation between the author and one Palamedes, "who is as great a rambler in his principles as in his person, and who has run over, by study and travel, almost every region of the intellectual and material world" (*ECPM*, 324). Palamedes attempts to trick his friend, by reporting—as the moral principles of a strange country called Fourli—some of the actual practices and incidents of Greek and Roman moral life, including the practice of exposing infants and (as an incident) the assassination of Caesar. He describes these as strange and bizarre customs which are approved by the natives, in order to show how utterly unaccountable are the moral judgments of different nations and cultures.[18] After discovering Palamedes' artifice, Hume responds that "there are no manners so innocent or reasonable, but may be rendered odious or ridiculous, if measured by a standard, unknown to the persons." Is this Hume in relativist dress? He accuses Palamedes of having "no indulgence for the manners and customs of different ages. Would you try a Greek or Roman by the common law of England? Hear him defend himself by his own maxims; and then pronounce." This is indeed a surprise. Hume proceeds to show Palamedes how strange the modern chivalric code, or the practice of dueling, must appear to a sensible Greek or Roman. Apparently he responds in this fashion because he assumes that Palamedes intends to praise modern morals at the expense of those of the ancients. But Palamedes denies any such aim. "I only meant to represent the uncertainty of all these judgments concerning characters; and to convince you, that *fashion, vogue, custom, and law, were the chief foundation of all moral determinations*" (*ECPM*, 333; emphasis added).

Here, then, we have the relativist thesis stated with utmost clarity. Palamedes professes his astonishment at the difference between Greek and French manners, especially because "these two people are supposed to be the most similar in their national character of any in ancient and modern times." If these differ so drastically, how could we ever expect to find natural or universal standards of moral judgment? Hume answers, "By tracing matters, replied I, a little higher, and examining the first principle, which each nation establishes, of blame or censure. The Rhine flows north, the Rhone south; yet both spring from the *same* mountain, and are also actuated, in their opposite directions, by the *same* principle of gravity. The different inclinations of the ground, on which they run, cause all the difference of their courses."

Hume devoted the entire *Enquiry concerning the Principles of Morals* to elucidating precisely the "principle of gravity" in the case of morals. In "A Dialogue" he undertakes to show Palamedes that the differences in morals which he has raised as examples are superficial and that they can be accounted for by careful consideration of the principles which underlie them. One example will suffice. The two fundamental moral principles Hume treats in the second *Enquiry* are usefulness and agreeableness, and in each case the criterion may have reference either to ourselves or to others. Together these principles account for our moral judgments. The four principles are occasionally, if not frequently, in tension with each other, with the result that a subtle shift in perspective can account for a considerable difference in moral judgments. In the case of French gallantry, for example, as opposed to the close confinement in which Greeks kept women and families, Hume has this to say: "Our neighbors, it seems, have resolved to sacrifice some of the domestic to the sociable pleasures; and to prefer ease, freedom, and an open commerce, to strict fidelity and constancy. The ends are both good, and are somewhat difficult to reconcile; nor need we be surprised, if the customs of nations incline too much, sometimes to the one side, sometimes to the other" (*ECPM*, 335). He can trace the principles underlying different moral judgments to the same sources; they are consistent with human capacities and needs wherever found and thus are grounded in nature and not merely convention. That human beings will always differ on such points, or that they may reason badly, bothers Hume not at all: "that they all reason aright with regard to this subject, more than with regard to any other, it is not incumbent on any moralist to show. It is sufficient, that the original principles of censure or blame are uniform, and that erroneous conclusions can be corrected by sounder reasoning and larger experience" (*ECPM, 336*).

In tracing the differences in customs and standards of taste, it is helpful to look at diverse political circumstances, differences in wealth or natural endowments, geography, and so on. For example, Hume says, "we may observe, that, as the difference between war and peace is the greatest that arises among nations and public societies, it produces also the greatest variations in moral sentiment, and diversifies the most our ideas of virtue and personal merit" (*ECPM, 337*).[19] He contrasts different nations which emphasize to different degrees the useful and the agreeable, or the self-regarding over the other-regarding virtues. Sometimes these differences can be explained by tracing them to "an early bias" of the mind—for example, the Swiss bias toward industry and practical arts. Hume never denies that this sort of philosophical investigation of morals is open to objections or that it requires a particularly sensitive and discerning intelligence. His aim is not to discover an explanation of such definitive rigor that agreement to it can be compelled. He is not teaching *the* system of morality, but inquiring into the general principles which—together with the diverse circumstances in which human beings find themselves—explain the various actual systems of moral judgments, bringing them under the rubric of a philosophic account of morals.

Healthy Judgment

We now return to the question raised earlier but not satisfactorily answered: Can we say what constitutes the healthy state of judgmental faculties? Hume devotes considerable attention to this in "Of the Standard of Taste," and it is worth sketching briefly the salient points of his account. He begins from the crucial feature of his rejection of relativism, namely, the common sense denial of "the principle of the natural equality of tastes" (*E*, 231). Once we admit there are different degrees of good judgment in arts, literature, or morals, we still need to identify the characteristics of good taste and judgment. The foundation of Hume's account is what he calls a "natural delicacy" of taste: The cause of a great deal of disagreement about taste is "the want of that *delicacy* of imagination, which is requisite to convey a sensibility" of inner emotions or distinctions. "This delicacy every one pretends to: Every one talks of it; and would reduce every kind of taste or sentiment to its standard" (*E*, 234). But Hume appeals—by the use of a story about wine tasting from *Don Quixote*—to our ordinary experience in taste. Everyone is aware that some palates are more discriminating and some ears are more finely attuned to subtleties in speech or music; it is a small step to the notion that this is true for all kinds of taste. "Where the organs are so fine, as to allow nothing to escape them; and at the same time so exact as to perceive every ingredient in the composition: This we call delicacy of taste, whether we employ these terms in the literal or metaphorical sense" (*E*, 235). Hume speaks chiefly in terms of the perception of beauty and the qualities in works of art. But the principle applies equally to discernment in moral sentiments. To judge the moral flavor of human actions is to exercise in sensitive discrimination of "beauty or deformity" of a different kind: our moral judgments rest in part on the sentiments, which are what taste is all about.

The possession of such natural delicacy of taste is, however, not enough. "Though there be naturally a wide difference in point of delicacy between one person and another, nothing tends further to encrease and improve this talent, than *practice* in a particular art" (*E*, 237). In terms of moral judgment, this suggests the necessity for wide exposure to different cultures, to different circumstances of human life, and thus recommends the study of history.[20]

To these features of healthy organs of taste, Hume adds two others which speak for themselves. The proper exercise of taste requires that the judge "preserve his mind free from all *prejudice*, and allow nothing to enter into his consideration, but the very object which is submitted to his examination." This is especially important for the critic "of a different age or nation," who, by allowing himself to judge "full of the manners of his own age and country, rashly condemns what seemed admirable in the eyes of those" he is concerned with. "His taste evidently departs from the true standards; and of consequence loses all credit and authority" (*E*, 239). The last requirement is what Hume calls "good sense," that is, the employment of reason to check the influence of prejudice. "Reason, if not an essential part of taste, is at least requisite to the operations of this latter faculty" (*E*, 240).

Hume suggests that the coincidence of all the conditions requisite for healthy judgment will necessarily be quite rare, because the possible defects are so common: "Under some or other of these imperfections, the generality of men labour; and hence a true judge in the finer arts is observed, even during the most polished ages, to be so rare a character: Strong sense, united to delicate sentiment, improved by practice, perfected by comparison, and cleared of all prejudice, can alone entitle critics to this valuable character; and the joint verdict of such, wherever they are to be found, is the true standard of taste and beauty" (*E*, 241).

At this point Hume responds with a question on behalf of the reader: "But where are such critics to be found? By what marks are they to be known? How distinguish them from pretenders? These questions are embarrassing; and seem to throw us back into the same uncertainty, from which, during the course of this essay, we have endeavoured to extricate ourselves" (*E*, 241). But surely it is not so difficult to think that we can discern human beings who are themselves more discerning, less prejudiced, of wider experience than others. As to exactly how the best critics are to be distinguished, "if we consider the matter aright," Hume tells us, "these are questions of fact, not of sentiment. Whether any particular person be endowed with good sense and a delicate imagination, free from prejudice, may often be the subject of dispute," but in principle the dispute can be resolved once we accept the distinctions to which Hume directs our attention. It is enough to have proved, he says, "that the taste of all individuals is not on an equal footing" (*E*, 242), and few who possess even rudimentary common sense would deny this.[21]

One may object that Hume speaks throughout the essay only of judgments of taste, as in art, and not of moral judgments. We have blurred the distinction, partly because on Hume's account moral judgments are at least partly matters of sentiment, as are judgments of beauty. But for Hume the principle which explains aesthetic judgment is important in judgments about all sorts of matters, including the sciences. On Hume's account, in fact, if we compare the place of such a principle in matters of sentiment (in artistic beauty and morals) with its place in science, the advantage, for reliability and decisiveness, rests with the former.

> In reality, the difficulty of finding, even in particulars, the standard of taste, is not so great as it is represented. Though in speculation, we may readily avow a certain criterion in science and deny it in sentiment, the matter is found in practice to be much more hard to ascertain in the former case than in the latter. Theories of abstract philosophy, systems of profound theology, have prevailed during one age: In a successive period, these have been universally exploded: Their absurdity has been detected: Other theories and systems have supplied their place, which again gave place to their successors: And nothing has been experienced more liable to the revolutions of chance and fashion than these pretended decisions of science. (*E*, 242)

What vitiates the claim of the speculative sciences to a solid and reliable ground is their very abstractness, or their distance from the shared and solid ground of common life. The closeness of ordinary judgments of taste and sentiment to common life supplies their relative stability and helps to guarantee their reliability. Matters of taste and sentiment are, at the highest level, fairly consistent: "Though a civilized nation may easily be mistaken in the choice of their admired philosopher, they never have been found long to err, in their affection for a favourite epic or tragic author" (*E*, 243). Thus the speculative character of speculation deprives it of the grounding in common life which characterizes the standard of taste Hume has articulated.[22] In Hume's words, "the case is not the same with moral principles, as with speculative opinions of any kind." The former are relatively hard to change, while speculative opinions "are in continual flux and revolution" (*E*, 246).

Natural and Moral Evidence

A passage from the first *Enquiry* elucidates Hume's suggestion that the "constant and universal principles of human nature" are discovered by historical inquiry. It is another passage which bears a striking resemblance to the later Wittgenstein's suggestion that the features of natural human languages are undergirded by the natural conventions called "forms of life" by Wittgenstein.[23] "Should a traveller, returning from a far country, bring us an account of men, wholly different from any with whom we were ever acquainted; men, who were entirely divested of avarice, ambition, or revenge; who knew no pleasure but friendship, generosity, and public spirit; we should immediately from these circumstances, detect the falsehood, and prove him a liar, with the same certainty as if he had stuffed his narration with stories of centaurs and dragons, miracles and prodigies" (*EHU*, 84).

Hume's point is simply that human beings characteristically exhibit not only certain qualities of character but certain constellations of them, and that we are quite confident as regards the broad outlines of the moral universe based on our experience of human characters in common life. The moral no less than the physical universe is common to all human beings. In both, the regional differences are dwarfed by common general principles. This is part of the Humean argument that we reason about moral regularities in the same manner as about natural or physical ones. "*Natural* and *Moral* evidence link together, and form only one chain of argument" (*EHU*, 90), he writes. "The same experienced union has the same effect on the mind, whether the united objects be motives, volition, and actions; or figure and motion. We may change the names of things; but their nature and their operation on the understanding never change" (*EHU*, 91).

Despite differences in the manners of different ages, to which Hume is quite sensitive, certain regularities in human life are undeniable; languages supply us with evidence of this. "Among different languages, even where we cannot suspect the least connexion or communication, it is found, that the words, expressive of ideas, the most compounded, do yet nearly correspond to each other: a certain proof that the simple ideas, comprehended in the compound ones, were bound together by some universal principle, which had an equal influence on all mankind" (*EHU*, 23). In an appendix to the second *Enquiry* Hume compares Livy's biographical picture of Hannibal, with its balanced picture of virtues and vices, to "the character of Alexander the Sixth, to be found in Guicciardin," and suggests that the latter "is a proof that even the moderns, where they speak naturally, hold the same language with the ancients" (*ECPM*, 320–21).

Since the general shape of the human situation is manifest in common life, common life is the ground for any moral investigation (moral in the Humean sense), and no acceptable theory may transform or eliminate its fixed features. "Where would be the foundation of *morals*, if particular characters had no certain or determinate power to produce particular sentiments, and these sentiments had no constant operation on actions? And with what pretence could we employ our *criticism* on any poet or polite author, if we could not pronounce the conduct and sentiments of his actors either natural or unnatural to such characters and in such circumstances?" (*EHU*, 90). Unfortunately philosophy—in its usual character, at least—has a tendency to distort, by reduction, the language (and with it the orientation) of common life. In his richly suggestive article "Hume's Historical Theory of Meaning," Donald Livingston has argued that it is a tendency of philosophy, or at least of modern philosophy, to try "to reduce the language of common life to some favored theoretical language. This sort of reduction is usually also part of a program to *ontologize* the theoretical language and to hold that reality can be grasped by it alone, common language being, at best an inadequate approximation."[24] He goes on to show how this is the basis of the Cartesian doctrine of "double existence" and is manifested in a wide variety of philosophical projects in the last three centuries which reject the perspective of common sense or common life. "Hume's philosophical method," Livingston maintains, "with the theory of meaning internal to it, is designed to check the tendency of philosophers to ontologize theoretical language and to rescue the language of common life from the category of 'illusion.' "[25] Hume's philosophy is not only grounded in common life, but "leaves everything as it is," to quote Wittgenstein. The prescientific consciousness or common sense is "methodized and corrected" by philosophy but not rejected.

It has recently been suggested that, whereas the shared features of common life may once have been adequate to delineate the principal landmarks of the moral landscape, this is no longer the case in the twentieth century. The disintegration of a moral consensus, this argument runs, has deprived us of the possibility of any genuine moral philosophy. In a recent study which makes this argument Richard Bernstein considers the claims of a variety of "hermeneutical" or "phenomenological" approaches in the human sciences, and in an appendix he prints a letter from Hans Georg Gadamer responding to his argument in terms evocative of Hume.

Gadamer maintains that the loss of moral consensus is in fact a problem only among philosophers, an artifact of philosophy.[26] Hume would not be surprised. Philosophers who complain that there is no longer enough "substance" in common life on which to base moral philosophy are probably only in need of an introduction to the "many honest gentlemen, who being always employ'd in their domestic affairs, or amusing themselves in common recreations, have carried their thoughts very little beyond those objects which are everyday expos'd to their senses" (*T*, 272). These "do well to keep themselves in their present situation," Hume continues, "and instead of refining them into philosophers, I wish we cou'd communicate to our founders of systems a share of this gross earthy mixture, as an ingredient, which they commonly stand much in need of" (ibid.). The problem is not with human understanding, in general, but with philosophic reasoning which gets out of touch with common life and then seeks to set itself up as an authority. This Humean argument, I believe, goes a long way toward explaining the character of all Hume's later writings, in both style and substance.

For all his emphasis on common life, Hume is not concerned with finding a moral philosophy or science of human nature which will serve as a practical guide. He turns to history because he is concerned to understand the human condition, to discover the principles, both natural and moral, which illuminate human life. David Fate Norton has pointed out that philosophical skepticism has a long traditional association with a certain kind of history, "a history on which the cogency of the skeptical claims about the weakness and fallibility of the human mind depend. Thus one finds many skeptics compiling a history of human opinion. . . . The point of such a history is to reveal the multiplicity of man's opinions as well as something about his nature—what his ideas are and how he comes to hold them and to hold them as true."[27]

This seems to be an accurate description of the kind of philosophic history which accurately depicts the moral landscape. For Hume, however, claims about "the weakness and fallibility of the human mind" were not "based on" a study of history but came directly from his philosophical investigation, and came in particular from the acute embarrassment caused in philosophy by its confrontation with common life. Common life or experience, once it became for Hume the touchstone of philosophy, pushed history into the preeminent place it occupies in all Hume's later work. A philosopher may "amaze and confuse" himself with profound reasonings, but "the first and most trivial event in life will put to flight all his doubts and scruples, and leave him the same, in every point of action or speculation, with . . . those who never concerned themselves in any philosophical researches" (*EHU*, 160). Philosophy does not change the world in any way, according to Hume; it discovers only "the whimsical condition of mankind, who must act and reason and believe; though they are not able, by their most diligent enquiry, to satisfy themselves concerning the foundation of these operations" (ibid.).

In his essay "The Sceptic," Hume considers at some length whether philosophy can be expected to benefit us in practical terms. The essay, perhaps his most beautiful, teaches us not to expect much from philosophy, "the *medicine of the mind,* so much boasted." Even if philosophy can help us to see what is valuable, we must ourselves value something in order to find happiness in it, and this is what philosophy cannot teach. "No man would ever be unhappy, could he alter his feelings. . . . But of this resource nature has, in a great measure, deprived us. The fabric and constitution of our mind no more depends on our choice, than that of our body" (*E*, 168). Not only the "ignorant and thoughtless part of mankind" are in this situation. "Even upon the wise and thoughtful, nature has a prodigious influence. . . . The empire of philosophy extends over a few; and with regard to these too, her authority is very weak and limited" (*E*, 169). We must not expect much, then, from philosophy, in the way of practical results. The furthest Hume will go is to suggest that "perhaps, the chief benefit, which results from philosophy, arises in an indirect manner, and proceeds more from its secret, insensible influence, than from its immediate application" (*E*, 170).

If philosophy is of little or no practical use, however, and if it more-over has a tendency to amaze and confuse, not to say torment us, why do philosophers engage in it? What can explain the philosophizing of Hume, who was so concerned with the problematic aspects of philosophy? The answer is found in a number of hints scattered through his writings, and the answer helps to confirm that Hume did not abandon philosophy for history but understood himself to be improving philosophy—or keeping it honest—by the addition of "this gross earthy mixture." The closing sentence of "The Sceptic" is this: "Even to reason so carefully concerning [life], and to fix with accuracy its just idea, would be overvaluing it, were it not that, to some tempers, this occupation is one of the most amusing, in which life could possibly be employed" (*E*, 180). Philosophy, for Hume, is rewarding in itself, so long as its feet are on the ground of common life.

7 "The Gradual Progress of Improvement": History and Political Economy

The rise, progress, perfection and decline of art and science, are curious objects of contemplation, and intimately connected with a narration of civil transactions. The events of no particular period can be fully accounted for, but by considering the degrees of advancement, which men have reached in those particulars.

—Hume, *History of England*

With this chapter we turn our attention from the nature of philosophy to Hume's understanding of society, in particular his understanding of historical progress toward the kind of society he calls civilized or cultivated, because it is marked by freedom and toleration, among other things.

Ancients and Moderns

We have already suggested, and will again in chapter 9, that in important respects Hume's teaching about philosophy or reason resembles that of classical political philosophy: Hume shares with Plato and Aristotle, for example, the practice of keeping in the forefront the beginning points for philosophy, namely, common life or ordinary speech about the things in

109

question; he shares with the ancients a rejection of scientific or abstract philosophizing in favor of what I have called "literary" philosophy; he does not expect philosophy to be justified by its utility nor marked by apodictic certainty; and he persists in the classical view that neither human life nor political life is or could be made rational, so that philosophy is always at least potentially dangerous to civic life. "It seems then," he accuses the unnamed interlocutor in section 11 of the first *Enquiry*, "that you leave politics entirely out of the question, and never suppose, that a wise magistrate can justly be jealous of certain tenets of philosophy, such as those of Epicurus, which denying a divine existence, and consequently a providence and a future state, seem to loosen, in a great measure, the ties of morality, and may be supposed for that reason, pernicious to the peace of civil society" (*EHU*, 133–34). This side of Hume, the epistemological side, recalls the principles of ancient political philosophy.[1]

But this is not an adequate picture. Notwithstanding our earlier reservations about calling Hume a figure of the Enlightenment, however, it would be absurd to claim that he is somehow classical or that he is not in major respects on the side of the moderns in the quarrel between ancients and moderns.[2] As Mossner writes with admirable clarity, "Hume's series of comparisons between the ancient and modern civilizations serves to build up piecemeal a formidable case for modern civilization in which mankind, in general, is characterized by more humanity, more moderation, more decency, and more politeness; government and society, by more liberty, more stability, more commerce, more industry, more comforts of life."[3] One of the challenges to scholars of Hume is how to reconcile his admiration for modern society with his profound skepticism about the foundations of the science on which it is based and with which it is inextricably bound up.

Whether or to what degree Hume is a conservative has long been argued.[4] Anthony Quinton includes Hume in his catalog of conservatives in *The Politics of Imperfection*, the title of which expresses forcefully the compelling grounds for doing so: Hume's deep reservations about the "ignorance and weakness of understanding" (*EHU*, 76) or what Burke later called "the fallible contrivances" of human reason, led him to doubt the efficacy of rational schemes for reform in politics, or the prospect of much political progress altogether.[5] Although such conservatism is often closely tied to some form of religious faith, which is notably absent in Hume's case, Quinton is correct in his characterization of this side of Hume's political thought.

But it is equally fair to speak of *The Politics of Progress*, as does Hiram Caton,[6] and to include Hume along with Adam Smith and other proponents of the modern commercial republic, whose emphasis on trade and commerce—with the attendant virtues of industry and thrift, for example—they believed would improve the condition of humankind. This progressive outlook emphasizes reason, toleration, and peace as the concomitants of enlightened trade and commerce. At the fringes such a view fades into the more radical expectations for equality and liberty associated later with the French Revolution and even to the millenarian projections of nineteenth-century reformers. With the latter, again, Hume has nothing whatever in common. The two sides of his thought, captured by the phrases "politics of imperfection" and "politics of progress," seem difficult to reconcile. As Sheldon Wolin has written, "to have fathered squabbling children is always something of an embarrassment, but particularly so when one is, like Hume, temperamentally averse to taking sides."[7] Yet both sides are undeniably present in Hume, and neither is adscititious. How can they be reconciled?

The conventional explanation, common to a spate of recent studies, approaches the question historically and locates Hume at the point in the seventeenth century where the radical revolt against organicist views of society was itself becoming entrenched as orthodoxy.[8] Much can be learned from such an explanation, but it has the grave defect of all historicist explanations, namely, that it deprives Hume's views of any possibility of permanent or transcendent significance. Hume's views, on such an account, not only must be studied in historical context, they *only* make sense in the context in which they are presented.[9] Thus Wolin writes that "Hume's position was symptomatic of the change taking place in English liberalism around the middle of the eighteenth century," and later, "Hume was representative of this changing temper, which prized the gains made possible by the upheavals of the previous century, and sought to preserve both the institutional achievements and their social undergirding."[10] Hume's forceful defense of the primacy of liberty and property, for example, is understood as a product of his historical position, and appropriate to it. But we wish to take seriously the possibility that Hume's understanding of man and society is part of a "science of human nature" meant to be true for all times and places. For reasons examined in the previous chapter, Hume—himself a very great historian—seems a poor candidate for "historicization," for the type of explanation which reduces a set of principles to the level of products of particular historical circumstances. Hume's teaching about the fundamental elements of decent social order should be taken seriously as a recommendation of what is best for human beings simply, not merely those in the middle of the eighteenth century.

If we are to approach Hume in this spirit we need an account of the superficial paradoxes of his thought which shows the internal coherence of his understanding of both humanity and the conditions and institutions which he recommends as best for such creatures. If Hume teaches the importance of property and liberty, and if his political science is truly a science in his own understanding of the term, we must at least consider the possibility that these are as important in the last decades of the twentieth century as they were in the middle decades of the eighteenth. Is there a teaching valid for all times?

The *History of England*

As I have already suggested, no one could be more alive to the immense variety of human social and political experience than Hume with his vast learning. He devotes an entire essay ("Of National Character") to the basis of this variety, asking specifically whether moral or physical causes play the greater role. In it he writes that "the manners of a people change very considerably from one age to another; either by great alterations in their government, by the mixtures of new people, or by that inconstancy, to which all human affairs is subject" (*E*, 205–6). The *History of England* can be read as the documentary evidence for that claim, since it is a study of precisely such a revolution in the manners of the English during seventeen centuries, tracing all these causes and more. Custom may be "the great guide of human life," but customs change and are grounded in circumstances and nature. Moreover, "though nature produces all kinds of temper and understanding in great abundance, it does not follow, that she always produces them in like proportions, and that in every society the ingredients of industry and indolence, valour and cowardice, humanity and brutality, wisdom and folly, will be mixed after the same manner" (*E*, 203). The challenge to philosophical history—and indeed to practical statesmanship—is to discover the circumstances and institutions which promote industry, valor, humanity, and wisdom rather than their opposites, or at least which allow these to predominate in what must inevitably be a mixture of virtues and vices.

In general Hume teaches that English history is the story of progress from conditions in which only one of these virtues—valor—has a place toward a state of society in which the other three can and often do flourish beside it. The history of any nation, either ancient or modern, if traced back far enough will discover a society characterized by ignorance, superstition, and brutality. Hume repeatedly describes such ages as "rude," "turbulent," "barbarous and illiterate," "rough and licentious," "ignorant and barbarous" (*History*, 1.14, 24, 17, 185, 51n, 53). "The only virtues which can have place among an uncivilized people, where justice and humanity are commonly rejected," he writes in the volume on the Saxons, are "valour, and love of liberty" (1.15). This is not yet to judge between the civilized nations of ancient or modern times, however, which is a separate and more difficult question.[11]

Whatever else it may be, the *History of England* is a demonstration of the superiority of civilized society over earlier stages of development, but in it Hume also traces the complicated mechanism of progress by which the civilized condition is reached. In this narration Hume tries to elucidate precisely the social and political institutions and practices in which the excellence of modern civilization is located. That is, the *History* shows why inferior social arrangements are inferior, by showing what life was like in earlier ages, materially and morally, even as it explores how earlier modes of life were transformed. Thus by following closely Hume's account of "the gradual progress of improvement" we can also discover the grounds of his claim for the superiority of modern to ancient civilization, or more precisely of liberal commercial society to ancient republicanism. If Hume's teaching in the *History* is a teaching for all times, it may be of more than scholarly interest to us to examine a philosophical defense of the sort of society which is today attacked from many quarters as alienating and inhumane, corrupt and vicious.

The key principle in Hume's *History* seems to be a largely unstated premise, a premise made explicit only once in the entire six volumes, to my knowledge. That passage (2.519), which serves as the epigraph to this chapter, maintains that "the rise, progress, perfection and decline of art and science, are curious objects of contemplation, and intimately connected with a narration of civil transactions. The events of no particular period can be fully accounted for, but by considering the degrees of advancement, which men have reached in those particulars" (2.519). But to call this a premise is wrong, since to do so begs the question of the superiority of developed society. It is, rather, the conclusion of Hume's *History,* and in fact it comes in the concluding pages of the last volume he wrote, the volume which ends with an account of the brief reign of Richard III (1485). It is not merely an artifact of the reverse order in which the *History* was composed.[12] He concludes this second (last-written) volume, in 1762, with a brief essay which begins "Thus we have pursued the History of England through a series of many barbarous ages; till we have at last reached the dawn of civility and sciences, and have the prospect, both of greater certainty in our historical narrations, and of being able to present to the reader a spectacle more worthy of his attention" (2.518). But in 1759 Hume had written, in his discussion of the laws of Henry VII in the first of the Tudor volumes, that "thus a general revolution was made in human affairs throughout this part of the world; and men gradually attained that situation, with regard to commerce, arts, sciences, government, police, and cultivation, in which they have ever since persevered. Here therefore commences the useful, as well as the more agreeable part of modern annals" (3.67).[13]

A careful student of the *History* therefore has a double task: he must discover more precisely what the superiority of modernity consists in, and he must unravel Hume's account of the "revolution" in human affairs which led to it. The former is the easier task, because we have the *Essays* and the *Enquiry concerning the Principles of Morals* at our disposal; the latter must depend more on the *History*, and the difficulties are multiplied because the relevant passages must be found among many hundreds of pages narrating historical transactions of all kinds, from the martial to the marital, involving every aspect of domestic, ecclesiastical, and political life. What we seek is a Humean "theory of development," as it would be called today, presenting an orderly account of what Hume termed the "moral cause" which transforms societies, the links which connect certain institutions, such as property ownership, with practices, such as chivalry, husbandry, or entail, and with the various virtues and vices which result from these together.

The Primacy of War and Arms

Our beginning point is the condition of society Hume calls barbarous or savage, that rude state which he suggests is not even of much interest to us: "the sudden, violent, and unprepared revolutions, incident to Barbarians, are so much guided by caprice, and terminate so often in cruelty, that they disgust us by the uniformity of their appearance" (*History*, 1.3–4). It suffices to describe the state of the early Britons. Most were nomadic; "they were clothed in the skins of beasts: They dwelt in huts. . . . They shifted easily their habitation, when actuated either by the hopes of plunder or the fear of an enemy. . . . And as they were ignorant of all the refinements of life, their wants and their possessions were equally scanty and limited" (ibid., 1.5). The description of these ancestors need detain us no longer than it detains Hume. Successive invasions by Romans and Saxons change the picture but little, despite the

Saxon virtues and the rudimentary political institutions they introduced.[14] The almost total lack of security suppressed any progress in
other areas. This is a principle which Hume defends as true in all ages.
Where no benefit can arise from application or industry, "a habit of
indolence naturally prevails. The greater part of the land lies uncultivated" (*E*, 261). Men are led in such conditions to apply themselves only
to the arts of war, and their rude state allows very little skill even here.
Describing the conditions in Britain in the ninth century, Hume reports
that "the Saxons, though they had been so long settled in the island, seem
not as yet to have been much improved beyond their German ancestors,
either in arts, civility, knowledge, humanity, justice, or obedience to the
laws. Even Christianity, though it opened the way to connexions between
them and the more polished states of Europe, had not hitherto been very
effectual, in banishing their ignorance, or softening their barbarous
manners" (*History*, 1.50–51).

Even by the time of the Norman Conquest, more than a millennium
after the starting point of Hume's *History*, conditions are nearly as dismal
as at the beginning, at least in respect to the cardinal principle of development—the rule of law. In his first appendix, devoted to the "Anglo-
Saxon Government and Manners," Hume writes that "among that military and turbulent people, so averse to commerce and the arts, so little
enured to industry, justice was commonly very ill administered, and
great oppression and violence seem to have prevailed. These disorders
would be encreased by the exorbitant power of the aristocracy and
would, in their turn, contribute to encrease it" (ibid., 1.166–67). This
introduces the next stage of development, which may be considered both
a setback and an advance. What prepares the way for the ultimate escape
from the cycle of licentious barbarism is actually a step away from the
rule of law. "Men, not daring to rely on the guardianship of the laws,
were obliged to devote themselves to the service of some chieftain, whose
orders they followed even to the disturbance of the government or the
injury of their fellow-citizens, and who afforded them in return protection from any insult or injustice by strangers" (ibid., 1.167). This is the

core of the system Hume calls feudalism, and the crucial stage of Hume's theory of development is the story of how its hold on society is broken.

Viewed in one way, the feudal system crystallizes the problems of the earlier condition by fixing them institutionally. But the Norman Conquest which brought the feudal system also introduces the first glimmerings of civilization to the Anglo-Saxons, whom the conquerors themselves spoke of as barbarians (ibid., 1.185). The Anglo-Saxons were "in general a rude, uncultivated people, ignorant of letters, unskilled in the mechanical arts, untamed to submission under law and government, addicted to intemperance, riot and disorder." Despite their "best quality"—military courage—their conduct was undisciplined, unfaithful, and always marked by a "want of humanity." Only the conquest "put the people in a situation of receiving slowly from abroad the rudiments of science and civilization, and of correcting their rough and licentious manners" (ibid.).

Even before the feudal system proper was introduced, the problems it institutionalized were present. They stem from one fundamental condition: the paramount importance of war in rude and barbarous times. Speaking of the jurisprudence, if it can be described as such, of the ancient English or Saxons, Hume offers the following characterization: "Such a state of society was very little advanced beyond the rude state of nature: Violence universally prevailed, instead of general and equitable maxims: The pretended liberty of the times, was only an incapacity of submitting to government: And men, not protected by law in their lives and properties, sought shelter, by their personal servitude and attachments under some powerful chieftain, or by voluntary combinations" (ibid., 2.521–22).

In such a condition the want of law is equated with the want of liberty and the radical insecurity of property. In fact property can scarcely be said to exist. In the "ancient state of Europe," as Hume puts it, "the far greater part of the society were everywhere bereaved of their *personal* liberty, and lived entirely at the will of their masters" (ibid., 2.522). The feudal system institutionalized this by the principle that "the King was

the supreme lord of the landed property: All possessors, who enjoyed the
fruits or revenue of any part of it, held those privileges, either mediately
or immediately, of him; and their property was conceived to be, in some
degree, conditional" (ibid., 1.461). The barons held their property from
the king in the same manner as the vassals from the barons (and indirectly from the king). All relations were subordinated to military requirement, the principle underlying the entire system. If the vassal re-
fused obedience or so much as failed to attend on or do fealty to his lord,
"he forfeited all title to his lands" (ibid., 1.477). Such specious liberty or
property is little better than the prefeudal liberty of the Anglo-Saxons,
who in fact lived under a system with the same military imperative as
feudalism, though it lacked the terminology of feudalism:

> On the whole, notwithstanding the seeming liberty or rather licen-
> tiousness of the Anglo-Saxons, the great body even of the free
> citizens, in those ages, really enjoyed much less true liberty, than
> where the execution of the laws is the most severe, and where
> subjects are reduced to the strictest subordination and dependance
> on the civil magistrate. The reason is derived from the excess itself
> of that liberty. Men must guard themselves at any price against
> insults and injuries; and where they receive not protection from
> the laws and magistrate, they will seek it by submission to superi-
> ors, and by herding in some private confederacy, which acts under
> the direction of a powerful leader. And thus all anarchy is the
> immediate cause of tyranny, if not over the state, at least over
> many of the individuals. (Ibid., 1.168–69)

Lack of liberty was not the only deplorable consequence of the subordination of every consideration to arms and defense. The feudal government was equally prejudicial to "the true liberty even of the military
vassal." But "it was still more destructive of the independence and
security of the other members of the state, or what in a proper sense we
call the people." The greater part of these were, as Hume notes, "*serfs,
and lived in a state of absolute slavery or villainage*" (ibid., 1.463). The

"immense possessions of the nobility" retarded, first of all, any improvements in the arts of agriculture; the "precarious state of feudal property" in general meant that "industry of no kind could then have place in the kingdom" (ibid., 1.484). Even the property of the military vassals could hardly be called secure. Compared to the people, the military tenants were "better protected, both by law, and by the great privilege of carrying arms." But even these "were, from the nature of their tenures, much exposed to the inroads of power, and possessed not what we should term in our age a very durable security" (ibid., 1.476).

The insecurity of property and want of liberty (really two sides of the same coin) precluded the development of trade and commerce, and the lack of economic progress in turn contributed to insecurity.

> The languishing state of commerce kept the inhabitants poor and contemptible; and the political institutions were calculated to render that poverty perpetual. The barons and gentry, living in rustic plenty and hospitality, gave no encouragement to the arts, and had no demand for any of the more elaborate produce of manufactures: Every profession was held in contempt but that of arms: And if any merchant or manufacturer rose by industry and frugality to a degree of opulence, he found himself but the more exposed to injuries, from the envy and avidity of the military nobles. (Ibid., 1.463–64)

In Saxon times in particular, there was virtually no escape from this condition. Anyone in the lower ranks of society was condemned to remain there. Despite two statutes among the Saxon laws which, as Hume notes, seem to provide an opportunity for change, Hume suggests that they were ineffective in practice (ibid., 1.169). The feudal system did little to improve things, and in fact the right of primogeniture, which came in with the feudal law, added to the problem "by producing and maintaining an unequal division of private property" (ibid., 1.486). On the other hand, the feudal system proper, by virtue of its "legalization" of the system of vassalage, land holding by tenure, and primogeniture, introduced the means by which the system would gradually be changed.

Hume's Account of the Disintegration of Feudal Order

Hume's theory of development has permanent significance because the features of society at the time of the Norman Conquest are not peculiar to that age. The conditions marked by lawlessness, insecurity of property, want of liberty, both personal and civil, and suppression of commerce and industry are not unknown in the contemporary world. Hume's account of the means of escape from this deplorable state is of particular interest to us insofar as it does not depend on miracles or on circumstances so singular that they are unlikely to be encountered again. At the same time we should be aware, as is Hume, of the essential fragility of all decent civil order and of its dependence on particular circumstances and accidents. His deep appreciation for the framework of English constitutionalism and for the institutions of liberal commercial society is proportionate to the value of these in relation to other forms of social order.

Hume's account of the "gradual progress of improvement" from the dismal condition of feudal society is very complicated. To present it intelligibly I will divide his remarks under three headings and ask the reader to bear in mind that it is impossible to do this tidily: the various explanations overlap at some points, and some loose ends cannot be tied up neatly. Nevertheless Hume presents this account with notable consistency, even though in some cases many hundreds of pages separate his comments in different volumes of the *History*. The three parts of his account vary according to their degree of specificity to English circumstances and in the degree to which they are fortuitous, according to the distinction Hume draws in one of the essays: "What depends on a few persons is, in a great measure, to be ascribed to chance, or secret and unknown causes: what arises from a great number may often be accounted for by determinate and known causes." Thus "to judge by this rule, the domestic and the gradual revolutions of a state must be a more proper subject of reasoning and operation than the foreign and the violent, which are commonly produced by single persons, and are more influenced by whim, folly, or caprice, than by general passions and interests" (*E*, 112). The largely domestic revolution we are considering here is not without an admixture of foreign causes, however.

Of the three parts of Hume's account, one has to do with England specifically because it is based partly on the special circumstances of the introduction of the feudal law by the Norman Conquest. A second portion is not specific to England, but dependent nonetheless partly on historical accident—namely, the discovery or recovery in 1130 of the Roman law in the form of the Pandects of Justinian and the train of events this set in motion. The third is a general "naturalist" explanation of the decline of feudalism based on tendencies in human nature. This last, of course, is universal in its operation, but Hume suggests it was not of sufficient force to overturn feudalism in the absence of other factors.

Montesquieu's *L'Esprit des Lois* may have taught Hume to look for circumstances peculiar to English civilization which could explain the development of its remarkable liberal commercial society as early as the eighteenth century. It is certain that Hume found the key in the Norman Conquest. Not that the Normans could be said to have brought the seeds of development with them, though Hume does suggest in one sentence that the conquest "put the people in a situation of receiving slowly from abroad the rudiments of science and cultivation, and of correcting their rough and licentious manners" (*History*, 1.185). Only by contrast with the barbarous manners of the Saxons did the Normans add anything: and even then the conquest acted only indirectly in the special circumstances of England and combined with other factors to transform these "military and turbulent people" into something approaching a civilized people or a people capable of civilization. The Normans themselves were, "during this age, so violent and licentious a people that they may be pronounced incapable of any true and regular liberty; which requires such improvement in knowledge and morals, as can only be the result of reflection and experience, and must grow to perfection during several ages of settled and established government" (ibid., 1.254).[15]

The conquest served to generate a special kind of tension in English feudalism, as a result of the fact that "England of a sudden became a feudal kingdom" (ibid., 1.461). That is, the exigencies arising from the manner in which the feudal system was introduced into England generated a heightened tension between king and barons, beyond the tension between king and barons inherent in any feudal arrangement. Indeed in the absence of the principle of hereditary authority, which is not "so easily subverted," the most common course for feudal systems is the degeneration "into so many independent baronies," with the loss of "the political union, by which they were cemented," and the sacrifice to the barons of "both the rights of the crown and the liberties of the people" (ibid., 1.464).

There is thus an incipient natural alliance between king and people, and in England special circumstances helped both. The first circumstance was only temporary. "The first Kings of the Norman race were favoured by another circumstance, which preserved them from the encroachments of their barons. They were generals of a conquering army, which was obliged to continue in a military posture, and to maintain a great subordination under their leader, in order to secure themselves from the revolt of the numerous natives, whom they had bereaved of all their properties and privileges" (ibid., 1.464–65). This result of the conquest helped William and his immediate successors to resist the barons, but it ceased to operate after about a century, and its effect was entirely obliterated under the despicable King John, who was compelled by his barons to acknowledge the Great Charter in 1215. In the meantime, however—during the century and a half following the conquest—the Norman kings were in a position to promote such rudimentary liberties or interests of the people as existed at the time and thus to move the feudal system toward its dissolution.

The majority of society in ancient Europe, Hume tells us, were "bereaved of their *personal* liberty and lived entirely at the will of their masters." Everyone was either noble or slave; if the latter, one was "sold along with the land: The few inhabitants of cities were not in a better condition" (ibid., 2.522). This condition was the necessary result of the primacy of armed force and the "slender protection" afforded by law or anything else. "The first incident, which broke in upon this violent system of government, was the practice, begun in Italy, and imitated in France, of erecting communities and corporations, endowed with privileges and a separate municipal government, which gave them protection against the tyranny of the barons, and which the prince himself deemed it prudent to respect" (ibid., 2.522–23).[16] The granting of a charter to London by Henry I, upon his accession to the throne in 1100, "seems to have been the first step towards rendering that city a corporation," according to Hume (ibid., 1.278), although he notes that William at the conquest itself had "confirmed the liberties and immunities of London and the other cities of England" (ibid., 1.192).

If the special powers enjoyed by William and his successors allowed them to promote, however slightly, the liberties of the commons against the villenage practiced by the barons, another specifically English circumstance played its part in this rise of the boroughs; "affairs," as Hume puts it, "in this island particularly, took early a turn, which was more favourable to justice and to liberty." The precise circumstance favoring England was her geography. "Civil employments and occupations soon became honourable among the English: The situation of that people rendered not the perpetual attention to wars so necessary as among their neighbors, and all regard was not confined to the military profession" (ibid., 2.522). This has particular relevance to the development of the rule of law, a development owing a great deal to the fortuitous recovery of a code of Roman civil law, the Pandects of Justinian, in A.D. 1130.

The second part of Hume's account of the rise of the English system of liberty and decline of feudalism owes less to specifically English circumstances. He presents it as part of his account of how the "rise, progress, perfection, and decline of art and science" are "intimately connected with a narration of civil transactions" (ibid., 2.519). Hume suggests a cyclical view of history, or the "general revolutions of society," according to which "there is an ultimate point of depression, as well as of exaltation, from which human affairs naturally return in a contrary progress, and beyond which they seldom pass either in their advancement or decline" (ibid.). He cites the Roman age of Augustus as a peak of "the improvements of the human mind" and suggests it was followed by a long descent back into an ignorance and barbarism so profound that they overwhelmed "all human knowledge, which was already far in its decline; and men sunk every age deeper into ignorance, stupidity, and superstition; till the light of ancient science and history had very nearly suffered a total extinction in all the European nations" (ibid.). The nadir of this cycle, according to Hume, "may justly be fixed at the eleventh century, about the age of William the Conqueror." He sketches the change in the fortunes of Europe in the broadest possible strokes. "From that aera, the sun of science, beginning to re-ascend, threw out many gleams of light, which preceded the full morning, when letters were revived in the fifteenth century." The depredations of the northern pirates ceased gradually as they learned the arts of tillage and agriculture. The feudal governments were gradually reduced "to a kind of system; and though that strange species of civil polity was ill fitted to ensure either liberty or tranquillity, it was preferable to the universal licence and disorder, which had every where preceded it" (ibid., 2.520). A critical factor in the recovery of civilization, however, was one seldom noticed: "But perhaps there was no event, which tended further to the improvement of the age, than one, which has not been much remarked, the accidental finding of a copy of Justinian's Pandects, about the year 1130, in the town of Amalfi in Italy" (ibid.).

Why was this event so important? The system of law contained in this work answered a pressing need of one sector of the community, and as the system spread it undermined the entire feudal order. Hume's description is worth quoting at length:

> The ecclesiastics, who had leisure, and some inclination of study, immediately adopted with zeal this excellent system of jurisprudence, and spread the knowledge of it throughout every part of Europe. Besides the intrinsic merit of the performance, it was recommended to them by its original connexion with the imperial city of Rome, which, being the seat of their religion, seemed to

acquire a new lustre and authority, by the diffusion of its laws over the western world. In less than ten years after the discovery of the Pandects, Vacarius, under the protection of Theobald, Archbishop of Canterbury, read public lectures of civil law in the university of Oxford; and the clergy every where, by their example as well as exhortation, were the means of spreading the highest esteem for this new science. That order of men, having large possessions to defend, was, in a manner, necessitated to turn their studies towards the law; and their properties being often endangered by the violence of the princes and barons, it became their interest to enforce the observance of general and equitable rules, from which alone they could receive protection. (*History,* 2.520)

To appreciate the centrality of this recovery of law in Hume's account of the gradual progress of improvement is to locate the key to civilization itself, or the rise and progress of the arts and sciences. The recovery of legal science, however rudimentary, proved to be the decisive factor in breaking out of the feudal system which, with its subordination of all concerns to martial authority, effectively blocked any improvement in commerce, agriculture, and hence in the arts and sciences. Hume speaks quite clearly of the "jealousy entertain'd by the barons against the progress of the arts, as destructive of their licentious power" (ibid., 2.523n). Speaking of the rapid spread of the study of the newly recovered Roman law, Hume suggests that "it is easy to see what advantages Europe must have reaped by its inheriting at once from the ancients, so complete an art, which was also so necessary for giving security to all other arts, and which, by refining, and still more, by bestowing solidity on the judgment, served as a model to farther improvements" (ibid., 2.521).

The importance of this development can be seen by considering it as a trigger which released tendencies inherent in the "natural course of things" (*E,* 260), or in human nature and the physical circumstances of human life, tendencies which were thwarted by the preoccupation of the feudal system with what Hume calls the "military profession" (*History,* 2.522). "The gentry, and even the nobility, began to deem an acquain-

tance with the law, a requisite part of education" (ibid.). This opened the
way for the gradual rise of the commons, as men who had earlier been
virtual slaves began to achieve some independence. Under the feudal
order, "even the gentry . . . were subjected to a long train of subordination under the great barons or chief vassals of the crown; who, though
seemingly placed in a high state of splendor, yet, having but a slender
protection from the law, were exposed to every tempest of the state, and
by the precarious condition in which they lived, paid dearly for the
power of oppressing and tyrannizing over their inferiors" (ibid.). The
"somewhat stricter" execution of the public law, which gradually followed upon the study of this science, "bestowed an independence on
vassals, which was unknown to their forefathers. And even the peasants
themselves, though later than other orders of the state, made their escape
from those bonds of villenage or slavery, in which they had formerly been
retained" (ibid., 2.523).[17]

Property, Law, and Liberty

Precisely how did this liberation take place? Hume offers two
clear and general accounts of the feudal system, one dealing with its
formation, the other with its disintegration. By considering them together and paying particular attention to the role played by jurisprudence, the mechanism of progress can be unraveled more precisely. This
brings in what I earlier called the third, naturalist component of Hume's
account of the deterioration of the feudal system, and it leads directly to
the core of his claim of the superiority of modern liberal commercial
society.

In explaining how a stable system of "fiefs and tenures" developed,
Hume uses arguments grounded in common sense or common life to
show how "the idea of property stole in gradually upon that of military
pay" (ibid., 1.458). Where lands were first distributed as a reward for
service in conquest and held only on condition of continued military
service, there is not quite a fixed notion of property. But where lands are

cultivated, a natural logic intrudes itself. "The attachment, naturally formed with a fixed portion of land, gradually begets the idea of something like property, and makes the possessor forget his dependant situation. . . . It seemed equitable, that one who had cultivated and sowed a field, should reap the harvest." The result was that fief holdings, "at first entirely precarious, were soon made annual" (ibid.). But the same logic carried men several steps further: "A man, who had employed his money in building, planting, or other improvements, expected to reap the fruits of his labor or expence: Hence they were next granted during a term of years." Since "it would be thought hard to expel a man from his possessions, who had always done his duty," feudal chieftains soon insisted on holding their feudal tenures for life. The last step follows equally naturally: "It was found, that a man would more willingly expose himself if assured, that his family should inherit his possessions, and should not be left by his death in want and poverty: Hence fiefs were made hereditary in families" (ibid.), and so on. Although other schemes to induce martial loyalty are imaginable, Hume's account emphasizes the naturalness of this progression; it accords with human nature and the conditions of feudal life.

But the logic Hume uses here to explain how the feudal property system was stabilized or "how these feudal dependancies" were "corroborated" (ibid., 1.459) bears a striking resemblance to the logic that accounts for its later disintegration, which he deals with in his summary of the first two volumes of the *History*. We learn here, as has already been suggested, that the spread of arts and sciences—and particularly the science of jurisprudence—was a general source of liberty and released feudal villains from their bondage. At first the villains were virtual agricultural slaves to the "military posture" of the chieftain, whose readiness had to be constantly maintained. They were occupied

> entirely . . . in the cultivation of their master's land, and paid their rents either in corn and cattle and other produce of the farm, or in servile offices. . . . In proportion as agriculture improved,

and money encreased, it was found, that these services, though
extremely burdensome to the villain, were of little advantage to the
master; and that the produce of a large estate could be much more
conveniently disposed of by the peasants themselves, who raised it,
than by the landlord or his bailiff, who were formerly accustomed
to receive it. (Ibid., 2.523)

The result was the introduction of the more convenient practice of
paying rent instead of services, and later indeed of money rents rather
than those in kind; "and as men, in a subsequent age, discovered, that
farms were better cultivated where the farmer enjoyed a security in his
possession, the practice of granting leases to the peasant began to prevail,
which entirely broke the bonds of servitude, already much relaxed from
the former practices" (ibid., 2.524). (The Soviet Union is struggling to
resist this lesson today, even as the Chinese seem to be learning it reluc-
tantly.) The system of villenage, as Hume notes, thus "went gradually
into disuse throughout the more civilized parts of Europe: The interest of
the master, as well as that of the slave, concurred in this alteration"
(ibid.). And as the distinction between freeman and villain disappeared, the political aspect of modern Europe began to take shape.
"Thus *personal* freedom became almost general in Europe; an advantage
which paved the way for the encrease of *political* or *civil* liberty"
(ibid.).

How can the same reasoning concerning the convenience of property
ownership and inheritance explain both the formation and dissolution of
the feudal land tenure system? The crucial factor is the development
of law following the recovery of the Pandects of Justinian. During the
ages when the feudal system was solidifying, as Hume points out repeatedly, military concerns were paramount because there was no
effective law. Indeed the "judiciary" itself, such as it was, was constituted
largely by the military chieftains; as is "unavoidable to all nations
that have made slender advances in refinement," these men "every
where united the civil jurisdiction with the military power" (ibid.,
1.459–60).

Law, in its commencement, was not an intricate science, and was more governed by maxims of equity, which seem obvious to common sense, than by numerous and subtile principles, applied to a variety of cases by profound reasonings from analogy. An officer, though he had passed his life in the field, was able to determine all legal controversies which could occur within the district committed to his charge; and his decisions were the most likely to meet with a prompt and ready obedience, from men who respected his person, and were accustomed to act under his command. (Ibid., 1.460)

Since judicial authority was combined with military command and both were attached to an hereditary fief holding, all were together transmitted by inheritance to each chieftain's posterity. The feudal lords were able to "render their dignity perpetual and hereditary. . . . After this manner, the vast fabric of feudal subordination became quite solid and comprehensive" (ibid.). The tendencies which solidified this system operated so long as law and justice were virtually identical to the chieftain's word, and this was the natural condition where military considerations were paramount, where "men, not protected by law in their lives and properties, sought shelter, by their personal servility and attachments, under some powerful chieftain; or by voluntary combinations" (ibid., 2.521–22).

But the beginning of the development of law as an independent science, which Hume dates in the middle of the twelfth century, broke the hold of the military chieftain. The church, for one, was deeply interested in securing its property by means other than military force; an independent civil law afforded it the opportunity. In England particularly, as we saw above, affairs "took very early a turn, which was more favorable to justice and to liberty" (ibid., 2.522). The study of the law as a science paved the way for the escape from the vicious hold of the feudal system itself, by freeing property from the fief system or, more to the point, establishing the security of property *independent of military vassalage*.

It is now possible to assess why Hume's account of the disintegration of the feudal order is so important to an understanding of the general teaching of the *History:* here, at the first origins of the "gradual progress of improvement," the crucial element of liberal commercial order, of civilized or refined society, appears with the greatest clarity, unconfused by the variety of circumstances and institutions which cloud matters when civilized society is more fully developed. The critical first element is the rule of law, or what would today be called an independent judiciary and a science of jurisprudence which separates questions of justice from considerations of military loyalty. When law replaces military force, the security of property—which Hume admits was secure enough before— is no longer dependent on one's loyalty to a chieftain. The results of this development include, most importantly, the beginning of the gradual rise of the commons, which was the natural accompaniment to what Hume calls the "introduction and progress of freedom" (ibid.) and the gradual development of commerce.

He illustrates the connection between these two factors with a story. During the reign of Henry VII, Hume writes, "there scarce passed any session . . . without some statute against engaging retainers, and giving them badges or liveries; a practice by which they were, in a manner, inlisted under some great lord, and were kept in readiness to assist him in all wars, insurrections, riots, violences, and even in bearing evidence for him in courts of justice" (ibid., 3.75–76). This is of course a remnant of the system of military loyalty just referred to, and "this disorder, which had arisen during turbulent times, when the law could give little protec- tion to the subject, was then deeply rooted in England; and it required all the vigilance and rigour of Henry to extirpate it." He took vigorous steps to eliminate the practice, making it illegal. The story of Henry's severity, Hume suggests, merits praise though it is usually mistakenly taken as an instance of Henry's "avarice and rapacity."

> The earl of Oxford, his favorite general, in whom he always placed great and deserved confidence, having splendidly entertained him at his castle of Heningham, was desirous of making a parade of his magnificence at the departure of his royal guest; and ordered all

his retainers, with their liveries and badges, to be drawn up in two lines, that their appearance might be the more gallant and splendid. "My lord," said the King, "I have heard much of your hospitality; but the truth far exceeds the report. These handsome gentlemen and yeomen, whom I see on both sides of me, are surely your menial servants." The earl smiled, and confessed that his fortune was too narrow for such magnificence. "They are most of them," subjoined he, "my retainers, who are come to do me service at this time, when they know I am honoured with your majesty's presence." The King started a little, and said, "By my faith, my lord, I thank you for your good cheer, but I must not allow my laws to be broken in my sight. My attorney must speak with you." Oxford is said to have payed no less than fifteen thousand marks, as a composition for his offence. (Ibid., 3.76)

The feudal practice of service by personal loyalty, Hume suggests, maintained the common people "in a vicious idleness." He admits that "the encrease of the arts, more effectually than all the severities of laws," put an end to "this pernicious practice." That its gradual disappearance is more than a mere change in manners is very clear. "The nobility, instead of vying with each other, in the number and boldness of their retainers, acquired by degrees more civilized species of emulation, and endeavored to excel in the splendour and elegance of their equipage, houses, and tables. The common people, no longer maintained in vicious idleness by their superiors, were obliged to learn some calling or industry, and become useful both to themselves and to others" (ibid.). The increase in personal liberty, then, was and is directly connected to the growth of commerce and, with it, of such commercial virtues as industry, honesty, and thrift. Hume goes further in the *Essays*, where he analyses the effects of "refinement in the arts" with great power and clarity. "In times when industry and the arts flourish, men are kept in perpetual occupation, and enjoy, as their reward, the occupation itself, as well as those pleasures which are the fruit of their labor. The mind acquires new vigour; enlarges its powers and faculties; and by an assiduity in honest industry, both satisfies its natural appetites, and prevents the growth of unnatural ones, which commonly spring up, when nourished by ease and idleness" (*E*, 270).

Commerce and the Arts

Once the feudal system had begun to lose its sway as a result of the spread of legal science or the art of jurisprudence, the arts themselves carried the revolution, or the "gradual progress of improvement," forward. The liberties even of the common people had been, in large measure, secured as early as the Great Charter in 1215, as Hume suggests; the effectiveness of the guarantees was not very great in practice, however. The charter had included some provisions for free commerce ("Merchants shall be allowed to transact all business, without being exposed to any arbitrary . . . impositions; . . . The goods of every free man shall be disposed of according to his will: If he die intestate, his heirs shall succeed to them . . ." [ibid., 1.444–45]), and Hume speaks of the nobles who extorted it from King John as "those generous barons." He praises them for including clauses which favored "the interests of the inferior ranks of men" (ibid.). Nevertheless he is at pains to show that, for example during the reign of Edward III, the charter itself was only a document and its provisions were not always followed in practice (ibid., 2.275): Why, Hume asks, since "this privilege was sufficiently secured by a clause of the Great Charter . . . is [it] so anxiously, and, as we may think, so superfluously repeated? Plainly, because there had been some late infringements of it, which gave umbrage to the commons." In the end, the progress of the arts, progress connected to the recovery of the art of Roman jurisprudence, and specifically the spread of a taste for luxury or "refinement in the arts" was what succeeded in transforming feudal society. Hume devoted considerable thought to this subject, and he wrote one of his best and most famous essays on it.[18] He concludes the report on Henry's reign, quoted above, by insisting that "it must be acknowledged, in spite of those who declaim so violently against refinement in the arts, or what they are pleased to call luxury, that, as much as an industrious tradesman is both a better man and a better citizen than one of those idle retainers, who formerly depended on the great families; so much is the life of a modern nobleman more laudable than that of an ancient baron" (ibid., 3.76–77).

Despite the great importance Hume accords to commerce and the close connection he sees between commerce and civilization, at least of the modern sort, he seems to believe that its spread is partly fortuitous. At the very least he suggests that attempts to promote commerce by specific legislation are unlikely to have much success. Speaking still of Henry VII, whose reign Hume regarded as very important in this regard, Hume writes that the king's "love of money naturally led him to encourage commerce, which encreased his customs; but, if we may judge by most of the laws enacted during his reign, trade and industry were rather hurt than promoted by the care and attention which were given to them" (ibid., 3.77). This theme had emerged already in the essay on commerce. Hume offers a number of examples of trade-retarding legislation under Henry VII (ibid., 3.77–80), and he makes an important general observation on the relationship between commerce and laws attempting to promote it. Henry VII was celebrated for his many good laws, and Hume admits that "several considerable regulations, indeed, are found among the statutes of this reign, both with regard to the police of the kingdom, and its commerce: But the former are generally contrived with much better judgment than the latter" (ibid., 3.74). The reason for this discrepancy is not difficult to see. A legislator concerned with justice need be guided only by "simple ideas of order and equity," Hume writes. "But the principles of commerce are much more complicated, and require long experience and deep reflection to be well understood in any state. The real consequence of a law or practice is there often contrary to first appearances" (ibid.). In this assessment Hume anticipates not only Adam Smith, with whom he shared so many other views, but also a number of modern economists who have assembled examples of government policies and legislation having effects opposite to those intended or anticipated. Hume's catalogue of Henry's misguided attempts at the legislation of economic behavior aims at showing the futility of resisting what he calls here the "natural course of improvement."

One law during the reign of Henry VII did have notably beneficial effects on commerce and indeed on the whole political order, and Hume even grants that Henry probably intended the results. This law, "the most important . . . in its consequences" of the entire reign, gave the nobility and gentry the "power of breaking the ancient entails, and of alienating their estates. By means of this law, joined to the beginning luxury and refinements of the age, the great fortunes of the barons were gradually dissipated, and the property of the commons encreased in England. It is probable, that Henry foresaw and intended this consequence; because the constant scheme of his policy consisted in depressing the great, and exalting churchmen, lawyers, and men of new families, who were more dependent on him" (ibid., 3.77).[19] Even here, the aim of the law was not to promote commerce but to alter the configuration of power in society. Commerce itself is best promoted indirectly or even negatively, that is, by removing obstacles or by assuring that it is not subordinated to other considerations, as it was under the feudal system. Hume believes that if one takes men as they are, given law and liberty, the "natural course of improvement" will lead to a commercial society in the absence of distorting factors (the ancient slave system, for example, or the powerful effects of superstition).

The crucial and original step in Hume's analysis is his claim that legal property rights should be understood as only an alternative to the feudal manner of securing property. Such security as property enjoyed under the feudal system was dependent entirely on personal loyalty and thus on the subordination of all other concerns to the military. Once the spread of an independent science of law undermined the hold of feudal chief-tains, the security of property could be combined with justice and personal liberty. The natural effect of this combination—though over a very long period of time—is, in Hume's view, the rise of commerce and trade. Hume suggests that even the principles enshrined in the Great Charter, though not fully effective in practice for centuries, "involve all the chief outlines of a legal government, and provide for the equal distribution of justice, and the free enjoyment of property; the great objects for which political society was at first founded by men" (ibid., 1.445). But he does not equate the natural course of things, by which human beings flourish, with the inevitable or even likely course of things: history teaches too many lessons to the contrary. The study of English history should teach us a regard for the fragility of the institutions of a decent political order. At the very end of the second volume of the *History of England*, the last Hume composed, he writes:

> Above all, a civilized nation, like the English, who have happily established the most perfect and most accurate system of liberty, that was ever found compatible with government, ought to be cautious in appealing to the practice of their ancestors, or regarding the maxims of uncultivated ages as certain rules for their present conduct. An acquaintance with the history of the remote periods of their government is chiefly *useful* by instructing them to cherish their present constitution, from a comparison or contrast with the condition of those distant times. (*History*, 2.525)

It also teaches, he adds, "the great mixture of accident which commonly concurs with a small ingredient of wisdom and foresight, in erecting the complicated fabric of the most perfect government." This, which is the culmination of lessons about law and justice, liberty and commerce, is the teaching for all times which we find in the early volumes of the *History of England*. It seems obvious and simple. He takes it further in the *Essays*, where he is concerned to show how the rise of commerce and refinement (or luxury) is inextricably bound up with "knowledge, industry, and humanity" and that these, in turn, are important and universal components of human well-being, not just in eighteenth-century England, but simply. He seeks to show, as he says, that "ages of refinement are both the happiest and most virtuous" (*E*, 269). In the next chapter we will examine this claim and explore two common misunderstandings which must be overcome in order to appreciate it fully.

"The Dismal Dress": Philosophy and Morals

Thus *industry, knowledge, and humanity,* are linked together, by an indissoluble chain, and are found, from experience as well as reason, to be peculiar to the more polished, and, what are commonly denominated, the more luxurious ages.

—Hume, *Essays*

In chapter 7 we examined Hume's account of the gradual and occasionally haphazard process by which, over several centuries, the conditions necessary for a refined or developed commercial society came into being. We have advanced the suggestion that this account is of more than historical importance, by virtue of its teaching about the "most perfect and most accurate system of liberty, that ever was found compatible with government"–the words Hume used to describe the eventual fruit of that process of development. Oddly enough we have broken off our consideration of the *History of England* just at the point where Hume announces that modernity truly begins, and where men "attained that situation with regard to commerce, arts, science, government, police, and cultivation, in which they have ever since persevered" (*History,* 3.81). In the face of Hume's suggestion that "whoever carries his anxious researches into preceding periods is moved by a curiosity, liberal indeed and commendable; not by any necessity for acquiring knowledge of public affairs, or the arts of civil government" (ibid., 2.82), how can our focus on the earlier period be justified?

The answer is that today many thoughtful people have doubts about precisely what for Hume at least is the central lesson of British history— the superiority of liberal commercial society over alternatives both ancient and modern. Hume's convictions on this score were not those of the unthinking patriot who prefers his own country's ways to all others without reflection.[1] He was aware of and had thought deeply about the chief alternatives to the type of society whose development he had traced. Opponents of the liberal commercial order that Hume admired directed their attacks from two sides, each based on a conception of virtue. Hume tried to show that each of these conceptions of virtue was based on a misunderstanding of human nature or the human condition or both. They had in common a similar weakness: neither was grounded solidly in common life. Each took its bearings, instead, from a philosophical or theological "system" which distorted the perspective of common sense.

Our focus on this issue should not be taken to suggest that the remainder of the *History* is not important for an understanding of the English political order. An appreciation of the British constitution, in particular, requires a careful study of the chief lesson of the two Tudor volumes—namely, that the gradual rise of the power of the commons depended on the suppression of the same powerful nobility who had extracted concessions from King John in the Great Charter. In Hume's words, "it required the authority almost absolute of the sovereigns, which took place in the subsequent period, to pull down these disorderly and licentious tyrants, who were equally averse from peace and from freedom, and to establish that regular execution of the laws, which, in a following age, enabled the people to erect a regular and equitable plan of liberty" (ibid., 2.525). If this is the chief lesson of the middle volumes of the *History,* the last two volumes instruct the reader concerning the great struggle prompted by the aspirations of the commons and exacerbated by the bloody and horrific religious factionalism of the seventeenth century. That there are useful lessons in these volumes will be clear to anyone who studies Hume's *History,* but for our immediate purpose the process of development we have already traced is most important.

Commercial Society and Virtue

A civilized society is one marked by refinements in sciences and the arts and one where relations among human beings are characterized by civility and humanity rather than by force and fraud. "Knowledge, industry, and humanity" constitute a triumvirate which will be present wherever refinement in the arts and sciences is found. The latter combination, in turn, is linked to or a product of commerce and trade, without which men can labor only for the bare necessities of life. Commerce and trade, in turn, require justice, liberty, and security as indispensable conditions. Although it is possible to have a kind of security without justice or liberty, as in the feudal order, in general this condition only obtains where everything is subordinated to the concern for survival: a condition Hume finds in Saxon times, for example, but one which has only the appearance of liberty with none of the genuine article. Justice and liberty require that the slavish subordination to a chieftain or military lord be replaced by a degree of individual autonomy, which can only be found where each man is entitled both to the fruits of his labor ("art or industry") and to equal protection of the law, a law independent of the personal authority of a chieftain. Thus individual property ownership and an independent judiciary with written—or at least nonarbitrary—laws, the constituents of what Hume calls "personal liberty," are prerequisites of civilized human society. As Hume summarizes the effects of the Magna Carta, "men acquired some more security for their properties and their liberties: And government approached a little nearer to that end, for which it was originally instituted, the distribution of justice, and the equal protection of the citizens" (ibid., 1.488).

All this is found in the *History,* but also, in distilled form, in the *Essays* —especially in the famous series of essays in political economy, beginning with "Of Commerce." This raises an interesting issue: since the

History was written long after the *Essays,* should we not suspect Hume of simply finding, in his survey of English history, what he thought he knew beforehand? When, for example, the *History* seems to confirm what Hume had written many years earlier in the essay "The Rise and Progress of the Arts and Sciences," should we suspect him of prejudging the facts?

Any such suspicion must result from confusion about Hume's interest in history in general and failure to distinguish between studying history and writing history in particular. That Hume was a serious student of the past from the time of his earliest writings and even before cannot be doubted; Mossner has demonstrated this beyond question, even if the ample evidence in Hume's letters left room for doubt, which it does not.[2] One of the earliest of the *Essays* recommends the study of history, and a famous passage in the first *Enquiry* suggests that history is the true laboratory for the researcher in the science of human nature (*EHU,* 83–84). Hume's research surely preceded his findings, and the *Essays* themselves are the results of his study of history. That the *History of England* confirmed Hume's earlier findings is no cause for surprise or suspicion if Hume was correct in his research. He himself notes that "it is universally acknowledged that there is a great uniformity among the actions of men, in all nations and ages, and that human nature remains still the same, in its principles and operations" (*EHU,* 83). The *History of England* differs from the *Essays* because it is particular where the *Essays* are general: it is a case study and traces events to accidents and particular circumstances, as well as to the general principles Hume explores in the *Essays.* A complete uniformity of human actions is not to be expected: "such a uniformity in every particular, is found in no part of nature" (*EHU,* 85). The general principles of human social life, including the principles manifested in the "gradual progress of improvement," hold in English history as much as everywhere else. We have traced out the most important of these with regard to the "gradual revolution in human affairs" which leads to a civilized society incorporating the arts and sciences and personal liberty. What conception of virtue belongs to civilization properly understood?

It should be no surprise that it is the conception of virtue presented by Hume in the *Enquiry concerning the Principles of Morals*. In this, the second enquiry, Hume suggests that a moral philosophy grounded in common life (as distinct from a philosophical moral system) teaches us that the virtues or estimable moral qualities are simply the qualities "useful or agreeable to the person himself or to others." The tone in which Hume advances this discovery is important. "It may justly appear surprising," he writes in the beginning of the concluding section, "that any man in so late an age, should find it requisite to prove, by elaborate reasoning," that virtue, or as he calls it "Personal Merit," can be described so simply and clearly (*ECPM*, 268). "It might be expected that this principle would have occurred even to the first rude, unpracticed enquirers concerning morals, and been received from its own evidence, without any argument or disputation" (ibid.). But this was not the case, and Hume suggests an explanation. Our understanding of virtue or the principles of morals has been distorted rather than clarified by the manner of philosophic enquiry, specifically by its failure to be grounded in common life. "It seems a reasonable presumption, that systems and hypotheses have perverted our natural understanding, when a theory, so simple and obvious, could so long have escaped the most elaborate examination" (*ECPM*, 268–69).

Hume's findings here coincide with his account of "the gradual progress of improvement" in the *History:* in both cases the distorting lens of a philosophical system has led to misunderstanding, and in both cases the cause is the same—namely, a misunderstanding of virtue. The principles of praise and blame used in common life are neither obscure nor contradictory, but moral theories have resisted or ignored them. As Hume explains at one point, "the very nature of language guides us almost infallibly" in forming judgments about which qualities deserve praise or blame (*ECPM*, 174). "However the case may have fared with philosophy, in common life these principles [the fruit of the *Enquiry*] are still implicitly maintained" (*ECPM*, 269).

Hume is convinced that the moral philosophy he proposes, which is solidly grounded in common life, is not only free of philosophical distortion but escapes or eliminates the tension between philosophy and common life. Why then should there by any resistance to it? And why should a historical "theory" which suggests "the gradual progress of improvement" in respect to such a moral theory meet with any objections? Notwithstanding the simplicity and power of Hume's account of virtue (and of the desirability of the liberal commercial society which promotes it), it has met and continues to meet with an astonishing degree of resistance. Let us try to state Hume's account more clearly, in preparation for examining contending views.

Hume's Account of Morality

According to Hume, the easiest way to understand the principles of morals is to trace them from their foundation, which is most easily seen by considering the object toward which the estimable qualities tend: the well-being of human individuals and society. He suggests that this will appear most clearly if we acknowledge that in all or most human beings there is at least a minuscule amount of what he calls "humanity," some "benevolence, however small . . . , some spark of friendship for humankind; some particle of the dove kneaded with our frame, along with the elements of the wolf and serpent" (*ECPM*, 271).

> Let these generous sentiments be supposed ever so weak; let them be insufficient to move even a hand or finger of our body, they must still direct the determination of our mind, and where everything else is equal, produce a cool preference of what is useful and serviceable to mankind, above what is pernicious and dangerous. A *moral distinction*, therefore, immediately arises; a general sentiment of blame and approbation; a tendency, however faint, to the objects of the one, and a proportionable aversion to those of the other. (Ibid.)

Hume makes no attempt to show that human beings are not frequently selfish or moved by such passions as avarice, ambition, or vanity. He simply denies that these are the foundations of morality. "The notion

of morals implies some sentiment common to all mankind, which recommends the same object to general approbation, and makes every man, or
most men, agree in the same opinion or decision concerning it" (*ECPM,*
272). Whether this entails some sort of "moral sentiment" first discovered by Hume (or perhaps Frances Hutcheson) need not concern us,
although this seems to me a highly dubious reading.[3] It is sufficient that
Hume traces morals to the sentiments arising from humanity which are
"not only the same in all human creatures, and produce the same approbation or censure; but they also comprehend all human creatures;
nor is there anyone whose conduct or character is not, by their means, an
object for everyone of censure or approbation" (*ECPM,* 273). Other
passions, of course, produce different sentiments in different individuals
according to their situation. Benevolence or humanity alone, however
faint, arouse in all mankind the same sentiments of approval or repug-
nance. That is why the sentiments "dependent on humanity," and not
those connected with any other passions, are the "origin of morals."
"Whatever conduct gains my approbation, by touching my humanity,
procures also the applause of all mankind, by affecting the same principle in them; but what serves my avarice or ambition pleases these passions in me alone, and affects not the avarice and ambition of the rest of
mankind" (*ECPM,* 274). The summary Hume offers is elegant and
concise:

> There is no circumstance of conduct in any man, provided it have
> a beneficial tendency, that is not agreeable to my humanity, how-
> ever remote the person, but every man, so far removed as neither
> to cross nor serve my avarice and ambition, is regarded as wholly
> indifferent by those passions. The distinction, therefore, between
> these species of sentiment being so great and evident, language
> must soon be moulded upon it, and must invent a peculiar set of
> terms, in order to express those universal sentiments of censure
> and approbation, which arise from humanity, or from views of
> general usefulness and its contrary. Virtue and Vice become then
> known; morals are recognized; certain general ideas are framed of

human conduct and behavior; such measures are expected from men in such situations. (Ibid.)

After thus presenting the foundations of morals or virtue, Hume makes one more attempt to "accommodate matters, and remove if possible every difficulty." He asks the reader to join him in supposing false all the reasoning he has just displayed and supposing that in tracing the principles of morals to the sentiments arising from humanity (or benevolence or sympathy—he uses all three terms) "we have embraced a wrong hypothesis" (*ECPM*, 276). Even on this supposition, according to Hume—that is, even if the qualities we approve or praise are not praised because we have a tendency to favor the good of mankind—we must still admit we praise them. To deny this is to deny the evidence of common life. "The preceding delineation or definition of Personal Merit must still retain its evidence and authority: it must still be allowed that every quality of the mind, which is *useful* or *agreeable* to the *person himself* or to *others*, or communicates a pleasure to the spectator, engages his esteem, and is admitted under the honourable denomination of virtue or merit." Hume goes on to adumbrate some of these qualities:

> Are not justice, fidelity, honour, veracity, allegiance, chastity, esteemed solely on account of their tendency to promote the good of society? Is not that tendency inseparable from humanity, benevolence, lenity, generosity, gratitude, moderation, tenderness, friendship, and all the other social virtues? Can it possibly be doubted that industry, discretion, frugality, secrecy, order, perseverance, forethought, judgement, and this whole class of virtues and accomplishments, of which many pages would not contain the catalogue; can it be doubted, I say, that the tendency of these qualities to promote the interest and happiness of their possessor, is the sole foundation of their merit? (*ECPM*, 277)

This list of virtues, though limited, includes, especially in the second and third parts, many qualities which men have little or no opportunity to develop or display in a savage state, or for that matter in conditions which do not include peace, order, security, and a degree of privacy or individual autonomy—the conditions recommended in Hume's account of the gradual progress of improvement in the *History*.

But *aren't* human beings capable of setting up other systems of morality if they wish? And aren't these to be accorded equal status with what Hume recommends? To the first question we must answer in the affirmative; Hume himself offers an example: "celibacy, fasting, penance, mortification, self-denial, humility, silence, solitude, and the whole train of monkish virtues" (*ECPM*, 270) have been elevated to a moral system by some. But to the second question Hume answers with a clear negative. Such a "moral system" is a perversion and could never be received "where men judge of things by their natural, unprejudiced reason, without the delusive glosses of superstition and false religion" (*ECPM*, 270). The natural, unprejudiced reason is precisely the capacity which runs into trouble in philosophical systems, and this seems to explain the fact that Hume's account of moral principles is at once so common sensical and so original: his philosophy is grounded in common life and eschews the systematizing and distorting inclinations characteristic of so many of his philosophical predecessors. The monkish virtues are seen by the ordinary man to "stupify the understanding and harden the heart, obscure the fancy and sour the temper." They properly belong among the vices, when judged by "natural, unprejudiced reason": "nor has any superstition force sufficient among men of the world, to pervert entirely these natural sentiments. A gloomy, hair-brained enthusiast, after his death, may have a place in the calendar; but will scarcely ever be admitted, when alive, into intimacy and society, except by those who are as delirious and dismal as himself" (ibid.).

Hume seems to have believed that an account of morals such as he offered, at once so simple and powerful, in accordance with common life, and moreover ratified by the "gradual progress of improvement" in human society, could scarcely admit of serious objections. In the conclusion to the *Enquiry*, he expresses his own conviction in the strongest terms. Despite his aversion to any "positive or dogmatical" tone in philosophy, he says, "I must confess, that this enumeration puts the matter in so strong a light, that I cannot, *at present,* be more assured of any truth, which I learn from reasoning and argument." Yet he confesses an almost ironical "diffidence and skepticism" because, as he puts it, an hypothesis accounting for morals which is "so obvious" must certainly, "had it been a true one, . . . long ere now, have been received by the unanimous suffrage and consent of mankind" (*ECPM,* 278). What can explain the resistance to it, or the failure to discover it? Indeed what can account for the astonishing degree of resistance, even today, to Hume's account of what constitutes a good society, an account which we have seen to be interwoven with his account of the virtues?

Misunderstandings of Virtue

Without seeking explicitly to answer these questions for our own times, let us look carefully at several passages in Hume's *Essays* which suggest the lines of his own thought concerning two related sources of resistance to the claim of the superiority of liberal commercial society and its virtues. These antagonists of his position have their roots in what might almost be called myths—the myth of superiority of the ancients and the myth of the viciousness of luxury. Both preclude wholehearted approval of the sort of society Hume admires and believes England to be. At least one, and perhaps both, of these myths continues to be powerful today.

First, how is the belief in the superiority of the ancients, which was widespread in the eighteenth century, connected to this discussion of virtue? The societies in question are the ancient republics of Greece and Italy, famous not only for letters but for their virtue. Hume admits that the ancient republics were quite different from modern ones. Ancient republics "were free states, they were small ones; and the age being martial, all their neighbors were continually in arms. Freedom naturally begets public spirit, especially in small states" (*E,* 259). Their chief and most splendid virtue seems indeed to have been an apparently selfless public spiritedness, or what Hume calls *amor patriae,* which made the ancient republics powerful and helped to protect their free and noncommercial way of life, their arts and civility. Many eighteenth-century writers, most notably Rousseau, expressed admiration for ancient republics, and the greatness of these republics was widely and correctly understood to be connected to their contempt for the merely commercial (as opposed to military) pursuit of wealth. This admiration emerged most often in the form of claims about the superior populousness of the ancient world.

In his brilliant article, already cited, E. C. Mossner established that Hume's longest essay, "Of the Populousness of Ancient Nations," constituted Hume's contribution to the controversy between ancients and moderns.[4] Hume himself explains why this apparently demographic issue has much greater importance: "in general, we may observe, that the question with regard to the populousness of ages or kingdoms, implies important consequences, and commonly determines concerning the preference of their whole police, their manners, and the constitution of their government" (*E*, 381). Hume calls attention to the ubiquitous human tendency to venerate what is ancient ("the humour of blaming the present, and admiring the past, is strongly rooted in human nature" [*E*, 464]) but suggests that such veneration is in this instance misplaced. Since in general "every wise, just, and mild government, by rendering the condition of its subjects easy and secure, will always abound most in people, as well as in commodities and riches" (*E*, 382), Hume's conviction of the superiority of modern commercial society requires that he show the belief in the greater populousness of ancient nations false or at least doubtful. In the course of his lengthy and ingenious analysis of the available figures on population, and in other essays, Hume introduces two related criticisms of ancient republicanism. The defects to which he calls attention are the reliance of ancient republics on slavery and the unnaturalness of their political institutions when considered in the light of natural human inclinations. Both of these are due in part at least, to an external circumstance: the primacy of war and the resulting overemphasis on martial qualities.[5]

"The chief difference," Hume writes, "between the *domestic* economy of the ancients and that of the moderns, consists in the practice of slavery, which prevailed among the former" (*E*, 383). This practice is itself unjust, and Hume castigates admirers of the civil liberty and virtue of the ancients for inconsistency: "whilst they brand all submission to the government of a single person with the harsh denomination of slavery, they would gladly reduce the greater part of mankind to real slavery and subjection." Any reasonable analysis will show that "human nature, in general, really enjoys more liberty at present, in the most arbitrary government of Europe, than it ever did during the most flourishing period of ancient times" (ibid.). Hume's argument depends on his inclusion—suggested by the use of the term *human nature*—of all human beings, masters and slaves, in the calculation. He shows that the modern practice of service for wages is both more equitable and produces superior virtue. In the ancient system there were no "checks" on the master, "to engage him in the reciprocal duties of gentleness and humanity"; even slave masters are corrupted by slavery. "In modern times, a bad servant finds not easily a good master, nor a bad master a good servant; and the checks are mutual, suitably to the inviolable and eternal laws of reason and equity" (*E*, 384). Claims about the superior virtue of the ancients require turning a blind eye to the destructive influence of domestic slavery on virtue, and not only with regard to slaves themselves.

In the essay "Of Commerce" Hume examines whether commerce contributes to the strength and greatness of a state. The question arises because admirers of the ancient republics maintain that their greatness was connected to their suppression of commerce, a suppression undertaken with the aim of maintaining a fit and ready military force. According to the ancient view, private wealth and even happiness are in conflict with public spirit and civic virtue. In the course of refuting this view Hume comments that "ancient policy was violent, and contrary to the more natural and usual course of things" (*E*, 259). In fact, he says, with reference to the "peculiar laws" by which Sparta was governed, "were the testimony of history less positive and circumstantial, such a government would appear a mere philosophical whim or fiction, and impossible ever to be reduced to practice." Sparta will seem a "prodigy" to anyone "who has considered human nature, as it displayed itself in other nations, and other ages" (ibid.). Though Roman principles were "somewhat more natural," even they could prevail only because an "extraordinary concurrence of circumstances," including above all considerations of survival in an age when a number of small states were continually in arms, made citizens "submit to such grievous burdens" (*E*, 259). "A continual succession of wars makes every citizen a soldier: he takes the field in his turn: and during his service he is chiefly maintained by himself. This service is indeed equivalent to a heavy tax; yet it is less felt by people addicted to arms, who fight for honor and revenge more than pay, and are unacquainted with gain and industry, as well as pleasure" (*E*, 259).[6]

But this is not the usual course of things, and "the less natural any set of principles are, which support a particular society, the more difficulty will a legislator meet with in raising and cultivating them" (*E*, 260). Even sovereigns, Hume suggests, "must take mankind as they find them." The best policy for a wise legislator is "to comply with the common bent of mankind and give it all the improvements of which it is susceptible." As we will see below, this often involves, according to Hume, balancing *vices* and not merely promoting virtue. A moral system, just as much as a legislator, must take human nature as it is. "Now, according to the most natural course of things, industry, and arts, and trade, increase the power of the sovereign, as well as the happiness of the subjects; and that policy is violent, which aggrandizes the public by the poverty of individuals" (ibid.). Mossner summarizes Hume's case against the ancient republics and their conception of virtue with the assertion that ancient manners "were unfavorable to the general welfare: these manners include the misunderstanding of liberty, the precariousness of property rights, the inhuman maxims of politics. . . . The inferiority of ancient manufactures and commerce did not contribute to the growth of luxury nor the general well-being of the masses of people."[7] This brings us neatly to the second of the myths Hume examines and explodes.

Luxury

Moral and political thinkers have widespread antipathy, amounting to prejudice, against luxury. Hume seems to see this prejudice as a deplorable kind of moralism, an ignorant moralism which is unwilling to scrutinize carefully the genuine and solid morality of common life. The prejudice against luxury continues to operate today, on both sides of the political spectrum. It has roots in secular egalitarianism, from which come calls for confiscatory taxes on the rich, and in some religious teachings which see commerce, and especially capitalism or free enterprise commerce, as sources of evil and exploitation.

There is a peculiar and mystifying tendency to attack luxury as the source of greed and avarice, a relationship common sense would reverse. The prejudice is fed by the strong historical association of ostentatious luxury with ages of stultifying social stratification and oppression. The luxury of magnificent palaces and the pomp and ceremony of a corrupt nobility, however, are examined very carefully by Hume in their relation to commerce, as we have seen. His advocacy of commercial society is based on his conclusion that stratification and nobility—not luxury—are obstacles to commerce, which in itself has a tendency to promote liberty and the rise of the commons, and thus to dissolve the stratification. (Consider the story about Henry VII fining the Earl of Oxford on account of his "retainers," in chapter 7 above.) Especially virulent strains of complaint about the viciousness of luxury are connected to religious fundamentalism, as may be seen from a consideration of the rantings of the late Ayatollah Khomeini or the more moderate warnings of decadence of Aleksandr Solzhenitsyn.[8]

These complaints and warnings are very close in spirit to the eighteenth-century prejudice against luxury which Hume examined in the essay originally introduced under the title "Of Luxury." The essay (whose name he changed to "Of Refinement in the Arts") begins as follows: "Luxury is a word of an uncertain signification, and may be taken in a good as well as a bad sense. In general it means great refinement in the gratification of the senses; and any degree of it may be innocent, or blameable, according to the age, or country, or condition of the person" (*E*, 268). He undertakes then to examine luxury dispassionately, noting that, since luxury may be either innocent or blameable, "one may be surprised at those preposterous opinions which have been entertained concerning it." Some men "of libertine principles" go so far as to praise even vicious luxury, whereas others represent luxury in any degree as "the source of all the corruptions, disorders, and factions, incident to civil government" (*E,* 269). The former, in their praise of luxury, "represent it as highly advantageous to society." Hume says his intention is to "endeavour to correct both these extremes," though by the end of the essay the reader finds that, however evenhanded Hume's analysis is, he has undercut the moralist position far more than the view of those who praise luxury. He will proceed, he says, by proving *"first,* that the ages of refinement are both the happiest and most virtuous; *secondly,* that wherever luxury ceases to be innocent, it also ceases to be beneficial; and when carried a degree too far, is a quality pernicious, though perhaps not the most pernicious, to political society" (*E,* 269). The last clause contains the catch: Hume suggests, at the end, that even vicious luxury is preferable to the alternatives. Though he is neither a libertine nor a severe moralist, and though he stops short of praising vicious luxury simply, Hume suggests that until all vices are eliminated from the human condition—an eventuality he does not look for—the vice even of vicious luxury may justly be endorsed or preferred to its alternatives.

Hume undertakes his first task, the proof that ages of refinement are happiest and most virtuous, by considering the effects of luxury in private and public life. He begins by asserting that human happiness consists of three ingredients (action, pleasure, and indolence), about which it is possible to disagree only about the proper proportions. "In times when industry and the arts flourish, men are kept in perpetual occupation; and enjoy, as their reward, the occupation itself, as well as those pleasures which are the fruit of their labor" (*E,* 270; unless otherwise noted, all subsequent references in this section are to this and the following ten pages). If in an attempt to prevent luxury one were to banish or discourage the refined arts, one would "deprive men both of action and of pleasure," and since indolence must fill the empty place, men will be less happy because even indolence, which may be enjoyable, can only be enjoyed as a respite from action and employment. Thus refinement in the arts contributes to happiness by promoting industry.

Not only are men inclined to be active and enjoy the satisfaction of active employment, but industry itself and the naturally concomitant refinements in mechanical arts "commonly produce some refinements in the liberal." Thus knowledge is promoted by refinement in the arts: "The spirit of the age affects all the arts, and the minds of men being once roused from their lethargy, and put into a fermentation, turn themselves on all sides, carry improvements into every art and science. Profound ignorance is totally banished, and men . . . cultivate the pleasures of the mind as well as those of the body." Thus refinement or luxury contributes to both industry and knowledge. Hume adds a third beneficial effect: men become more sociable, and with more sociability comes humanity. Only in "ignorant and barbarous nations" are men content to live in solitude or at a distance from others. When the arts flourish, men "flock into cities; love to receive and communicate knowledge; to show their wit or their breeding; their taste in conversation or living, in clothes or furniture." Whether from curiosity, which "allures the wise," or vanity or pleasure, men are drawn together and meet in an increasingly "easy and sociable" manner. The result is that, "beside the improvements which they receive from knowledge and the liberal arts, it is impossible but they must feel an increase of humanity, from the very habit of conversing together, and contributing to each other's pleasure and entertainment." Hume's summing up brings all three effects together: "Thus *industry, knowledge,* and *humanity,* are linked together by an indissoluble chain, and are found, from experience as well as reason, to be more peculiar to the more polished, and, what are commonly denominated, the more luxurious ages." To those three good effects Hume adds a fourth, almost as an afterthought: men will indulge less in excesses as they become more refined, since "nothing is more destructive to true pleasure than such excesses." Thus luxury or refinement in the arts, contrary to what severe moralists assert, actually promotes moderation.

In public life, the effects of refinement in the arts include a tendency to contribute to the strength and power of the society as a whole. "The increase and consumption of all the commodities, which serve to the ornament and pleasure of life, are advantages to society; because, at the same time that they multiply those innocent gratifications to individuals, they are a kind of *storehouse* of labour, which, in the exigencies of state, may be turned to the public service." This is the real answer to the charges that luxury and commerce are incompatible with public spiritedness: they supply an alternative to the direct public spirit the ancients promoted at such enormous cost; the public spirit of a commercial society exists in reserve only, but though less splendid it is preserved much more easily and is always there to be drawn on. Ancient public spirit was maintained only at great cost in terms of natural human inclinations and was thus fragile and not entirely reliable. Without refinement in the arts, according to Hume, that is, "in a nation where there is no demand for such superfluities, men sink into indolence, lose all enjoyment of life, and are useless to the public, which cannot maintain or support its fleets and armies from the industry of such slothful members." In addition to increasing the strength of the society, luxury and commerce contribute to wiser government by promoting improvements in the knowledge of "laws, order, police, discipline," which "can never be carried to any degree of perfection, before human reason has refined itself by exercise." By combating superstition and prejudice, advances in arts and sciences promote political decency. "Knowledge in the arts of government begets mildness and moderation, by instructing men in the advantages of humane maxims above rigour and severity, which drive subjects into rebellion." Hume was no doubt thinking here of the violent religious strife he was to write about so eloquently in the Stuart volumes of the *History*. [9] The spread of refinement or luxury softens the tempers of men, improves their knowledge and promotes humanity even in public life, and thus conspicuous humanity "is the chief characteristic which distinguishes a civilized age from times of barbarity and ignorance."

Hume maintains that commerce and the arts need not diminish a nation's "martial spirit" even though they tame men's ferocity; honor is a principle which becomes more important with civility, politeness, and refinement, and a sense of honor may promote courage just as well as does the anger characteristic of more brutal or savage ages.[10] He denies the claim that the decline of Rome was due to an effeminacy brought on by its embrace of luxury and refinement: though "all the Latin classics, whom we peruse in our infancy, are full of these sentiments, and universally ascribe the ruin of their state to the arts and riches imported from the East," Hume writes, "it would be easy to prove, that these writers mistook the cause of the disorders in the Roman state, and ascribed to luxury and the arts, what really proceeded from an ill-modelled government, and the unlimited extent of conquests." He might have added that the decline of Rome seems to strengthen his claim that the ancient republics had to distort human nature in order to achieve that public spirit which distinguished them, gloriously but briefly.

The final and perhaps most important claim concerning the effects of refinement in the arts is also the most general: "if we consider the matter in a proper light, we shall find, that a progress in the arts is rather favourable to liberty, and has a natural tendency to preserve, if not produce a free government." This is the core of the argument later traced in detail in the *History* (see chapter 7, above). In "rude unpolished nations" almost all labor is necessarily devoted to cultivation of the ground (or to fighting), which invariably results in two classes of men: peasants or serfs, who are often slaves and are fitted only for subjection, and a class of proprietors, or nobles, whom Hume calls "petty tyrants."

> But where luxury nourishes commerce and industry, the peasants, by a proper cultivation of the land, become rich and independent; while the tradesmen and merchants acquire a share of the property, and draw authority and consideration to that middling rank of men, who are the best and firmest basis of public liberty. These submit not to slavery, like the peasants, from poverty and meanness of spirit; and having no hopes of tyrannizing over others, like the barons, they are not tempted, for the sake of that gratification, to submit to the tyranny of their sovereign. They covet equal laws, which may secure their property, and preserve them from monarchical, as well as aristocratical tyranny.

Hume expresses amazement at the violent blame attached to luxury or refinement, in view of the role it has played in transforming English society by contributing to the rise of popular government. The lower house of Parliament is the mainstay of that government, and "all the world acknowledges, that it owed its chief influence and consideration to the encrease of commerce, which threw such a balance of property into the hands of the commons."

What though of the effects of luxury or refinement when it ceases to be "innocent"? The argument Hume offers here is almost devious, but it is so elegantly simple that one scarcely notices the real force of his conclusion. He has already warned the reader of its bearing by noting, and now repeating, that even vicious luxury, while a quality pernicious, is "perhaps not the most pernicious, to political society." "Vicious luxury" is taken to mean a "gratification" which "engrosses all a man's expence, and leaves no ability for such acts of duty and generosity as are required by his situation and fortune." That virtue is desirable and superior to vice Hume readily acknowledges. But if we are to speak of removing a vice—for example, the *indulgence* of a desire for some vicious luxury—is the alternative some virtue? If by banning a vicious luxury we could be assured that a man would employ the saving "in the education of his children, in the support of his friends, and in relieving the poor," then the benefit is self-evident. But what if by removing one vice we simply promote another, if by banning a luxury, we encourage a man to give way to indolence? "To say, that, without a vicious luxury, the labour would not have been employed at all, is only to say, that there is some other defect in human nature, such as indolence, selfishness, inattention to others, for which luxury, in some measure, provides a remedy; as one poison may be an antidote to another." Of course, as Hume admits, "virtue, like wholesome food, is better than poison, however corrected."

The comparison invites us to ask what course is open to us as reformers. Aside from bodily sickness, Hume suggests, "all other ills spring from some vice, either in ourselves or others; and even many of our diseases proceed from the same origin." To deny this is to maintain that this is the best of all possible worlds, a view to which Hume does not subscribe. Since our ills proceed from vice, he says, "remove the vices, and the ills follow. You must only take care to remove all the vices. If you remove part, you may render the matter worse. By banishing *vicious* luxury, without curing sloth and an indifference to others, you only diminish industry in the state, and add nothing to men's charity or their generosity." Hume leaves the reader to draw the conclusion and immediately obscures the issue by arguing against those who assert vice to be beneficial to society, which he calls a contradiction in terms. And rightly, for Hume is not praising vices. He shows that they stand in a complex relation to one another. With delightful irony he points out that he is contributing to a philosophical question and not a political one, and so underlines the irrelevance of his fastidious refusal to endorse a vice.

> I call it a *philosophical* question, not a *political* one. For whatever may be the consequence of such a miraculous transformation of mankind, as would endow them with every species of virtue, and free them from every species of vice; this concerns not the magistrate, who aims only at possibilities. He cannot cure every vice by substituting a virtue in its place. Very often he can only cure one vice by another; and in that case, he ought to prefer what is least pernicious to society. Luxury, when excessive, is the source of many ills; but is in general preferable to sloth and idleness, which would commonly succeed in its place, and are more hurtful both to private persons and to the public.

The proper understanding of luxury requires a comprehensive understanding of human nature and of the physical and moral circumstances of human life.[11] Hume's account has the advantage of its close agreement with common life or, as he puts it here, with a political perspective rather than the philosophic.

The Dismal Dress Falls Off

The careful reader of Hume's second *Enquiry* is alerted by a curious story related near the beginning of the work to the paradoxical originality of his account of the principles of morals. After opening section 2 ("Of Benevolence") with the admission that "it may be esteemed, perhaps, a superfluous task to prove, that the benevolent or softer affections are estimable" (*ECPM*, 176), Hume proceeds to tell of Plutarch's account of the death scene of Pericles, "the great Athenian statesman and general." His friends, thinking him "now insensible, began to indulge their sorrow . . . by enumerating his great qualities and successes, his conquests and victories," when Pericles, conscious throughout, remonstrated with them for forgetting "the most eminent" of the things for which he deserved praise—his benevolence, manifested in the fact that "no citizen has ever yet worn mourning on my account" (*ECPM*, 176–77). The story suggests what Hume himself means to teach, namely, that the fundamental importance of the "benevolent or softer affections" is largely unrecognized. If the position these occupy as the foundation of morality is sometimes misunderstood even in common life, in moral theories their importance has been totally neglected. Hume finds himself urging their importance on the reader in the next paragraphs, then pretends to catch himself doing something unnecessary: "But I forget, that it is not my business to recommend generosity and benevolence, or to paint, in their true colours, all the genuine charms of the social virtues" (*ECPM*, 177). As the story of Pericles itself shows, this is precisely what is necessary: Hume's moral theory is intended to bring moral philosophy or "speculation" into touch with the reality of moral judgments in practice, the foundation of which is benevolence or sympathy, despite the failure of moral theorists to recognize it.

Some forty pages later, in the section called "Why Utility Pleases," Hume elaborates further on this theme. "It seems so natural a thought," he begins, "to ascribe to their utility the praise, which we bestow on the social virtues, that one would expect to meet with this principle everywhere in moral writers, as the chief foundation of their reasoning and enquiry" (*ECPM*, 212). That we do not suggests something defective about moral theories; after all, "in common life, we may observe, that the circumstance of utility is always appealed to; nor is it supposed, that a greater eulogy can be given to any man, than to display his usefulness to the public, and enumerate the services, which he has performed to mankind and society" (ibid.). This is precisely what the friends of Pericles were doing, only Hume seems to suggest that they did not correctly understand the basis of their praise. Pericles' remonstrance was required to point it out.

That the defect is in philosophy becomes even clearer. Hume suggests that the "difficulty of accounting for" the effects of utility, or its contrary, "has kept philosophers from admitting them into their system of ethics, and has induced them rather to employ any other principle, in explaining the origin of moral good and evil" (*ECPM*, 213). Moral philosophy, embarrassed at its inability to explain this principle fully, has chosen to leave it out of consideration, according to Hume. "But it is no just reason for rejecting any principle, confirmed by experience, that we cannot give a satisfactory account of its origin, nor are able to resolve it into other more general principles" (ibid.). Hume appeals, as ever, to experience; where philosophical reason, with its tendency to systematize, is in conflict with common life Hume prefers the rough contours of the latter. Why men feel sympathy with their fellow creatures, or are inclined to display mild benevolence toward others, is perhaps not something we can explain rationally, but this is no reason, in Hume's view, to deny what the facts teach so plainly.

Some philosophers have begun from this principle of utility, however, and proceeded too far in the opposite direction: "from the apparent usefulness of the social virtues, it has readily been inferred by skeptics, both ancient and modern, that all moral distinctions arise from education, and were, at first, invented, and afterwards encouraged, by the art of politicians, in order to render men tractable, and subdue their natural ferocity and selfishness, which incapacitated them for society" (*ECPM*, 214). These philosophers have held that all morality is purely conventional, since only thus can it be made consistent with theories which attempt to reduce all natural impulses to selfishness or self-regard. Hume dismisses this sort of "moral philosophy." Despite the admittedly "powerful influence" of education and convention, which may "frequently increase or diminish, beyond their natural standard, the sentiments of opprobrium or dislike," the claim that "*all* moral affection or dislike arises from this origin, will never surely be allowed by any judicious enquirer" (ibid.). Common life speaks sufficiently plainly here:

> Had nature made no such distinction, founded on the original constitution of the mind, the words, *honourable* and *shameful*, *lovely* and *odious*, *noble* and *despicable*, had never had place in any language; nor could politicians, had they invented these terms, ever have been able to render them intelligible, or make them convey any idea to the audience. So that nothing can be more superficial than this paradox of the sceptics; and it were well, if, in the abstruser studies of logic and metaphysics, we could as easily obviate the cavils of that sect, as in the practical and more intelligible sciences of politics and morals. (Ibid.)

The latter are more intelligible precisely because the proximity of our everyday experience makes overly reductive theories improbable on their face (though this has not discouraged philosophers from developing them). The social virtues "must, therefore, be allowed to have a natural beauty and amiableness, which, at first, antecedent to all precept or education, recommends them to the esteem of uninstructed mankind, and engages their affections" (ibid.). The basis of this esteem, Hume teaches, is the "public utility" of these virtues. "A creature, absolutely malicious and spiteful, were there any such in nature, must be worse than indifferent to the images of vice and virtue" (*ECPM*, 226).

We are now in a position to appreciate the genuine originality of Hume's moral philosophy. Its great complexity results from Hume's efforts not to distort the perspective of common life. Only in moral theories of the systematic kind is there an attempt to eliminate or reduce the complexity inherent in ordinary experience. But Hume claims an additional merit for his account of morals besides accuracy, located in the explanation it gives of our obligation to virtue. He undertakes in the last section of the *Enquiry*, "to inquire whether every man, who has any regard to his own happiness and welfare, will not best find his account in the practice of every moral duty" (*ECPM*, 278). If he can succeed in this, Hume writes, "we shall have the satisfaction to reflect, that we have advanced principles, which not only . . . will stand the test of reasoning and inquiry, but may contribute to the amendment of men's lives, and their improvement in morality and social virtue" (*ECPM*, 279). This is not an automatic effect of accurate moral theory, since as Hume admits "the philosophical truth of any proposition by no means depends on its tendency to promote the interests of society." In fact he suggests that a true or accurate theory, the effects of which would be pernicious, should not be made public at all. "The ingenuity of your researches may be admired, but your systems will be detested. . . . Truths which are *pernicious* to society, if any such there be, will yield to errors which are salutary and *advantageous*" (ibid.).

But Hume's account of the principles of morals does not suffer from any practical deficiency, and he contrasts it specifically with the moral theories offered by philosophers and theologians, both of which have misled us. "What philosophical truths could be more advantageous to society, than these here delivered, which represent virtue in all her genuine and most engaging charms, and make us approach her with ease, familiarity, and affection? The dismal dress falls off, with which many divines, and some philosophers, have covered her; and nothing appears but gentleness, humanity, beneficence, affability; nay, even at proper intervals, play, frolic, and gaiety" (ibid.). Hume's account of morals is accurate and offers its own justification, because it teaches that virtue is connected with happiness, that it accords with the natural inclinations to live in prosperity, congenially with others, and satisfied with the integrity of the decent ordinary man. It avoids the dangerous distortions of philosophic moral systems which teach that virtue is rigorous and austere. In Hume's account, which is consistent with his account of the desirability of liberal commercial society, virtue is relieved of the "dismal dress" which has so often covered her. "She talks not of useless austerities and rigours, suffering and self-denial." In this account virtue conduces to make "all mankind, during every instant of their existence, if possible, cheerful and happy; . . . The sole trouble which she demands, is that of just calculation and a steady preference of the greater happiness" (ibid.).

Hume claims the advantage of his moral theory consists in its unblinking acceptance of the actual desires and preferences of mankind—that is, in its entire accordance with common life, or at least with the principles implicit in it and discernible to a careful eye. Indeed, he asks, on what other ground can morality be recommended? "What theory of morals can ever serve any useful purpose, unless it can show, by a particular detail, that all the duties which it recommends are also the true interest of each individual?" (*ECPM*, 280). Examples can be adduced without limit; it would "surely be superfluous to prove," as Hume puts it, "that the virtues which are immediately useful or agreeable to the person possessed of them, are desirable in a view to self-interest." The case is the same with the companionable virtues: "Would you have your company coveted, admired, followed; rather than hated, despised, avoided? Can anyone seriously deliberate in the case?" (ibid.). This is not to suggest there are no conflicts or tensions between the various virtues, and Hume makes no such claim. In fact any theory which pretended to eliminate such tensions—which are inherent in common life and obvious to common sense—would be guilty of precisely the kind of systematizing distortion to which philosophical theories not grounded in common life are so prone.

Two lessons may be drawn from this performance. They appear if we ask who teaches that virtue is unpleasant or difficult, that it requires us to suppress the human inclination to prosperity and wealth, for example. "Many divines, and some philosophers" have tried to teach this, and we can trace their deficiency to denials of some aspect of common life. Common life or experience suggests we be moderate in our expectations of ourselves and other human beings; the moral systems of theologians and philosophers tend at least to make much greater demands on men. Whereas austere systems of morality call on men to suppress or eliminate any desire for wealth, Hume's account of morals suggests that the desire for wealth will be—and should be—governed or regulated by other considerations, such as the natural desire for esteem and good will. A second lesson is implicit here as well: we ought to make no attempt to systematize the complexity of common life by subordinating to one rule or one goal the multiplicity of (sometimes) conflicting practical ends. A moral system which proclaims the superiority of pleasure as an end, for example, begins to lose touch with common life by its attempt to ignore or diminish the existence of other considerations, such as integrity or esteem of others. Among Hume's essays is a set of four which take the names of ancient sects of philosophy, and in a note to the first, "The Epicurean," Hume explains that his intention in "this and the three following essays" is "to deliver the sentiments of sects that naturally form themselves in the world and entertain different ideas of human life and happiness" (*E*, 138). Each presents a persuasive account, but each is guilty of what might be called reductive distortion, which is why Hume identifies them as sects. His own account of the principles of morality makes no attempt to reduce the complexity of the moral universe of common life; it has, in fact, room in it for each of the sects sketched so beautifully in these essays.

Something about Hume's account of the principles of morals is strongly reminiscent of the *Nicomachean Ethics* of Aristotle. Like Aristotle Hume repeatedly emphasizes the dependence of his ethics on common life or ordinary speech about moral things. Like Aristotle Hume suggests that living properly or virtuously is rewarding in itself and that, given the proper external circumstances or good fortune, virtue is closely connected to happiness (of the garden-variety sort, that is, as prephilosophically understood). Like Aristotle Hume gives an important place to moderation ("why collect arguments to evince that . . . excesses of pleasure [are] hurtful. . . . These excesses are only denominated such, because they are hurtful" (*ECPM*, 280)). And like Aristotle Hume examines both private and public or social virtues and, refusing to subordinate one to the other, leaves them in all the complexity and potential tension in which they appear to us in common life. Paradoxically, in view of all these similarities, Hume's account of morals is deeply modern. It might be described as a *Nicomachean Ethics* for liberal commercial society, an ethics consistent with the political situation of modern man.

We must end the chapter with a problem raised by Hume's insistence that in his account of moral virtues the "dismal dress" falls off and that it is unnecessary to offer any external account of moral obligation since virtue recommends herself. The problem brings us full circle in our account of Hume's philosophy and points to the issue discussed in the next chapter. We began in chapter 2 from the observation that Hume was deeply troubled by the apparently insuperable tension between reason or philosophy and common life and suggested that his understanding of philosophy—and indeed his philosophy itself—was transformed as a result of his confrontation with that tension. We have now arrived at an understanding of his moral philosophy in which all tension seems to have disappeared, though some might say that philosophy has disappeared, leaving the maxims of common life to reign supreme. Is there no tension between philosophy thus understood and common life? Surely Hume has not forgotten the issue raised so explicitly in the first *Enquiry,* in particular in the section "Of a Particular Providence and of a Future State," where he professes to admire "the singular good fortune of philosophy, which, as it requires entire liberty above all other privileges . . . received its first birth in an age and country of freedom and toleration" (*EHU,* 132). He reports there a dialogue with an unnamed friend who proposes much what Hume has just seemed to propose—that between philosophy rightly understood and the requirements of society there is no tension at all. But there Hume maintains a position quite different, in view of the conflict between philosophy and religion.

Philosophy teaches us that we cannot know anything about a deity and that religious doctrines about an afterlife where virtue will be rewarded are without foundation. Philosophy also teaches us that such doctrines are not necessary to promote virtue because virtue promotes itself. Hume's friend argues that once the latter tenet is clear, it must be evident that philosophy is no threat and should not require an age of "freedom and toleration" in order to flourish. Hume replies in the following words:

> You conclude, that religious doctrines and reasonings *can* have no influence on life, because they *ought* to have no influence; never

considering, that men reason not in the same manner you do, but draw many consequences from the belief of a divine Existence, and suppose that the Deity will inflict punishments on vice, and bestow rewards on virtue, beyond what appear in the ordinary course of nature. Whether this reasoning of theirs be just or not, is no matter. Its influence on their life and conduct must still be the same. And, those who attempt to disabuse them of such prejudices, may, for aught I know, be good reasoners, but I cannot allow them to be good citizens and politicians; since they free men from one restraint upon their passions, and make the infringement of the laws of society, in one respect, more easy and secure. (*EHU*, 147)

Even if Hume's philosophic account of morals is in no tension with society or political life, philosophy herself may still be dangerous because "certain tenets of philosophy . . . seem to loosen . . . the ties of morality, and may be supposed, for that reason, pernicious to the peace of civil society" (*EHU*, 133–34). The problem which must be confronted is in the tension between philosophy and religion.

9 "The Surest Foundation": Philosophy and Religion

Hume is conventionally understood to have been an opponent or critic of both religion in general and Christianity in particular. Superficial evidence for this view is easy to find in his writings, and the identification of Hume with the Enlightenment helps to obscure the real character of his views. But Isaiah Berlin has noted the peculiar fact that Hume was the "patron saint" of a group of German "anti-rationalists and fideists" in the decades after the *Treatise* was translated into German, which suggests that the view of Hume as a rationalist of the Enlightenment may be too simple.[1] Although Berlin suggests that Hume would have been horrified by the use the irrationalists made of his doctrines, this judgment depends on assimilating Hume to the standard Enlightenment viewpoint of antipathy to religion, a step which may be too hasty.

At least some of the great thinkers behind the modern conception of liberal society believed that their most urgent task was to supply a critique of religion. This critique was intended to liberate political life from the influence of religious myth or superstition, and from the pernicious effects of Christianity in particular, through a literal "enlightenment" from what Hobbes called "the Kingdom of Darkness."[2] The project of the Enlightenment was advanced in a spirit of temerity which must surprise us, not only in the light of the recent developments to which Solzhenitsyn directs our attention, but also from a brief consideration

164

of the prevailing view in the centuries prior to the conception of the Enlightenment. In sharp contrast to the classical understanding, the new opponents of "superstition" entertained the most extravagant hopes for political life. Thus Hobbes wrote, "The Light of human minds is Perspicuous Words, but by exact definitions first snuffed, and purged from ambiguity; *Reason* is the *pace;* Encrease of *Science,* the *way;* and the Benefit of mankind, the *end.*"[3] The new understanding—one might call it a faith—rejected outright the classical view of piety as the strongest support of common morality. Cicero had expressed this classical view as follows: "I do not even know, if we cast off piety towards the Gods, but that faith, and all the associations of human life, and that most excellent of all virtues, justice, may perish with it."[4] Such doubts about the viability of atheistic civil life led the classical thinkers to conclude that theology was in need of defense, which was in turn to be supplied by philosophy, or rather, by political philosophy. Precision is necessary here because the enemy of piety was itself thought to be another kind of philosophy, namely natural philosophy or physics. The atheism which was associated with the natural philosophers (as pointed out by Socrates in Plato's *Apology of Socrates*) claimed that the cosmos consists of nothing but matter and as such is utterly or radically indifferent to the existence of human beings—and hence a fortiori to their moral requirements or conduct.[5] Political philosophy, using rhetoric, attempted to show that such a view did not successfully account for the whole of human experience and was, moreover, destructive of civilized human life.

The modern thinkers to whom Solzhenitsyn traces our ills reversed this classical stance. The new science saw the danger to man as proceeding not from physics but from religious enthusiasm or superstition. The latter, by the clear light of reason, was seen to be responsible for enormous human suffering, in the form of spiritual torment and material misery. A clear and reliable moral teaching was needed in order to replace the claims of superstition. It would be grounded not on piety or faith but on a scientific understanding of the natural requirements of human existence. Reason alone was to supply the foundation, in the form of a quasimaterialist interpretation of the universe, which revealed that the only genuine standards for human conduct arise from the need of the individual to preserve his or her natural or material being. These considerations suggest that, if we wish to come to terms with the charges of Solzhenitsyn, we must begin by examining some portion of this critique of religion, a critique first advanced in the name of healthy politics and sound morality, but which has led us—if he is correct—hopelessly far away from both.

Within the modern liberal tradition, the most powerful and original thinker to address these issues with the necessary energy and insight is Hume, who considered the issue of religion more openly and directly than any other modern thinker, with the possible exception of Spinoza. Two brief but important works of Hume proclaim his interest by their very titles: *The Natural History of Religion* and *Dialogues concerning Natural Religion*. Moreover, as Hume was a member—the ranking member—of the Scottish Enlightenment, we may expect him to approach religion in precisely the skeptical or critical frame of mind we wish to examine. Indeed, *The Natural History of Religion* has long been regarded as simply an antireligious work.[6] In this work Hume disparages all "popular religions." He finds that they tend, without exception, either toward melancholy and ignorant superstition or toward fanatical and ignorant enthusiasm, between which there is little to choose. "Every bystander will easily judge (but unfortunately the bystanders are few) that, if nothing were requisite to establish any popular system, but exposing the absurdities of other systems, every voter of every superstition could give a sufficient reason for his blind and bigotted attachment to the principle in which he has been educated" (*NHR*, 57). The tenor of his remarks here is reminiscent of the more guarded observations of Hobbes.[7]

In the *Dialogues concerning Natural Religion* Hume's views are less clear.[8] Despite the obscurity of his own position here, the *Dialogues* most certainly cannot be taken as supportive of customary religious teachings, popular or otherwise. As one commentator points out, in regard to the theological claim for the existence of God, "no volume in the literature has subjected the argument from design to more extended and acute criticism than Hume's *Dialogues*. No criticism of the ontological argument has been more widely accepted than his dictum that 'Whatsoever we conceive as existent, we can also conceive as non-existent' (*D*, 189)."[9] Such skeptical arguments seem to locate Hume squarely in the modern camp, where, along with Hobbes and others, he is to be understood as deeply critical of the pernicious effects of religious faith on political and moral life.

The Problem of How to Read the *Dialogues*

Even a casual reader of the secondary literature on these two "theological" works of Hume would be struck by the disagreement over his views or intentions. The obstacle to achieving clarity about these matters is not so much *The Natural History of Religion* as the *Dialogues*, and the chief obstacle is the very form of this work—that is, Hume's rhetoric or resort to "politic speech." We are not accustomed to this type of philosophical writing, as Hume himself notes in the prologue to the *Dialogues:* "Though the ancient philosophers conveyed most of their instruction in the form of dialogue, this method of composition has been little practised in later ages, and has seldom succeeded in the hands of those who have attempted it" (*D*, 127). That the issue of how to write philosophy is of special importance in coming to terms with Hume's thought has been suggested repeatedly in this study. One may add to this the evidence of Hume's great admiration for Cicero, the greatest of the Latin masters of rhetoric. Hume's *Dialogues*, in fact, are explicitly modeled on Cicero's great work, *De Natura Deorum*, "On the Nature of the Gods." In Hume's *Dialogues* as in Cicero's we find the greatest philosophical themes under consideration: piety and reason, belief, science, skepticism, politics, and religion. The work contains Hume's teaching on the most important questions.

But what is that teaching? The importance of Hume's *Dialogues concerning Natural Religion* is exceeded only by their inaccessibility, if we are to judge by the disagreement among scholars as to what he intended to convey in this work. Chief among the effects of this problem of the form of the *Dialogues* is the humility it recommends to any student of the work. Some of the finest interpreters of Hume have attempted to unravel the teaching of the *Dialogues,* yet there is little consensus.[10] Since the *Dialogues* were published only posthumously (Hume had worked on them for more than two decades), Hume himself speaks only in the work itself, and not in his own name there. The work consists of a long conversation among three principal interlocutors, narrated by a young auditor named Pamphilus. The three characters are Demea, a believer, Philo, the radical skeptic, and Cleanthes, who takes a sort of middle position against the other two. Demea and Philo, together in an uneasy alliance, hold that the nature of the Divine Being is wholly mysterious. From the first, scholars of the *Dialogues* have assumed their central task to be determining which character is the vehicle for Hume's own views of religion.[11]

The controversy over who speaks for Hume seems to have been, on the whole, fruitless and has given rise to a "second stage" of interpretation, which can be expressed as the attitude that "it seems wisest to proceed on what is in any case surely the safest assumption; namely, that it is the *Dialogues* itself which serves as Hume's spokesman." But those who have advanced this claim typically read Hume as solving a personal problem by liberating himself from all religious convictions and thus showing others the way to a mitigated skepticism or agnosticism.[12] Nothing but our own predispositions compels us, however, to understand Hume's undertaking in either of these ways. Hume's own religious views need not be the main issue: we have only to pay attention to Hume's model for the *Dialogues* to find a hint on this matter. Cicero warns readers in the beginning of *De Natura Deorum* that "those men who desire to know my own private opinion on every particular subject, have more curiosity than is necessary."[13] Surely it is no coincidence that Hume's views in the *Dialogues* are so obscure.

What has been forgotten in the case of Hume is that he was a *political* philosopher. We are prompted to this conclusion by the striking resemblance between Hume's last great work and the philosophic work of a preeminently political man, the statesman and orator Cicero. This suggests that Hume was seeking in the *Dialogues concerning Natural Religion* not to liberate himself or resolve a personal philosophical problem but to come to terms with a problem of vastly larger scope, a political problem. We may say, following Mossner, that the *Dialogues* is a work about much more than religion, and I wish to suggest here that it represents for us a recovery or reconstitution of the ancient task of political philosophy, for which Hume precociously detected a need, perhaps a century before other thinkers.

Hobbes, whom we have singled out among the founders of the modern liberal understanding for his trenchant critique of religion, had already claimed, a century before Hume, to have successfully established morality on a new scientific foundation. As a result, one of the tasks of political philosophy (as understood, for example, by Plato), was eliminated. That task was the defense of a kind of civic theology from the attacks of the young men who listened to the atheistic natural philosophers or physicists. For Plato the *need* for philosophy was not its primary justification: as the highest or best way of life it needed no justification from utility. But it needed to make a home for itself in an otherwise hostile political community, and by showing its usefulness it could make such a home. This state of affairs was transformed by Hobbes in two decisive respects: First, reason becomes nothing more than the servant of the passions,[14] and so philosophy is justified *only* insofar as it is the instrument of practical needs; and second, religion or theology no longer requires rhetorical *defense* by philosophy but instead becomes the object of philosophical attack. Indeed, political philosophy in the ancient sense, to the extent that any residue of it survives at all, should in Hobbes' view be absorbed into the new scientific psychology of man modeled on Galileo's physics.[15] The activity of *reflecting* on the human phenomena was no longer a danger to healthy civic life, but neither was it necessary any longer. Society was to be based on scientific reason in a narrow sense: only clear and demonstrably true principles were to be part of the new civic foundations. Moral principles of lesser clarity or more disputability—such as we find in the books of "the old moral philosophers"—were to be banished along with superstition and the Kingdom of Darkness.[16]

Hume's reflections on this state of affairs, together with his long study of the ancient writers whom Hobbes debunks, seem to have led him to see a danger here.[17] The new science itself appeared to him to rest on a kind of faith, a belief in principles for which no rational justification except our acceptance of them can be found. The danger which Hume must have seen here is similar to, but not the same as, the danger which classical philosophy attempted to counteract so as to supply a justification for its place in the city. The threat to healthy civic life in Hume's case comes less from physics or atheistic materialism than from the excessive skepticism on which modern science claims to be grounded. The danger of this skeptical posture is in its debunking not only of all religion but, what is worse, of the common sense grounding of moral principles. Hume seems to think that intransigent skepticism or Pyrrhonism contributes not the *death* of religion—as Hobbes apparently hoped or thought—but to its *debasement*, into forms of superstition or enthusiasm worse than those Hobbes loathed. But even aside from the effects of such skepticism on religious doctrines, it poses a danger to *all* morality, if the science on which it is ostensibly grounded reveals itself finally as only another form of groundless faith, a kind of "religion of skepticism" which has no purchase on life.

Thus Hume's *Dialogues* (together with the dialogue comprising chapter 11 of the *Enquiry concerning the Principles of Morals*) can be read as a forewarning of the dangers of scientific reason as later exposed by Kant and especially Nietzsche. If this view is correct, we may describe the *Dialogues* as an attempt to restore the theological-political teaching of ancient political philosophy. Hume wishes to defend healthy political life from what he perceives to be a threat, and in so doing he can restore to primacy the philosophic—as opposed to the narrowly scientific—life.[18] What better way to accomplish this classical task than with the tools of classical rhetoric? And what better tool than the classical dialogue, as used above all by Plato and Cicero?[19] Philosophy as Hume conceives it can become in this context a moderator in the otherwise dangerous or destructive battle between the new political science and vulgar or popular religion.

In the light of these considerations, it seems wise for us to look at the *Dialogues* again, as a work of political philosophy, a work whose political dimension must be kept in sight. We must read Hume's dialogues as we read Plato's: informed by our awareness that they present not so much Hume's own religious convictions as his reflections about the place of religion in our lives and about the relation of religion or theology to science, reason, politics, and philosophy.

The Teaching of the *Dialogues*

Hume himself does not speak in the *Dialogues* except for the title and one note—of ambiguous status—appended to the text near the end of part 12.[20] The entire work is written in the first person; the speaker is a young man named Pamphilus, who relates a long conversation he has witnessed but in which he took no part. The first question, then, especially to anyone familiar with Cicero's *De Natura Deorum* (which is manifestly the model for Hume's work in a number of respects)[21] is: Why doesn't Hume narrate in his own name? Two of Hume's major characters—Philo and Cleanthes—have the same names as did teachers of two of Cicero's three characters. One might reasonably expect Hume to follow Cicero in pretending to report a conversation he has himself witnessed, which would permit him—following Cicero—to make a judgment at the end. The usual explanation for Hume's departure from his model is that Hume had to be very circumspect in his approach "to such a momentous subject as religious belief."[22] But this is not persuasive, in view of Hume's already published views excoriating popular religions, not to mention that the *Dialogues* was not published (on the advice of Hume's friends) until after his death.[23] This suggests that Hume had some other reason for the introduction of Pamphilus as narrator. In particular we must inquire what about this character makes him appropriate where Hume himself would not have been. This is one of the first indications of the political character of this work: the *Dialogues* is not a discussion among philosophers only, since a young man is present. Hume emphatically directs our attention to this fact in the first sentence of the dialogue. Thus we need to pay careful attention not only to the arguments but to the characters—who says what to whom.

I believe it is a general failing of current readings of the *Dialogues* that the work is treated as being of exclusively philosophical or theological interest, rather than as an example of political philosophy. Current readings ignore the obvious question: Why should a thinker who wrote treatises and essays clearly and well write this as a dialogue? As if in anticipation of such reflections, Hume has his narrator open the prologue with some observations concerning the dialogue form, noting that "though the ancient philosophers conveyed most of their instruction in the form of dialogue, this method of composition has been little practiced in later ages, and has seldom succeeded in the hands of those who have attempted it" (*D*, 127). We are thus alerted to a possible connection between this work and the works of the ancients, in particular the ancients known to us as political philosophers, since these authored such dialogues. When does a writer need to employ the dialogue to convey his teaching? Not, we are told by Pamphilus, when he has a "system" to deliver. A system, we learn, is associated with "regular argument" and "proofs," such as we expect, for example, in the new sciences with which Hobbes attempted to replace the old political philosophy.

Pamphilus continues: "There are some subjects, however, to which dialogue-writing is peculiarly adapted, and where it is still preferable to the direct and simple method of composition." We are given a general formula: any "point of doctrine" is suited to a dialogue, if it is both "obvious" and "so important" that "it cannot be too often inculcated," or on the other hand so "obscure and uncertain, that human reason can reach no fixed determination with regard to it" (*D*, 127–28). Pamphilus uses both these criteria to justify a dialogue as the appropriate vehicle for considering the subject of natural religion where, "happily, these circumstances are all to be found" (*D*, 128). By this he means that the *"being* of a God" is obvious and important, while the *"nature* of that divine being" is obscure and uncertain. This may also apply on another level, as we will see below. Evidence from other works justifies formulating Hume's views as follows: it is an unavoidable feature of human life that religious belief will exist in some form; what is open or indeterminate is the form of that religious belief, or the nature of the principles religious men will espouse.[24] At one level the *Dialogues* seem to direct us along these lines to a political consideration of the problem of natural religion.

One final point must be noted in connection with this peculiar passage in the prologue, in light of the drama of the *Dialogues* themselves. Pamphilus observes here, with innocent charm, that "reasonable men may be allowed to differ, where no one can reasonably be positive: Opposite sentiments, even without any decision, afford an agreeable amusement" (*D*, 128). Although this observation might be taken as an indication of his own less than philosophic nature, it is sharply at odds with the action which follows. At the end of part 11, Demea, offended and unhappy, finds an excuse to leave the company, when he can no longer tolerate his interlocutors' point of view (*D*, 213), and the field is left to Cleanthes and Philo. While even before this there is no doubt that Demea is not a reasonable man, the refutation of Pamphilus' claim goes deeper. There is a kind of warning here. Not only are some men not reasonable, but the discussion of certain questions is sometimes not amusing or agreeable. When Pamphilus says that such discussions unite "the two greatest and purest pleasures of human life, study and society," he alludes to the classical understanding of philosophy.[25] The ensuing drama with Demea, then, suggests that study, philosophy, or philosophic dialogue are not unquestioned blessings in human life: to some they are unpleasant or dangerous. We need to see more about what sort of man Demea is, in order to grasp Hume's teaching.

Only one paragraph of the prologue remains. We have been directed to think, in the first five paragraphs, about the way Hume chose to present this "instruction," and Pamphilus even suggests that we join in the dialogue: "if the subject be curious and interesting [as in the present case], the book carries us, in a manner, into company, and unites the two greatest and purest pleasures of human life, study and society" (*D*, 128). Now he sets the scene we are to join. Pamphilus names the interlocutors and explicitly calls our attention to their characters: "The remarkable contrast in their characters still further raised your expectations; while you opposed the accurate philosophical turn of CLEANTHES to the careless skepticism of PHILO, or compared either of their dispositions with the rigid inflexible orthodoxy of DEMEA" (*D*, 128).[26]

We are thus alerted to the need to pay attention to more than the arguments themselves. What sorts of men are the speakers? It is helpful here to recall the participants in Cicero's dialogue. There, too, we find three speakers and an auditor, and the resemblance is striking in several respects. The problematic view of the gods in Cicero's account is presented by the Epicurean, Velleius, who gets the worst of the argument.[27] The others are Lucilius Balbus, the stoic, whom Cleanthes resembles (and this resemblance is reinforced by the narrator's final judgment, which in both cases pronounces in favor of the moderate argument—"the most probable" in Cicero, "still nearer to the truth" in Hume), and Cotta, who is clearly the model for Philo (Cicero tells us, in fact, that Cotta's teacher was a certain Philo, as the teacher of Balbus was a Cleanthes).

The obvious similarities in these two characters compel us to reflect on the third. The Epicurean is missing from Hume's dialogue and has been replaced by a pious divine. Is this meant to suggest, as I have already said, that (for Hume) the theological problem of the arguments of Epicurean physics has been replaced by the problem of the zealous piety which Demea seems to represent? Hume could have introduced an Epicurean, as he does in chapter 11 of the *Enquiry concerning Human Understanding,* where Hume reports a supposed conversation or dialogue and presents Epicurus himself giving an imaginary defense of his philosophy before the Athenian assembly, claiming that it must ultimately be harmless because it cannot affect the real foundations of virtue, which are to be found in the observation of common life. Parts of that dialogue are nearly identical with passages in the *Dialogues* now under consideration, and we will return to this similarity below.[28] But the substitution here of Demea for the Epicurean Velleius suggests that Hume believes the problem of religion has shifted its ground. Most modern thinkers—such as Hobbes, whom we have mentioned—would have made this substitution, in the belief that the danger to healthy civic life is not physics (of the Epicurean or any other sort) but irrational religious belief or superstition. We must not, however, assume that this obvious step is the whole of Hume's teaching, because he hints both in the *Dialogues* and elsewhere (*NHR; EHU* 12) that there is another problem.

In the first part of the *Dialogues* Hume sets the stage for the remainder of the work by his careful presentation of the political problem for which almost the whole of the rest of the work is an extended denouement. At the end of part 1, the issue hangs delicately suspended, and only at the opening of part 2 is there an indication of where the dialogue is headed. The crux of the issue is the alliance formed between Philo and Demea.

The central theme of part 1 is the relation of reason or scientific skepticism to common life, which includes religious belief as well as accepted opinions of all kinds. Before the discussion turns to this central theme, however, the topic itself is introduced. Pamphilus narrates: "After I joined the company, whom I found sitting in CLEANTHES'S library, DEMEA paid CLEANTHES some compliments, on the great care which he took of my education, and on his unwearied perseverance and constancy in all his friendships" (*D*, 130). We are thus reminded of Pamphilus' youth; now we begin to see why Hume does not narrate in his own name, following Cicero. The dialogue begins literally on the topic of education, and the entire discussion is carried on in the presence of a young man who is, as he intimates at the close of the prologue, "all ears" concerning the things said. The importance of this is confirmed by Demea's much later expression of strong indignation, when he objects to "such principles [being] advanced, supported by such an authority, before so young a man as PAMPHILUS" (*D*, 145). The issue which shadows the dialogue from the opening page, then, is the nature of education in piety and theology appropriate to young men.

We glimpse, at the very beginning, the character of Demea. He praises Cleanthes warmly for his loyalty to an old friend, whose son he is educating "in every useful branch of literature and science." He admires not only his "constancy" but his "industry" and "prudence"; Demea is a man with admiration for the ordinary or homely virtues. His concern with the education of the young is matched by his reliance on traditional views, which he immediately demonstrates by communicating to

Cleanthes a "maxim," founded "on the saying of an ancient," which, Demea says, "I have observed with regard to my own children" (*D*, 130). The maxim teaches that a student should be exposed to "the science of natural theology" only at the end of his education, because "none but a mind, enriched with all the other sciences, can safely be entrusted with it." This is the point of entry for the main issue of the *Dialogues*. Philo enters with a question, put to Demea in a tone of ironical piety: "Are you so late in teaching your children the principles of religion? Is there no danger of their neglecting or rejecting altogether, those opinions, of which they have heard so little during the whole course of their education?" Demea hastily explains that he only postpones the study of natural theology as a *science:* "to season their minds with early piety is my chief care." And this provokes him to reveal, with almost palpable indignation, a deep antipathy to reason and philosophy. He tells the others that, while teaching his children the sciences, he remarks on "the uncertainty of each part, the eternal disputations of men, the obscurity of all philosophy, and the strange, ridiculous conclusions which some of the greatest geniuses have derived from the principles of mere human reason." By calling attention to this, he eliminates any danger from "that assuming arrogance of philosophy" (*D*, 130–31).

From the point of view of Hume, or indeed any philosopher, such sentiments are unfortunate but understandable. The hostility of modern philosophy to religious dogma could not be expected to provoke any other response. With an ironic appeal to the reasonableness of Demea's approach, Philo now states, in a speech of some forty lines, a skeptical manifesto which will become the core of his position. "Your precaution," he tells Demea, "of seasoning your children's minds with early piety, is certainly very reasonable; and no more than is requisite, in this profane and irreligious age" (*D*, 131). The surest remedy against the destruction of the principles of religion, he notes, is ignorance. But those who are exposed to a little science are fired with enthusiasm, and soon "think nothing too difficult for human reason." Thus they, "breaking through all fences, profane the inmost sanctuaries of the temple." And here he appeals to Cleanthes to agree with him, that, "after we have abandoned ignorance, the surest remedy, there is still one expedient left to prevent this profane liberty." The expedient he proposes becomes the object of the controversy which I believe is Hume's central concern in this work:

> Let DEMEA's principles be improved and cultivated: Let us become thoroughly sensible of the weakness, blindness, and narrow limits of human reason: Let us duly consider its uncertainty and needless contrarieties, even in subjects of common life and practice: Let the errors and deceits of our very senses be set before us; the insuperable difficulties, which attend first principles in all systems; the contradictions, which adhere to the very ideas of matter, cause and effect, extension, space, time, motion; and in a word, quantity of all kinds, the object of the only science, that can fairly pretend to any certainty or evidence. When these topics are displayed in their full light, as they are by some philosophers and almost all divines; who can retain such confidence in this frail faculty of reason as to pay any regard to its determinations in points so sublime, so abstruse, so remote from common life and experience? (*D*, 131)

Hume has brought us almost immediately to the heart of the issue of natural theology. A rigorous and thoroughgoing skepticism erases any foundation, in reason, for the substantive principles of religion. The narrator, Pamphilus, reports on the company: "When PHILO pronounced these words, I could observe a smile in the countenances both of DEMEA and CLEANTHES. That of DEMEA seemed to imply an unreserved satisfaction in the doctrines delivered: But in CLEANTHES's features, I could distinguish an air of finesse; as if he perceived some raillery or artificial malice in the reasonings of PHILO" (*D*, 132).

In the passage just cited, we begin to witness the drama of the *Dialogues:* the relations among the characters are already complicated, and we glimpse the lines of the dramatic and philosophic problem to which the characters of the interlocutors are the key. Philo, the "careless skeptic," is not pious in any sense Demea would recognize, and any doubts on this score will shortly be resolved. Cleanthes is aware of this already, but Demea is not so perceptive. Only at the end of the drama will he realize Philo's true position. In the penultimate section we find this, directed at Philo: "Hold! Hold! cried DEMEA: Whither does your imagination hurry you? I joined in alliance with you, in order to prove the incomprehensible nature of the divine Being, and refute the principles of CLEANTHES, who would measure everything by a human rule and standard. But now I find you running into all the topics of the greatest libertines and infidels [Hume changed "sceptics" to "infidels"]; . . . Are you secretly, then, a more dangerous enemy than CLEANTHES himself?" (*D*, 212–13). Immediately after this, an indignant Demea leaves the conversation entirely, and in part 12 Hume presents a friendly conversation between Cleanthes and Philo. But at the point we have reached in part 1, the relations among the three are not yet fixed, the lines of argument have not been drawn. Cleanthes next attempts to expose Philo's "malice," and he seems to assume not only that he and Demea are natural allies, but that Demea will know it.

Cleanthes suggests mildly that the skepticism Philo has expressed is too radical, that he is claiming a skepticism so strong that it cannot be sustained in common life:

> Whether your scepticism be as absolute and sincere as you pretend, we shall learn bye and bye, when the company breaks up: We shall then see, whether you go out at the door or the window; and whether you really doubt, if your body has gravity, or can be injured by its fall; according to popular opinion, derived from our fallacious senses and more fallacious experience. And this consideration, DEMEA, may, I think, fairly serve to abate our ill-will to this humourous sect of the sceptics. If they be thoroughly in earnest, they will not long trouble the world with their doubts, cavils, and disputes: If they be only in jest, they are, perhaps, bad railliers, but can never be very dangerous, either to the state, to philosophy, or to religion. (*D*, 132)

It is important to note Hume's insertion of the state as one proper object of concern here. This is not merely an issue between philosophy and theology; radical skepticism may have serious political implications as well.

Cleanthes' characterization of Philo's skepticism as tendentious is countered by the latter, who nevertheless admits that such skepticism cannot be applied always and everywhere. Even a skeptic "must act, I own, and live, and converse like other men; and for this conduct he is not obliged to give any other reason than the absolute necessity he lies under of so doing" (*D*, 134). But Philo holds to his skepticism as soon as we leave that realm of necessity. "When we look beyond human affairs and the properties of the surrounding bodies," Philo insists, we are reaching beyond our grasp, and this applies specifically, he makes clear, in "theological reasoning." We can know nothing of things beyond the immediate world of "common sense and experience." We may recall in this connection Hobbes' clear statement along the same lines in *Leviathan:* "Whatsoever we imagine, is *Finite.* Therefore there is no Idea, or conception of anything we call *Infinite.* . . . When we say anything is infinite, we signifie onely, that we are not able to conceive the ends, and bounds of the thing named; having no Conception of the thing, but of our own inability. And therefore the Name of *God* is used, not to make us conceive him (for he is *Incomprehensible;* and his greatnesse, and power are unconceivable;) but that we may honour him."[29] We thus also witness, in Demea's agreement with Philo, his unwitting approval of the doctrines of Hobbes, one of the principal objects of vilification by modern divines.[30]

Demea expresses his assumed agreement with Philo in terms which suggest a posture of humility uncharacteristic of Hobbes. The nature of God, he affirms, is "altogether incomprehensible and unknown to us. The essence of that supreme mind, his attributes, the manner of his existence, the very nature of his duration; these and every particular, which regards so divine a Being, are mysterious to men. *Finite, weak, and blind creatures, we ought to humble ourselves in his august presence, and, conscious of our frailties, adore in silence his infinite perfections*" (*D*, 141; emphasis added). We have already seen how Philo's skepticism can result in a view which is similar in its implications to Demea's, at least in its unwillingness to seek to understand the divine in terms which bear any relation to human life. Thus Philo can explain away the usual theological practice: "Wisdom, thought, design, knowledge; these we justly ascribe to him; because these words are honourable among men, and we have no other language or other conceptions, by which we can express our adoration of him" (*D*, 142).

Against this view Cleanthes attempts to establish grounds in experience to justify human belief in not only the existence of the Deity but "his similarity to human mind and intelligence" (*D*, 143). He attempts to hold to a kind of middle ground between the abject and humble piety of Demea and the philosophical skepticism of Philo. Philo and Demea find themselves together in argument against Cleanthes, and this drama is the key to Hume's political point, which seems to be that there is a considerable danger in the easy alliance of skeptical reason (read *modern natural science*) with dogmatic piety of the kind which eschews any possibility of our knowing anything about the divine being. The only kind of religion this can leave us with is one which depopulates the world of God or the gods, or at least of gods with any relation to human moral life. We find in this alliance only the "God" of modern science and its more thoughtless practitioners: this God "exists" but has no meaning for us, answers no prayers, produces no miracles, and neither rewards justice nor punishes injustice in any afterlife.

According to Philo, in his first response to Cleanthes' objections to his skepticism, "all sceptics pretend, that, if reason be considered in an abstract view, it furnishes invincible arguments against itself" (*D*, 135). We have already seen Hume's familiarity with this point—a familiarity no doubt contributing to the impression that Philo speaks for Hume. "We could never retain any conviction or assurance, on any subject, were not the skeptical reasonings so refined and subtle, that they are not able to counterpoise the more solid and natural arguments, derived from the senses and experience" (*D*, 135). Usually, in other words, the skeptical arguments—such as those which deny the solidity of apparently solid objects—do not touch us directly or affect our commonsense views. But in the case of theology, where common life or experience is not in a position of direct "counterpoise," our confidence in ordinary opinion or plain sense is unjustified, our arguments from common life lose their advantage, and "the most refined skepticism comes to be on a footing with them, and is able to oppose and counterbalance them" (*D*, 135). This is Philo's argument for radical skepticism in theological matters.

But is it true to say that skeptical arguments in theological matters touch us as they cannot in matters of common life? We must draw here on Hume's *Natural History of Religion* to supplement the indications he gives us in the *Dialogues*. Cleanthes responds to this argument from Philo by raising an issue which anticipates the most serious philosophical investigations of the twentieth century, examinations of the phenomenological ground of science. He distinguishes two kinds of skepticism, which may fairly be said to characterize Demea on the one hand and Philo on the other. The first is "a kind of brutish and ignorant skepticism," which

> gives the vulgar a general prejudice against what they do not easily understand, and makes them reject every principle which requires elaborate reasoning to prove and establish it. This species of scepticism is fatal to knowledge, not to religion; since we find, that those who make greatest profession of it, given often their assent, not only to the great truths of theism, and natural theology, but even to the most absurd tenets, which a traditional superstition has recommended to them. They firmly believe in witches; though they will not believe nor attend to the most simple proposition of Euclid. But the refined and philosophical sceptics fall into an inconsistency of an opposite nature. They push their researches into the most abstruse corners of science; and their assent attends them in every step, proportioned to the evidence which they meet with. They are even obliged to acknowledge, that the most abstruse and remote objects are those which are best explained by philosophy. Light is in reality anatomized: The true system of the heavenly bodies is discovered and ascertained. But the nourishment of bodies by food is still an inexplicable mystery: The cohesion of the parts of matter is still incomprehensible. (*D*, 136–37)

The political problem alluded to earlier arises from the conjunction of these two forms of skepticism, or rather from the irresponsible exercise of that "refined and philosophical" skepticism which Philo represents. This may be seen from the following considerations. Cleanthes attempts to defend a theology which understands the Divinity in human terms as wise or intelligent, for example, or as representing a perfection of the higher human faculties, above all mind. Both pious mystics, as he calls Demea (*D*, 158), and "skeptics or atheists" refuse their assent to this characterization, for different reasons. The "refined and philosophical" skeptics are unwilling to characterize the Divinity as wise or intelligent, and they refuse on the ground that human reason can give us no guidance here.

Philosophically Philo may have the better of this argument, but Hume has reminded us both directly and by his rhetoric of another perspective—the perspective of political philosophy. That Philo compares himself at one point in the *Dialogues* to the sort of man who "has himself no fixed station or abiding city, which he is ever, on any occasion, obliged to defend" (*D*, 187) is no accident. We may say that Philo's philosophic suspension of conviction is suitable only to a man with "no abiding city." The political problem arises from the fact that human beings seem to be so constituted that most at least will believe, willy-nilly, in some principles of religion.[31] The question is, thus, in which principles? Genuine skepticism as a way of life is impossible, except perhaps for a very few, and even for them, only in reflection and not in action (see *D*, 132–34). It is incompatible with a political community because it leads to a loss of will (of the sort charged against liberal democracies by Solzhenitsyn?). Human nature is such that men are bound to live by their beliefs and opinions. Hence the political question is, what beliefs? If Philo's skepticism teaches us that we can know nothing and thus encourages humility, it too easily contributes to the kind of dogmatic—and in effect skeptical—humility Demea represents. Such a skepticism, which Cleanthes characterizes as "brutish and ignorant," is not inconsistent with a fervent belief in witches. In the *Natural History of Religion* this is much more explicit (compare the views Hume describes with the sentiments of Demea, above):

> Where the deity is represented as infinitely superior to mankind, this belief, though altogether just, is apt, when joined with superstitious terrors, to sink the human mind into the lowest submission and abasement, and to represent the monkish virtues of mortification, penance, humility, and passive suffering, as the only qualities which are acceptable to him. But where the gods are conceived to be only a little superior to mankind, and to have been, many of them, advanced from that inferior rank, we are more at our ease, in our addresses to them, and may even, without profaneness, aspire sometimes to a rivalship and emulation of them. Hence activity, spirit, courage, magnanimity, love of liberty, and all the virtues which aggrandize a people. (*NHR*, 52)

A radical skepticism may thus encourage melancholy, dread, and awe, and result in a debasing and slavish worship. Philo's skepticism may contribute not to a reserved and philosophical faith but to the most blind and abject superstition imaginable. "Whatever weakens or disorders the internal frame promotes the interests of superstition: And nothing is more destructive to them than a manly, steady virtue, which either preserves us from disastrous, melancholy accidents, or teaches us to bear them. During such calm sunshine of the mind, these spectres of false divinity never make their appearance. On the other hand, while we abandon ourselves to the natural undisciplined suggestions of our timid and anxious hearts, every kind of barbarity is ascribed to the supreme Being" (*NHR*, 73).

Hume thus seems to suggest that a politically responsible theology would foster, or make us look up to, a "manly, steady virtue," and a calm reasonableness. That is, it would support and encourage the human virtues as we can recognize them in common life. But there is no purely philosophical foundation—or grounding in science or reason—for these qualities, and in that sense Philo is correct. Yet Hume seems to teach that there is another prudence than the purely philosophical which deserves our attention. To live life properly or well, some beliefs are better than others. From the standpoint of political philosophy it is possible to prefer manly virtue to abject piety, and to show—although perhaps not prove—good reasons for defending the sort of theology that encourages the former and not the latter. The problem Philo presents is not too *much* reason as much as it is unpolitical or irresponsible reason. Cleanthes is helpless to counteract this, because Philo cannot be simply overcome in argument.

The relations among the characters mirror the political problem as Hume seems to understand it. Philo, the Pyrrhonist or radical skeptic, by undermining the claims of moderate reason (Cleanthes), leaves the field free for the worst sorts of belief, personified by the blind pious mysticism of Demea. Philo carelessly or maliciously provokes Demea to think his enemy is Cleanthes; Cleanthes is powerless, once the issue is framed as Philo frames it, to prevail with his more moderate theology. Popular religion will ally itself, Hume tells us, with skepticism, when the latter seems to serve its purposes (see *D*, 139–40, 213). But if we wish for a theology in accord with the natural human moral qualities, as opposed to a popular religion marked by melancholy superstition or ignorant enthusiasm, we must be concerned that it *look up to* reason in some way. Cleanthes urges the following on the interlocutors: "Contemplate the whole and every part of it. . . . The curious adapting of means to ends, throughout all nature, resembles exactly, though it much exceeds, the productions of human contrivance; of *human design, thought, wisdom,* and *intelligence*. Since therefore the effects resemble each other, we are led to infer, by all the rules of analogy, that the causes also resemble; and that the Author of nature is somewhat similar to the mind of man" (*D*, 143; emphasis added).[32]

Let us return to the point from which we set out in our consideration of part 1. We may summarize what we have suggested is Hume's teaching as follows. A healthy civic life is threatened in modern times from two directions, and not from one as the classical writers appear to have believed.[33] In Cicero's or Plato's view, Epicurean physics or natural philosophy is the danger against which theology is in need of defense. In the *Enquiry concerning Human Understanding*, as we have noted, Hume reports the delivery by one of Hume's companions of an "apology" on behalf of Epicurus, in which it is argued that "all the philosophy, therefore, in the world, and all the religion, which is nothing but a species of philosophy, will never be able to carry us beyond the usual course of experience, or give us measures of conduct and behavior different from those which are furnished by reflections on common life . . . nor have the political interests of society any connexion with the philosophical disputes concerning metaphysics and religion" (*EHU*, 146–47). The last point, however, is contradicted by the teaching of the *Dialogues*, as well as objected to by Hume in the passage in question. For Hume, what philosophers say will not stop men's believing in *something;* but the political question is not thereby settled, because, although what philosophers teach may not stop men from believing, it can affect what they believe, and thus a *political* philosophy is called for.[34] Hume tries to show in the *Dialogues* that, while in an obvious sense Demea is the problem (he literally replaces the Epicurean from Cicero's dialogue), there is another problem in philosophy's neglect of the political responsibility it had once accepted in order to insure its own survival (see *EHU*, 133–34). Merely exposing Demea to mild ridicule—and provoking his departure—is no solution. There will be human beings like Demea in any society, because not everyone can live purely by reason. Demea has many of the characteristics of good solid citizens: he cares about education of the young, admires "prudence and industry," and cherishes the ways of the past (*D*, 130). The views Philo represents may be said to threaten the very existence of a decent polity, even if they are acceptable to narrow philosophical reason.

But why should philosophy care about polity—why should philosophy become *political* philosophy? Hume seems to suggest most clearly in the *Enquiry concerning Human Understanding*, but also in the *Natural History of Religion*, that philosophy will become political if it wishes to preserve an environment where it can be carried on. There Hume admires "the singular good fortune of philosophy," in receiving "its first birth in an age and country of freedom and toleration" (*EHU*, 132); at present, he believes, matters are not so favorable. His companion responds that Hume's admiration is misplaced. "This pertinacious bigotry, of which you complain, as so fatal to philosophy, is really her offspring, who, after allying with superstition, separates himself entirely from the interest of his parent, and becomes her most inveterate enemy and persecutor" (*EHU*, 133). That is, when superstition is allied with philosophy (Demea with Philo?), the result is an intransigent dogmatism, beside which a more reasonable philosophy has no place. Philosophy must become political philosophy to guarantee its own survival, as the classical thinkers had taught. We may say that Hume is attempting to restore this philosophical project, the need for which Hobbes claimed he had eliminated.

That this concern was not new to Hume in the *Dialogues* is evidenced by the little noticed epigraph he placed on his earliest work, the *Treatise of Human Nature*. The words come from Tacitus: *Rara temporum felicitas, ubi sentire, quae velis; & quae sentias, dicere licet* (Seldom are men blessed with times in which they may think what they like, and say what they think).

10 Conclusion

Many opinion shapers today profess to be worried about the resurgence of fundamentalist Christian sects in the United States. Some of the fundamentalists seem to be turning their backs on science. As the celebrated Harvard paleontologist Stephen J. Gould said in a recent lecture, this at the least bodes ill for the education and training of the scientists of the future. But meanwhile the very journal in whose pages Gould's essays often appear—*The New York Review of Books*—gives space to philosophers and literary critics who believe that science itself is only another mythmaking activity. Richard Rorty has expressed this position with admirable clarity: "The literary artist's awareness that he is making rather than finding, and more specifically the ironic modernist's awareness that he is responding to texts rather than to things, puts him one up on the scientist."[1] One consequence is that literary artists (philosophically sophisticated ones, at any rate) view "the scientist as naive in thinking that he is doing something *more* than putting together ideas, or constructing new texts."[2]

But for the most part scientists are not worried. Their enterprise rolls on, adding success after success to a record of achievements now centuries long. This is as it should be: what scientist can resist a chuckle as he reads of his naivete, his mythmaking, in articles composed at the keyboard of a personal computer? Modern natural science is an unqualified success; as far as the life of the mind is concerned, this is the central fact of our time. Natural science sets the standard for all forms of what was once known as rational inquiry. Social sciences strive to apply the methods of chemistry and physics to their own subject matter, as their very language attests. Many graduate programs in political science have dispensed with courses in "philosophy of social science"—common only a decade ago—and replaced them with required sequences in "research design." After all, no physicist needs to study philosophy of science to get on with physics, and even if he wants to, he will find such a course over in the philosophy department.

The robust condition of the natural sciences is not, it seems to me, a cause for worry. We must worry, rather, about the declining state of our understanding of the things—perhaps the one thing—the natural scientists do not tackle. By this I mean the questions fundamental to any comprehension of our situation as human beings, including the question of the good or how we should live. To raise this or related questions is to open the issue of whether there is a human nature, or whether human beings are part of nature. This question indeed remains open and can be treated as settled only by our neglecting it. Natural scientists happily go their way but cannot give an account of their activity itself, or of its goodness for man. How did we arrive at this state of affairs, in which no one is wrestling with the fundamental questions the greatest minds of the past addressed, questions the confrontation with which was once the highest occupation of the greatest thinkers?

I have argued in this book that the issues of what we can have knowledge of, or attain truth about, were implicit in the earliest formulations of what modern natural science is and does. Hume is important to us precisely to the extent that our problems today revolve around the enterprise of modern natural science as the paradigm of genuine knowledge. To an amazing degree, Hume addresses the very issues at the core of the problems of our time, captured by the slogan "abandonment of truth." If Hume is correct, the abandonment by philosophy of any attempt to ask the fundamental questions has its roots not as Nietzsche was to claim in the rationalism of Socrates, but rather in the success of one particular account of what the method of modern natural science produces. By studying Hume's philosophical confrontation with that account, we can learn much that is needed today to reopen the fundamental questions.

In the preceding chapters we have tried to trace the "problem of reason" as Hume confronted it. We saw that it arises from the separation of science from experience attempted, or at least announced, by Hume's great predecessors. The insuperable difficulties to which this leads brought to light for Hume what he called the "strange infirmities" of the understanding, which in turn compel us to admit the necessity of grounding science itself in "common life," in the prescientific facts of human existence. Our belief in the "necessary connexion of cause and effect," on which scientific explanation rests, is simply a fact of human nature, of the way we are constituted. That "all knowledge resolves itself into probability" meant, for Hume, not that philosophical truth is impossible to attain but that science or philosophy should be moderate in its claims. Indeed physicists and chemists are moderate in their pretensions to truth: it has not been natural scientists who introduced the "abandonment of truth," but philosophers—system builders, as Hume would say—who did not pay sufficient attention to common life. Hume teaches that once we moderate our expectations we realize we can attain truth about the nature of things, though many things, especially those involving human beliefs and passions, are vastly complicated, and the truth about them is beyond the capacity of all but the most patient and skeptical inquirers, possessed of the finest sensibilities and the most extensive experience.

The problem of reason today, or what some call the crisis of reason or the crisis of Western rationalism, has its center not in the natural sciences but in the humanities, where the fundamental questions were once addressed. Philosophers have in a sense been paralyzed by the successes of natural science and have retreated into isolation. If Hume is correct, however, this was unnecessary. Philosophy needs to do what it has always done—attend to what is highest in man, make a place for decency, resist the bigotry and fanaticism to which our century has been particularly prone. By asking too much from rational inquiry we have become Pyrrhonists; we have succumbed to what Hume calls "false philosophy."[3] If I read Hume correctly, his quarrel is primarily with his modern predecessors, who pretend to have overcome the limitations of philosophy, limitations of which the greatest ancient thinkers were at least aware. Socrates' knowledge of his own ignorance is justly famous as the key to this man's life.

Hume's achievement was to denigrate the claims of modernity, on the one hand, while elevating its achievement, on the other. He exposes the claims of the new science—its announcement of liberation from the limitations of prudence and fallibility—as too ambitious. We are still limited in the same old ways when we reason. Thus Hume makes philosophy in the old sense both possible and necessary; philosophy is still an opportunity to explore limits, to wonder, to be open to the mysteries of human existence, including the fundamental mystery of the desire to know. It is not that science does not produce or discover the truth, but that truth is not quite what some—including those who proclaimed the new method—take it to be. The search for truth, even about the human things, need not be abandoned if we moderate our standards of what constitutes the truth. As for the critics of science today, those following Nietzsche, Hume's argument undercuts their insistence that science is only a myth and thus undercuts the relativism which follows from it. The assertion that modern science is simply mythmaking is not only preposterous on its face but also an indication of the irrelevance of the humanities today.

I have suggested that Hume's exposure of the strange infirmities of the understanding restores an earlier conception of philosophy. Philosophy, for Hume, is not instrumental; he is not trying to do anything except to understand. Hence Hume's philosophy does not purchase power or clarity at the cost of complexity. It does not reduce to simples, as Hobbes had taught that it must. One result is the unsystematic character of Hume's writings. He refuses to build from a relatively simple state of nature where human beings are viewed reductively, as individuals, merely because we can be most certain of this aspect of our being. For Hume, humans are social beings, as well as individuals, and if that complicates matters, so be it. He refuses to arrive at a simple picture of the goals of civil order by building systematically from a social contract, because much that is important to man is likely to be missed by such a procedure. Man is best understood, for Hume, by examining the soul and the passions—and the principles of morals—as they appear in common life, in history, rather than by means of an abstract scheme or system. In fact, Hume suggests, human nature is such that man's latent sociability is expressed more in some historical circumstances than others: it is "peculiar to ignorant and barbarous nations" for men to live with their fellows in a "distant manner," but the more the "refined arts advance, the more sociable men become" (*E*, 271). "They flock into cities; love to receive and communicate knowledge; to show their wit or their breeding; their taste in conversation or living, in clothes or furniture." What is the status of such an observation? How recognize its truth if we try to take our bearings only from what men are like in the rudest or most primitive circumstances? Thus the unsystematic character of Hume's philosophy merely reflects the complexity of the human universe.

Hume's attempt to ground philosophy in ordinary life did not result from an antirational devotion to practice or action at the expense of thoughtfulness. Hume opposes overly skeptical philosophy, but only because it exemplifies ill-grounded and unbalanced reason. Hume displays a curiously unmodern understanding of philosophy as an activity or way of life worth pursuing for its own sake. He embodies for us an echo of the classical spirit, connected with what we have suggested is his attempt to restore the status of political philosophy. Unlike his modern predecessors, Hume hopes for very little practical payoff from the powers of human reason. He seems to have rediscovered the pleasures of philosophy and so de-emphasizes its utility.

But the classical approach to philosophy in Hume's thought is not carried over to admiration for ancient societies themselves or their political structures. Hume has no reverence for the ancient republics, as we have seen. He believed them to have been full of injustice and to have sacrificed too much (and too many) to the political and even tyrannical ambitions of the few. His admiration for liberal commercial society, especially the English sort, "the most perfect and most accurate system of liberty that was ever found compatible with government," makes him inescapably modern.

What might the encounter with Hume's understanding of the world do for us as students of human nature and society? Aside from inviting us to wrestle with the fundamental questions, Hume's legacy can help us as social scientists in a number of ways. We would be wise to stop aping the procedures of physics, for example. The mathematical tools of natural science are powerful because of their abstraction, but abstraction is also a danger. We do not live—in common life—in the world of the physicist, for whom abstraction is the only access to molecules, photons, and DNA. When we use this technique to penetrate the surface of common life—life as lived by human beings with passions and beliefs to which we do have immediate access—we risk losing touch with the very things we seek to comprehend. This contrast is all to the advantage of studies of the human world, because we lose our bearings there only if we willfully cast them off. In political science or morals, as Hume calls it, to begin "from scratch" would be to ignore the very things—the implicit articulation of a moral universe—that will allow us to know when we have got something right.

Hume's investigation into the foundations of science teaches that the knowledge produced by a physicist is not different in any way from the knowledge of a moral philosopher. Both kinds of knowledge resolve themselves into probability, which is all that we can have. To think that our studies of politics will somehow attain to a new level of truth if we make them sound like physics is to mistake the grounds of knowledge, and meanwhile to cut ourselves off from common life, which is what we are trying to give an account of. Human beings, as Hume knew, are sometimes reasonable, but also deeply irrational. Our very science depends on a kind of belief (in causation) which is simply a fact about human beings. The irrationality of so much of our lives is one explanation for why human history has produced so few decent or admirable societies.

A sensible social science must begin from the categories of judgment—good or bad, decent or indecent, just or unjust—which are embedded in every human language and thus are in a sense natural to us as human beings. The social scientist has the task of studying the record of human activity to articulate what is good, and why. Thus for Hume it is not mysterious that a social scientist should try to work out the political principles (which are surely *not* self-evident) important in good social orders: "knowledge, industry, and humanity," for example, or liberty and the rule of law. These are goods. Prosperity, refinement, and the courage necessary to defend them, all pointing toward the pleasures of speech and the arts—these can be reasonably argued for, and Hume does so. Want, poverty, slavery, fanaticism, self-mortification and domination—these are bad for human beings and society, though they have been very common in history and remain so today. There is plenty here for social science to study, merely in investigating the conditions for the good things and the reasons for the frequency of the bad. A social science taking its guidance from Hume would resemble old-fashioned history. It would not attempt to be value-free any more than Hume does in his *History of England*, or for that matter in the *Enquiry concerning the Principles of Morals*.

The human world is vastly complicated, at least as complicated as the world of the chemist. Hume believed that "to balance a large state or society, whether monarchical or republican, on general laws, is a work of so great difficulty, that no human genius, however comprehensive, is able, by the mere dint of reason and reflection, to effect it" (*E*, 124). But we may hope that such a balance is not beyond human power to comprehend. The task of the human sciences is as easy to state as it has proven difficult to accomplish: to seek an understanding of what is good for mankind. Hume's most profound reflections help remove some of the obstacles obscuring that possibility from our sight.

Notes

Chapter 1: Introduction

1 Bacon, *Great Instauration*, 26.
2 For an extended discussion of these issues see Allan Bloom, *The Closing of the American Mind* (New York: Simon and Schuster, 1987).
3 Thomas Main, *American Spectator* 16 (June 1983).
4 There is clear warrant for this suspicion in Socrates' admission to Cebes in *Phaedo* at 96a6–9: "When I was young, Cebes, I had an extraordinary passion for that branch of learning which is called natural science; I thought it would be marvellous to know the causes for which each thing comes and ceases and continues to be. . . . At last I came to the conclusion that I was uniquely unfitted for this form of inquiry. I will give you a sufficient indication of what I mean. *I had understood some things plainly before, in my own and other people's estimation; but now I was so befogged by these speculations that I unlearned even what I had thought I knew*" (Penguin Classics, Tredennick translation; emphasis added).
5 Hobbes, *Elements of Law, Epistle Dedicatory.*
6 Anthony Earl Cooper, 3d Earl of Shaftesbury, *The Moralists, A Philosophical Rhapsody,* Treatise 5, in *Works,* Vol. 2, part 1, sect. 1, p. 189. (N.p. 1709).
7 One example from Descartes: "the poetry [of the ancients] makes one imagine many events to be possible which are not so at all, and even their most faithful histories, if they do not change or increase the value of things to make them more worthy of being read, at least almost always omit the lowest and least illustrious circumstances surrounding them; thus it happens that the rest does not appear as what it is, and that those who regulate their morals from examples they take from it are apt to fall into the extravagances of the knights of our romances, and to conceive designs that surpass their capabilities." From *Discourse on the Method* I, cited in Carnes Lord, *Education and Culture in the Political Thought of Aristotle* (Ithaca: Cornell University Press, 1982), 21.

8   Shaftesbury, *Moralists*, 191.

9   There is an extensive literature concerned with the nature and place of philosophy today, and I presume some familiarity with it on the part of the reader. Much of it stems from the philosophical reflections of Ludwig Wittgenstein, but the central figure on the contemporary scene is probably Richard Rorty. See his *Philosophy and the Mirror of Nature* (Princeton: Princeton University Press, 1979); *Consequences of Pragmatism;* and his recent *Contingency, irony, and solidarity.* See also Hiley, *Philosophy in Question*. I return to this in chapter 2.

10 I have in mind "Of the Populousness of Ancient Nations," "Of Taxes," "Of Interest," etc. See Rotwein, *David Hume*. For the method of citing Hume's works, see the list of works cited in the text which precedes chapter 1.

11 See, e.g., Garry Wills, *Inventing America* (New York: Random House, 1978). See also Craig Walton, "Hume and Jefferson on the Uses of History," in *Hume,* ed. Livingston and King, 389–403; J. G. A. Pocock, "Hume and the American Revolution: The Dying Thought of a North Briton," in Norton, Capaldi, and Robison, *McGill Hume Studies,* 325–44; Douglass Adair, "'That Politics May Be Reduced to a Science': David Hume, James Madison, and the Tenth Federalist" in Livingston and King, *Hume,* 404–17; James Moore, "Hume's Political Science and the Classical Republican Tradition" in *Canadian Journal of Political Science* 10 (1977):809–39.

12 Though Hume himself identified the *ECPM* as "in my own opinion . . . of all my writings . . . incomparably the best" ("My Own Life," in *E,* xxxcvi). I return to this in chapter 3.

13 This view has, I believe, been effectively refuted by David Miller in his excellent *Philosophy and Ideology in Hume's Political Thought,* but from an approach quite different to that taken here.

14 See Miller, *Philosophy and Ideology,* 5–10, on this.

15 See Friedrich Nietzsche, *Birth of Tragedy,* trans. and ed. Walter Kaufmann (New York: Vintage, 1967), esp. sec. 15. Related sources include Edmund Husserl, *The Crisis of European Sciences and Transcendental Phenomenology,* trans. David Carr (Evanston, Ill.: Northwestern University Press, 1970), and his essay "Philosophy and the Crisis of European Man," in *Phenomenology and the Crisis of Philosophy,* trans. Quentin Lauer (New York: Harper and Row, 1965); Leo Strauss, "Political Philosophy and the Crisis of Our Time," in *Post-Behavioral Perspectives,* ed. George Graham and George Carey (New York: D. McKay, 1972), and *The City and Man,* (Chicago: University of Chicago Press, 1964), chapter 1; Aleksandr Solzhenitsyn, "A World Split Apart," *National Review,* July 7, 1978, 836–55.

Chapter 2: Science and Truth

1   See Gillespie, *Hegel, Heidegger, and the Ground of History,* 8–12, 18.

2   Condorcet, *Selected Writings,* 211.

3 Thomas Hobbes, *Leviathan*, ed. C. B. Macpherson, (Harmondsworth, England: Penguin, 1968), chap. 46. Hereafter cited in text by either chapter or chapter and page.

4 MacIntyre, *After Virtue*, 78.

5 Ibid., 77.

6 It is of course possible and sometimes useful to distinguish between "empirical" and "empiricist." Thus David Thomas writes: "post-empiricist philosophy seeks to be empirical without being empiricist" (*Naturalism and Social Science*, 3–4). But since the meaning of these terms is precisely what is in question here, perhaps for the moment confusion is preferable.

7 Thomas Hobbes, among others, is explicit on this (*Leviathan*, 46.682–83). See also note 7 to chapter 1.

8 See, e.g., Bacon, *Of the Dignity and Advancement of Learning*, 399: "Neither ought a man to make scruple of entering and penetrating into these holes and corners, when the inquisition of truth is his sole object. . . . For it is esteemed a kind of dishonor upon learning for learned men to descend to inquiry or meditation upon matters mechanical, except they be such as may be thought secrets of art or rarities and special subtleties." See also 360. In *New Organon*, 83, Bacon complains of an "opinion or conceit, which though of long standing is vain and hurtful; namely, that the dignity of the human mind is impaired by . . . experiments and particulars, subject to sense and bound in matter" (356).

9 See, e.g., MacIntyre, *After Virtue*, 76; cf. Thomas, *Naturalism and Social Science*, 2–4.

10 Actually Bacon's notion is considerably more sophisticated: see *New Organon*, 95. Those who have handled sciences have been either men of experiment or men of dogmas. The men of experiment are like the ant: they only collect and use; the reasoners resemble spiders, who make cobwebs out of their own substance. But the bee takes a middle course: it gathers its material from the flowers of the garden and of the field, but transforms and digests it by a power of its own. Not unlike this is the true business of philosophy, for it neither relies solely or chiefly on the powers of the mind, nor does it take the matter which it gathers from natural history and mechanical experiments and lay it up in the memory whole, as it finds it, but lays it up in the understanding altered and digested. Therefore from a closer and purer league between two faculties, the experimental and the rational (such as has never yet been made), much may be hoped.

11 Thomas, *Naturalism and Social Science*, 2. This same point is often made in terms of a distinction between "correspondence" and "coherence" views of theory. In the case of the former, we view our theoretical account as corresponding to "the way things are." A coherence theory has as a criterion of success only its own coherence—that is, how it hangs together and makes sense of theory-guided "facts," while recognizing it is only one way of viewing "things" (obviously even our language gets us in trouble here). See Hiley, *Philosophy in Question*, 124–142; Rorty, *Contingency, irony and solidarity*, 3–16.

12 Strauss, *Natural Right and History*, 176.

13 See Kuhn, *Structure of Scientific Revolutions*.

14   See especially his *Consequences of Pragmatism* and his recent *Contingency, irony, and solidarity.*

     In addition, especially as it relates to this study, the reader should consult Hiley, *Philosophy in Question.* Hiley wrestles with the alternative posed by philosophical Pyrrhonism and treats Hume fairly extensively, though from a slightly different perspective from that taken here. I agree with much of what Hiley says in this thoughtful book but find his treatment of Hume less than clear. He argues against a straw Hume in some places (Hume "underrates Pyrrhonism" [26], "What Hume missed" [27]), but then comes back to say that "Hume's own position turned out to be far more at home in the older Pyrrhonist tradition" (31). I find the latter view more compelling, as will become clear below.

15   Rorty, *Consequences of Pragmatism,* 139.

16   Ibid., 140. See also Rorty, *Contingency, irony, and solidarity,* chaps. 1–3.

17   Descartes, *Discourse on the Method,* esp. parts 1–3; see discussion in chapter 4 below.

18   See Danford, *Wittgenstein and Political Philosophy,* 20–33.

19   Hobbes to geometry, Descartes rather more to mathematics in general, though he mentions "geometrical analysis and algebra" (*Discourse on the Method* II, 9), the latter disparagingly. See also 11.

20   Locke, *Essay concerning Human Understanding,* 4.3.18. Cf. Danford, *Wittgenstein,* 65–69.

21   Solzhenitsyn, "World Split Apart," 840.

Chapter 3: Hume's First Formulation of the Problem of Reason

1   Huxley's nineteenth-century biography of Hume gives us an instance of this influential view. According to Huxley, in fact, Hume exhibits "no small share of the craving after mere notoriety and vulgar success, as distinct from the pardonable, if not honorable, ambition of solid and enduring fame" (Huxley, *Hume,* 11). And the view continues to surface: a recent commentator notes, in an account of the history of pragmatism, that "while Berkeley and Kant were called by Truth to solve Locke's problem, Hume followed literary fame and fortune" (H. S. Thayer, *Meaning and Action: A Critical History of Pragmatism* [Indianapolis: Hackett, 1968], 25).

2   Stewart, *Moral and Political Philosophy of David Hume,* 17.

3   The shift is from what Hume himself later called "The positive Air" which prevails in his *Treatise* to a position of more moderate hopes. A good summary of the relevant literature is found in Noxon, *Hume's Philosophical Development,* 153–57.

4   Miller, *Philosophy and Ideology,* 9.

5   See "My Own Life" (*E,* xxxviii), where Hume speaks of living in a "philosophical manner." As Hume wrote to Montesquieu, "I have consecrated my life to philosophy and to fine letters" (*Letters,* 1.138). Elsewhere he opposes "philosophical" to "political" (see *E,* 280).

6   See Livingston, *Hume's Philosophy of Common Life,* 214. Livingston's views are very close to those expressed here.

7   This view is beginning to find more support. The best monograph on this issue is still Noxon, *Hume's Philosophical Development*, a very careful study which contains a good summary of the historical debate.

8   Ernest Campbell Mossner's excellent biography is the standard reference. The reference here is to his claim that the earliest essays, written in 1741, "are to be regarded as a *literary experiment*" (Mossner, *Life of David Hume*, 140).

9   See Letwin, *Pursuit of Certainty*, 3ff.

10 Smith, *Philosophy of David Hume*, 532.

11 See also Flew, *David Hume*, 11–12; cf. Noxon, *Hume's Philosophical Development*, 154–57.

12 See, e.g., Thomas Hobbes, *De Cive*, Epistle Dedicatory, (ed. Sterling Lamprecht [New York: Appleton-Century-Crofts, 1949]), *Elements of Law*, Epistle Dedicatory, and *Leviathan*, 46. A discussion of Hobbes' optimism is found in Danford, *Wittgenstein and Political Philosophy*, chaps. 2–3. See also Russell, "Hume's *Treatise* and Hobbes's *The Elements of Law*," 51–63.

13 The *Philosophical Essays* (a reworking of book 1 of the *Treatise*) went through several editions under this title. Hume did not acknowledge himself the author in the first two editions, though apparently did so with the third, which was published as Mossner tells us "within three years" of the first (1748). I have so far been unable to discover when or why the title was changed, though it was surely Hume's idea, perhaps to match the other recasting from the *Treatise*, the *ECPM*, which first appeared in 1751. See Mossner, *Life of David Hume*, 174, 223–24.

14 Ibid., 141.

15 Hume may only have been referring, however, to scholastic thought and particularly that of the so-called Cambridge platonists. But see the discussion of *T*, book 1, part 4 (below), which employed similar constructions. See Mossner, *Life of David Hume*, 140–42.

16 I am indebted to Donald Livingston for the suggestion that I include a reference to this passage here. As he points out, "Hume also in several places says his moral and political philosophy follows the ancients not the moderns."

17 See, above all, Stewart, *Moral and Political Philosophy*, 328, "daring voyage of discovery." The expression is echoed, perhaps unconsciously, in Miller, *Philosophy and Ideology*, 9, "voyage of discovery in spirit of high ambition."

18 Cf. Descartes, *Discourse on the Method*, 35, 37. Descartes emphasizes separation of imagination (and sense) from *reason*. See chapter 4 below.

Chapter 4: Hume's Predecessors and the Problem of Reason

1   Thomas Hobbes, *The Elements of Law*, ed. Ferdinand Tönnies (London: Frank Cass, 1969), part 1, chap. 2, para. 4. Hereafter cited as *EL* by part, chapter, and paragraph, respectively.

2   Leo Strauss, *Natural Right and History*, 175.

3   Ibid., 174.

4   Ibid., 174–75.

5   Descartes, *Discourse on the Method* 2, 16.

6   Ibid.

7   Strauss, *Natural Right and History*, 175.

8   Ibid.

9   This view in its modern form can be found in the writings of early twentieth-century physicists, in particular (see Duhem, *Aim and Structure of Physical Theory*, 169), and was anticipated clearly by, among others, Nietzsche. But as Strauss has shown, Hobbes presented such a view more than three centuries ago. As Strauss points out, "We understand only what we make. Since we do not make the natural beings, they are, strictly speaking, unintelligible. According to Hobbes, this fact is perfectly compatible with the possibility of natural science. But it leads to the consequence that natural science is and will always remain fundamentally hypothetical. Yet his is all we need in order to make ourselves master and owner of nature. Still, however much man may succeed in his conquest of nature, he will never be able to understand nature. The universe will always remain wholly enigmatic" (*Natural Right and History*, 174).

10   The following passage is sufficient (note the identification of poetry with "fancies"): "I esteemed eloquence highly, and I was in love with poetry; but I thought both were natural gifts of the mind rather than fruits of study. Those who reason most powerfully, and whose thoughts are best digested so as to be made clear and intelligible, are still the best able to urge their proposals, even though they speak only *bas breton* and have never learnt rhetoric. And those whose fancies are most pleasing and who can express them with the greatest embellishment and sweetness would not fail to be the best poets, though unacquainted with the *Ars Poetica*" (Descartes, *Discourse on the Method* 1, 11).

11   Descartes, *Discourse on the Method* 5, 35.

12   Ibid., 37.

13   Ibid., 5, 52. Cf. also Bacon, *The Great Instauration*, 24.

14   Locke, *Essay concerning Human Understanding*, book 2, chap. 11, sect. 11. I have used the "complete and unabridged" edition by Alexander Campbell Fraser (New York: Dover, 1959), in two volumes. Hereafter cited as *Essay*, followed by book, chapter, and section number.

15   Bishop Berkeley, *A Treatise concerning the Principles of Human Knowledge*, ed. Colin M. Turbayne (Indianapolis: Bobbs-Merrill, 1957), Intro., para. 7. Hereafter cited as *PHK* by part and paragraph number.

16   There are some significant parallels between Berkeley's enterprise and Wittgenstein's challenge to the positivist understanding of language in *Philosophical Investigations*. For a treatment of the latter, see Pitkin, *Wittgenstein and Justice* (Berkeley: University of Califor-

nia Press, 1971); and Danford, *Wittgenstein and Political Philosophy*. Cf. Antony Flew, "Was
Berkeley a Precursor of Wittgenstein?" in *Hume and the Enlightenment*, ed. William B.
Todd, 153–63.

17   Thomas Reid, *Essays on the Intellectual Powers of Man*, in *Thomas Reid's Inquiry and Essays*,
ed. Beanblossom and Lehrer (Indianapolis: Hackett, 1983), 174.

18   Ibid., 174–75.

19   See Capaldi, *David Hume*, 20–21, for a discussion of this issue.

20   As Reid puts it, "however absurd this doctrine might appear to the unlearned, who
consider the existence of the objects of sense as the most evident of all truths, and what no
man in his senses can doubt, the philosophers who had been accustomed to consider ideas
as the immediate objects of all thought, had no title to view this doctrine of Berkeley in so
unfavourable a light. . . . Thus we see that the new philosophy had been making gradual
approaches toward Berkeley's opinion; and, whatever others might do, the philosophers
had no title to look upon it as absurd, or unworthy of a fair examination," 166–67.

21   This will be discussed more extensively below. But see *EHU*, 149–51. Cf. Livingston,
Hume's Philosophy of Common Life, chap. 1.

22   Cf. Popkin, "David Hume: His Pyrrhonism and His Critique of Pyrrhonism," 53–98.

23   See Mossner, *Life*, 233, 319, 592.

24   As did Reid, who notes that "in the new philosophy, the pillars by which the existence of a
material world was supported, were so feeble that it did not require the force of a Samson to
bring them down; and in this we have not so much reason to admire the strength of
Berkeley's genius, as his boldness in publishing to the world an opinion which the unlearned would be apt to interpret as the sign of a crazy intellect. A man who was firmly
persuaded of the doctrine universally received by philosophers concerning ideas, if he could
take courage to call in question the existence of the material world, would easily find
unanswerable arguments in that doctrine" (*Essays on the Intellectual Powers of Man*, 169).

25   Cf. Reid, *Intellectual Powers*, 169–70.

Chapter 5: "One of the Most Sublime Questions"

1   George Davie observes that, "as seen by Reid, the great achievement of the deep-wrought,
sceptical arguments of *Treatise* I was to have brought into the open the fundamental flaw
that had entered into the intellectual structure of our civilization at the time of its birth in
Greece and that had not been exposed and eliminated by the great Cartesian reform—
namely, an excess of technical bias, which had, from the first, cut philosophy off from the
plain man by divorcing it from the realist standpoint of common sense." From "Husserl
and 'the as yet, in its most important respect, unrecognized greatness of Hume,'" 69–76.
This seminal article has received insufficient attention.

2   By far the most exhaustive study of Hume's account of causation is the recent *Hume and the Problem of Causation*, by Tom L. Beauchamp and Alexander Rosenberg. The arguments here are directed primarily to the concerns of academic philosophers. More general but still excellent accounts can be found in Laird, *Hume's Philosophy of Human Nature*, 84–126; Smith, *Philosophy of David Hume*, 121–24, 393–410; Stewart, *Moral and Political Philosophy of David Hume*, 33–38, 41–56; Capaldi, *David Hume*, 95–129.

3   See Beauchamp and Rosenberg, *Hume and the Problem of Causation*, 119–51.

4   See Smith, *Philosophy of David Hume*, 341.

5   For a full discussion of this principle and objections to it, see Donald Livingston, "Hume's Historical Theory of Meaning," in Livingston and King, *Hume*, 213–38.

6   Cf. *EHU*, 70–72; see chapter 4 above.

7   See chapter 1 of David Miller, *Philosophy and Ideology*, 19–39, which is entitled "The Natural Workings of the Human Mind." Cf. Livingston, *Hume's Philosophy of Common Life*, 15–33.

8   A most extensive treatment of Hume's reasoning here is the excellent discussion in Livingston, *Hume's Philosophy of Common Life*, 15–19, in the section entitled "The Transcendental Status of the Popular System."

9   For Hume this is no cause for despair. He is aware of the limitations of reason, and of senses, but he teaches us also that these are all we have to work with. With unfailing humor, he catches himself sometimes in philosophical enthusiasm (or dogmatism), as when, after announcing that all knowledge is in the end probability, he adds ironically: "I had almost said, that this was certain; but I reflect, that it must reduce *itself*, as well as every other reasoning, and from knowledge degenerate into probability" (*T*, 181).

10 See Smith, *Philosophy of David Hume*, 139–55, esp. 152–55; also David Fate Norton, *David Hume: Common-Sense Moralist, Sceptical Metaphysician* (Princeton: Princeton University Press, 1982), 14–20, 192–238; cf. D. D. Raphael, "Hume's Critique of Ethical Rationalism," *Hume and the Enlightenment*, ed. W. B. Todd, 14–29.

11 See Livingston, *Hume's Philosophy of Common Life*, 9–33, 91–111.

12 See Flew, *Philosopher of Moral Science*, 1–2.

13 One of the clearest treatments of this issue, and one in many respects parallel to that offered here, is in Norton, *Common-Sense Moralist*. Norton is unfortunately not as clear as he might be about the connection between what he sees as two "sides" of Hume's philosophy.

14 Perhaps the clearest account of this is in Plato's *Apology of Socrates*, implicit in the story of Socrates' questioning in response to the oracular pronouncement at Delphi. But the tension is also a theme in *Meno* and other dialogues.

15 Cf. the sections devoted to the "Reason of Animals" in both the *Treatise* (*T*, 176–79) and the first *Enquiry* (*EHU*, 104–8).

16 It seems strange that Mossner could think that in Hume's work "the sceptics (Bayle and Berkeley)" were "to be confirmed" (Mossner, *Life*, 104).

17　The phrase is used as a title in Laird's 1932 study, *Hume's Philosophy of Human Nature,* 84, and is now in common use.

18　See Richard H. Popkin, "David Hume: His Pyrrhonism and His Critique of Pyrrhonism," 53–98. Cf. Livingston, *Hume's Philosophy,* 9–33.

19　Among the considerable evidence for this assertion, consider Hume's reaction to Rousseau's publication of his "Profession of Faith of a Savoyard Vicar," in *Emile,* and the opprobrium that followed. Mossner quotes Hume from a letter to Mme de Boufflers: "I am not in the least surprized that it gave offence. He has not had the precaution to throw any veil over his sentiments; and as he scorns to dissemble his contempt of established opinions, he could not wonder that all the zealots were in arms against him. The liberty of the press is not so secured in any country, scarce even in this, as not to render such an open attack of popular prejudices somewhat dangerous" (*Letters* 1, 373–74). Quoted in Mossner, *Life,* 508.

20　A lucid account of "moderate scepticism" is to be found in Miller, *Philosophy and Ideology,* 35–39.

21　See the treatment of this theme and the discussion of "false" versus "true philosophy" in Livingston, *Hume's Philosophy,* 20–33.

22　See the wonderful passage on "Queen Reason" (my term) at *T,* 186–87, which Hume concludes with the statement that "the sceptical and dogmatical reasons are of the same kind, tho' contrary in their operation and tendency; so that where the latter is strong, it has an enemy of equal force in the former to encounter; and as their forces were at first equal, they still continue so, as long as either of them subsists; nor does one of them lose any force in the contest, without taking as much from its antagonist." Cf. *T,* 273: "A true sceptic will be diffident of his philosophical doubts, as well as of his philosophical conviction." Cf. the passage from Shaftesbury in the preface, above. We return to this theme of the easy alliance between radical skepticism and dogmatism in our consideration of the *Dialogues,* chapter 9, below.

Chapter 6: History and Relativism

1　Ludwig Wittgenstein, *Philosophical Investigations,* trans. G. E. M. Anscombe (Oxford: Basil Blackwell, 1968), 132. See Jones, "Strains in Hume and Wittgenstein," 191–209. There are many other parallels as well, including their views of the aim of philosophy, and of what Wittgenstein was to call "language games." See *EHU,* 38, 13, 84, 23; *ECPM,* 219n–20n ("We must stop somewhere in our examination of causes; and there are, in every science, some general principles, beyond which we cannot hope to find any principle more general"); cf. *T,* 224.

2　See Livingston, "Hume's Historical Theory of Meaning," in Livingston and King, *Hume,* 213–38, esp. 217–21. He discusses the notion at much greater length in *Hume's Philosophy of Common Life,* of which—as the title implies—it is the central claim.

3   But see Friedrich Nietzsche's discussion of the "objectivity" of historians, in *On the Advantage and Disadvantage of History for Life* (Indianapolis: Hackett, 1980), 33–38. Nietzsche, of course, goes much further than Hume.

4   The essay "Of the Study of History" was published in the first group of essays Hume wrote, in 1742. Mossner speculates (in my judgment, persuasively) that Hume's intention to write history dates from the mid–1740s, at least, well before he actually began to compose his *History of England* (Mossner, *Life*, 174–75).

5   I find it strange that "Of the Study of History," from which the quotation above comes, is not even mentioned by Duncan Forbes in *Hume's Philosophical Politics* and is dismissed as "frivolous" by Mossner in the biography, despite containing so important a key to understanding Hume's mature conception of his philosophic enterprise.

6   Norton, "History and Philosophy in Hume's Thought," in Norton and Popkin, *Philosophical Historian* xxxiii.

7   "Economics and the Mechanism of Historical Progress in Hume's *History*," in Livingston and King, *Hume*, 296.

8   See Gillespie, *Hegel, Heidegger, and the Ground of History*, chapter 1.

9   See Allan Bloom, *The Closing of the American Mind* (New York: Simon and Schuster, 1987), 25–43, 141–56.

10 *Letters* 2.230; cf. Mossner, *Life*, 318.

11 Stockton, "Economics and the Mechanism of Historical Progress," 296.

12 Mossner, *Life*, 318.

13 Ibid., 317–18; emphasis added.

14 Accounts of the basis of this view can be found in among others, Winch, *Idea of a Social Science* (London: Routledge and Kegan Paul, 1958) and Clifford Geertz, *The Interpretation of Cultures* (New York: Basic, 1973), esp. 3–33.

15 Hume himself, it should be noted, refuses to call moral judgments matters of sentiment only. In the opening sections of the second *Enquiry* Hume refers to the controversy "concerning the general foundation of Morals: whether they be derived from Reason, or from Sentiment" (*ECPM*, 17). It is clear, he tells us, that moral principles grounded on reason alone have no power to move us or to foster virtue: "is this ever to be expected from inferences and conclusions of the understanding, which of themselves have no hold on the affections nor set in motion the active powers of men? They discover truths; but where the truths which they discover are indifferent, and beget no desire or aversion, they can have no influence on conduct and behavior" (*ECPM*, 172). On the other hand, we do apply our reason to moral questions, so they cannot be only matters of sentiment. Sentiment or passion is a necessary *component* of moral judgment, but "in order to pave the way for such sentiment, and give a proper discernment of its objective, it is often necessary, we find, that much reasoning should precede, that nice distinctions be made, just conclusions drawn, distant comparisons formed, complicated relations examined, and general facts fixed and

ascertained" (*ECPM*, 173). Moral judgments must be based, then, on some combination of the two principles; they fall somewhere *between* matters of reason and those of sentiment. For the clearest discussion of this issue by Hume, see *ECPM*, 169–75 (section 1), and 285–94 (appendix 1).

16   I am thinking of course of A. J. Ayer's now classic *Language, Truth and Logic* (New York: Dover, N.D.). For an excellent account of Ayer, Stevenson, Weldon, and others with similar views, see Hanna Pitkin, *Wittgenstein and Justice* (Berkeley: University of California Press, 1972), 219–25.

17   An interesting comparison can be drawn here with Aristotle's discussion of the quality of judgment (and degree of precision) appropriate to particular subjects. See *Nicomachean Ethics*, book 1, Cf. Danford, *Wittgenstein and Political Philosophy*, chap. 6.

18   As an example of Palamedes' presentation, the following is representative: "Having heard Alcheic's virtue so extremely celebrated, I pretended to join in the general voice of acclamation, and only asked, by way of curiosity, as a stranger, which of all his noble actions was most highly applauded; and I soon found, that all sentiments were united in giving the preference to the assassination of Usbek. This Usbek had been to the last moment Alcheic's intimate friend, had laid many high obligations upon him, had even saved his life on a certain occasion, and had, by his will, which was found after the murder, made him heir to a considerable part of his fortune. Alcheic, it seems, conspired with about twenty or thirty more, most of them also Usbek's friends; and falling all together on that unhappy man, when he was not aware, they had torne him with a hundred wounds . . . this action of Alcheic's sets him far above Usbek in the eyes of all judges of merit; and is one of the noblest that ever perhaps the sun shone upon" (*ECPM*, 326).

19   We will examine this issue in more detail in the next chapter. Cf. the essay "Of National Characters" (*E*, 197–215).

20   Recall the passage quoted above from "Of the Study of History" (*E*, 566–67).

21   We may consider as an example the sort of discernment, experience, and objectivity necessary to a good practitioner of the physical sciences. No scientist would claim that all scientists are on an equal footing with regard to judgment: the great geniuses of the physics of recent centuries are sufficient evidence, if the annual selection of Nobel Prize winners were not already indication enough. But is this a reasonable example? Isn't Hume speaking of some sort of aesthetic judgment, judgment according to a "standard of taste" quite different from the criteria for judgment in physical science? There is ample evidence that in the construction of the greatest physico-mathematical theories, great theoretical physicists perceive, and judge according to, criteria which can only be described as more akin to aesthetic criteria than to anything else. Einstein's general theory of relativity is by some considered "probably the most beautiful of all existing physical theories. And Einstein himself wrote at the end of his first paper announcing his field equations, 'Scarcely anyone who fully understands this theory can escape from its magic'" (I draw heavily here on an

article entitled "Beauty and the Quest for Beauty in Science," by astrophysicist S. Chandrasekhar, in *Physics Today* [July 1979], 25–30). Heisenberg has left ample documentation of his conviction along these lines, and there are even cases where, when the beauty and truth of a scientific theory appear to conflict, the principle of beauty is preferred. Chandrasekhar relates an account of the physicist Hermann Weyl, who at one point in his work "became convinced that [his] theory was not true as a theory of gravitation, but still it was so beautiful that he did not wish to abandon it and so he kept it alive for the sake of its beauty." And it did turn out later that Weyl's initial instinct was correct, and the theory was eventually incorporated into quantum electrodynamics. "We have evidence, then, that a theory developed by a scientist, with an exceptionally well-developed aesthetic sensibility, can turn out to be true even if, at the time of its formulation, it appeared not to be so. . . . It is, indeed, an incredible fact that what the human mind, at its deepest and most profound, perceives as beautiful finds its realization in external nature" (27–28).

This is, of course, a far cry from the picture of the prosaic white-jacketed laboratory scientist working to verify another piece of a complicated "jigsaw puzzle." But the evidence is considerable from thinkers as diverse as Kepler, Einstein, Pauli, Boltzmann, Heisenberg, and of course Newton, on the issue of the beauty of physical theories. Chandrasekhar proceeds to ask "how one may evaluate scientific theories as works of art in the manner of literary or art criticism," and he goes on to adduce two criteria of a sort of scientific aesthetic, one from Francis Bacon and one from Heisenberg.

22   Oddly enough Hume's account seems to be perfectly consistent with Thomas Kuhn's, but so far is it from applying to moral systems (as frequently interpreted) that, if Hume is correct, the accuracy of Kuhn's description is restricted especially to the physical sciences, precisely because of their speculative character, that is, their *lack* of a grounding in the phenomena of ordinary human life. See Thomas Kuhn, *The Structure of Scientific Revolutions*.

23   See Danford, *Wittgenstein;* Cf. Pitkin, *Wittgenstein and Justice;* Stanley Cavell, *The Claim of Reason: Wittgenstein, Skepticism, Morality, and Tragedy* (New York: Oxford University Press), 1979.

24   Donald Livingston, in Livingston and King, *Hume,* 220. See also the more extended discussion in his more recent book, *Hume's Philosophy of Common Life.*

25   Ibid., 221. Livingston goes on to argue that "Hume's paradigm for understanding the language of common life is not theoretical inquiry but *historical* inquiry."

26   Part of his letter reads as follows: "Clearly your decisive argument is the collapse of all principles in the modern world, and I certainly agree with you that, if this were correct, my insistence on *phronesis* would be nothing more than pure declamation. But is this really the case? Don't we all then run the risk of a terrible intellectual hubris if we equate Nietzsche's anticipations and the ideological confusion of the present with life as it is actually lived with its own forms of solidarity?" In Richard J. Bernstein, *Beyond Objectivism and Relativism: Science, Hermeneutics, and Praxis* (Philadelphia: University of Pennsylvania Press), 1983.

27   Norton, "History and Philosophy in Hume's Thought."

Chapter 7: History and Political Economy

1   In a sense Hume was merely one of the first—of a great many—to react to what might be regarded as the Enlightenment's overly sanguine view of reason. He was to be joined almost immediately by Rousseau, whose *Discourse on the Arts and Sciences* (1750) is surely the strongest attack, at least rhetorically, on reason and the spread of science, based on the danger posed to morals by this development.

2   See Mossner, "Hume and the Ancient-Modern Controversy, 1725–1752," 139–53.

3   Ibid., 146.

4   See, for example, Sheldon Wolin, "Hume and Conservatism," in Livingston and King, *Hume*, 239–56; Craig Walton, "Hume and Jefferson on the Uses of History," in ibid., 389–403.

5   Quinton, *Politics of Imperfection*.

6   This is the title of a work in progress, parts of which I have seen as a result of private correspondence with Professor Caton, who teaches in Brisbane, Australia.

7   Wolin, *Politics*, 239.

·8   See, for example, Norton, *David Hume;* Wolin, *Politics;* Forbes, *Hume's Philosophical Politics*.

9   An especially clear case of this reasoning is found in the passage cited in the last chapter from Mossner, *Life*, 318: "Although Hume's *History* is not for our times, it is proper to turn to it for either of two reasons: to enjoy it as literature, or to learn from it how the greatest mind of the Enlightenment interpreted the past for his age."

10   Wolin, *Politics*, 254–55.

11   See Mossner, "Hume and the Ancient-Modern Controversy."

12   The first written (later volume 5), on the Stuarts, was published in 1754; in 1757 the second Stuart volume, (later volume 6); and in 1759 came the two Tudor volumes (later volumes 3 and 4). The final two volumes Hume wrote (volumes 1 and 2) were those devoted to the earliest period and were published in 1762.

13   See *The Letters of David Hume*, ed. J. Y. T. Grieg (Oxford: Clarendon, 1932), 1.249: Hume writes to publisher Andrew Millar that he is writing the history beginning with the reign of Henry VII and adds "It is properly at that Period modern History commences. America was discovered: Commerce extended: The Arts cultivated: Printing invented: Religion reform'd: And all the Governments of Europe almost chang'd." See also *Letters*, 1.251.

14   For a quite different but compelling view (which makes the Saxons sound nearly modern and civilized), see Paul Johnson, *A History of the English People* (New York: Harper and Row, 1985), originally published as *The Offshore Islanders* (London: George Weidenfeld and Nicholson, 1972).

15 In the original (1762) edition, this passage read somewhat differently: "they may be pronounced incapable of any true and regular liberty; which requires such a refinement of laws and institutions, such a comprehension of views, such a sentiment of honour, such a spirit of obedience, and such a sacrifice of private interests and connexions to public order, as can only be the result of. . . ."

16 In a note to this passage Hume writes that "the Kings, to encourage the boroughs, granted them this privilege, that any villain, who had lived a twelvemonth in any corporation and had been of the gild, should be thenceforth regarded as free" (2.444n). Cf. 1.409–10.

17 The process of liberation which follows or accompanies the development of the arts and sciences is contrasted by Hume with the course of events in Greek and Roman times, when the progress of the arts "seems . . . to have daily increased the number of slaves." The difference, he teaches, results "from a great difference in the circumstances" (2.523): where the Roman lords were interested in opulence and displays of wealth, and hence in domestic services of all kinds, the feudal barons, "being obliged to maintain themselves continually in a military posture, and little emulous of elegance or splendor, employed not their villains as domestic servants, much less as manufacturers; but composed their retinue of free-men, whose military spirit rendered the chieftain formidable to his neighbours."

18 "Of Refinement in the Arts" (*E*, 275–88). This essay comprises the second of the set of essays generally read today as political economy (see Mossner, *Life*, 269–71). It was originally entitled "Of Luxury" in the first edition of "Political Essays."

19 It is instructive to compare Hume's estimation of the importance of this change with the account offered by Tocqueville of the centrality of inheritance laws: "I am surprised that ancient and modern writers have not attributed greater importance to the laws of inheritance (fn.) and their effect on the progress of human affairs. . . . They should head the list of all political institutions, for they have an unbelievable influence on the social state of peoples" (Tocqueville, *Democracy in America* [New York: Anchor, 1969], 51–52).

Chapter 8: Philosophy and Morals

1 See for example Forbes, *Hume's Philosophical Politics*, 140–41. Speaking of Hume's cosmopolitanism, Forbes suggests "it is especially necessary to remember that Hume was not, as he still appears in some English and foreign writings, an Englishman, but belonged to the most European of all the communities of Europe—its law based on Roman law to a considerable degree, its people scattered all over Europe for centuries in the universities and the armies and in branches of Scottish families settled on the continent. These things cannot be weighed and measured, but Hume's love of France and French civilization is obvious to any reader of his letters, who will remember, for example, the long continued debate, which went on up to the last year of his life (II, 295), as to whether he would settle in France for good. As a 'citizen of the world' taking a metropolitan, European view of English politics and history, and a Francophile, therefore, as well as in his role of Newtonian

philosopher appealing to experience, Hume was offended by a theory of political obligation based on an experience so limited as to exclude the civilized absolute monarchies of Europe." Cf. 196ff.

2 Mossner, *Life,* 175–76; Cf. *Letters* 1.99, 1.109.

3 Claims of this kind have been made recently by those attempting to construe Hume as some sort of communitarian, who placed a central emphasis on sympathy and moral sense in human nature. See the account of Hume in Garry Wills, *Inventing America* (New York: Random House, 1978), 193–216, where Hume is assimilated to some sort of "moral sense school" to which Thomas Jefferson allegedly belonged ("The existence of a separate moral faculty, looking to gratification rather than to verification, allows Hume to treat morals without reference to his epistemological doubts").

A helpful corrective to this treatment can be found in a number of places, especially David Fate Norton, *David Hume: Common-Sense Moralist, Sceptical Metaphysician* (Princeton: Princeton University Press, 1982), 108–20, 126ff.

See also Capaldi, *David Hume,* 183–87. Capaldi shows both how and why Hume's restructuring of his thought after the *Treatise* led him to "the rejection of sympathy" as the main principle in moral transactions. Cf. James L. King, "The Place of the Language of Morals in Hume's Second *Enquiry,"* in Livingston and King, *Hume,* 343–61; see also note 15 to chapter 6, above.

4 Mossner, "Hume and the Ancient-Modern Controversy."

5 Views similar to Hume's (favoring commercial republics over ancient martial republics) are found in John Adams' *A Defence of the Constitutions of Government of the United States of America* (New York: Da Capo, 1971), esp. vol. 1, pp. 113–14, 212, 256–57. A careful reading of Montesquieu's *Spirit of the Laws* will find powerful coincident arguments. See Thomas L. Pangle, *Montesquieu's Philosophy of Liberalism* (Chicago: University of Chicago Press, 1973).

6 See Hume's note to this passage, a digression on the double meaning of the old Latin term for stranger, *hostis,* which also meant *enemy.* As Hume notes, "The more ancient ROMANS lived in perpetual war with all their neighbors" (*E,* 259n).

7 Mossner, "Hume and the Ancient-Modern Controversy," 151.

8 For Solzhenitsyn's views see his celebrated Harvard commencement address in 1978, "A World Split Apart," published in *National Review* (July 7, 1978, 836–55). But the view that commerce or capitalist society is hopelessly decadent is widespread today among political commentators. See Henry Fairlie's lament for the disappearance of public spirit (civic virtue) under Reagan, in "Citizen Kennedy" (*The New Republic,* February 3, 1986, 14–17). Fairlie complains that "With the idea of citizenship all but submerged in appeals to private pursuits, private satisfactions, the private sector, the most Reagan could hope to lead against a real enemy would be a herd of Gadarene swine."

9 The paradox that severity in government drives subjects to rebellion is treated analytically in one of Hume's *Essays.* See "Of the Liberty of the Press" (*E,* 9–13).

10 It is instructive to compare Hume's claims with the much lengthier discussion by Adam

Smith in book 5 of *An Inquiry into the Nature and Causes of the Wealth of Nations*. Cf. Haakonssen, *Science of a Legislator*, 93–98, 146, 159–62; and Winch *Adam Smith's Politics*, 103–120.

11   The issues Hume addresses here are explored in some of the literature of the recent "civic humanist" movement in historiography. See *Wealth and Virtue: The Shaping of Political Economy in the Scottish Enlightenment*, ed. Istvan Hont and Michael Ignatieff (Cambridge: Cambridge University Press, 1983); Cf. Pocock, *Virtue, Commerce and History;* and Winch, *Adam Smith's Politics*.

Chapter 9: Philosophy and Religion

1   Isaiah Berlin, "Hume and the Sources of German Anti-Rationalism," in *David Hume: Bicentenary Papers*, ed. G. P. Morice (Austin: University of Texas Press, 1977), 93–116.

2   In addition to Hobbes, one need only mention Machiavelli and Spinoza, whose critiques of revealed religion are well known. See Rousseau, *Social Contract* 4, viii, for a slightly different critique of Christianity. Cf. Strauss, *Natural Right and History*, 168–69. On the other hand, the view that Hobbes was an atheist is by no means universally accepted. On the convoluted subject of Hobbes' views concerning the Deity, see, e.g., Willis Glover, "God and Thomas Hobbes," in K. C. Brown, ed., *Hobbes Studies* (Cambridge: Harvard University Press, 1965); R. W. Hepburn, "Hobbes on the Knowledge of God," in Maurice Cranston and Richard S. Peters, eds., *Hobbes and Rousseau* (Garden City, N.Y.: Anchor, 1972), 85–108; Strauss, *What is Political Philosophy?* (New York: Free Press, 1959), 182–90; Samuel I. Mintz, *The Hunting of Leviathan* (Cambridge: Cambridge University Press, 1962), passim. It should also be noted that Hobbes' attack was primarily, though not exclusively, directed against the Roman Catholic Church.

3   Hobbes, *Leviathan*, 116.

4   Cicero, *De Natura Deorum*, or *On the Nature of the Gods* (London: George Bell and Sons, 1876), Bohn edition, translation ascribed to Benjamin Franklin, 2.

5   See Thomas Pangle, "The Political Psychology of Religion in Plato's Laws," in *American Political Science Review* 70 (1976), 1059–77. Cf. Plato *Laws*, book 10. This is not to say that the defense provided by philosophy was or could be successful, or that the motive for supplying it was piety or civic responsibility. Plato seems to suggest that political philosophy can use this need of the city to make a home for itself, without entirely refuting the claims of the atheists.

6   See H. E. Root's introduction to Hume's *Natural History of Religion* (Stanford: Stanford University Press, 1957), 9.

7   See Hobbes, *Leviathan*, 168: "And this Feare of things invisible, is the naturall Seed of that, which every one in himself calleth Religion; and in them that worship, or feare that Power otherwise than they do, Superstition."

8   A helpful and brief introduction to this work, and scholarship on it, is Mossner, "Hume and the Legacy of the Dialogues," in *David Hume: Bicentenary Papers*, ed. Morice, 1–22.

9   Keith Yandell, "Hume on Religious Belief," in Livingston and King, *Hume*, 109–25. Yandell's page reference is to the Norman Kemp Smith edition of the *Dialogues*, which is cited here also.

10   See James Noxon, "Hume's Agnosticism" in *Hume: A Collection of Critical Essays*, ed. V. C. Chappell (Garden City, N.Y.: Anchor, 1976) 362–63.

11   Thus, Noxon writes, "The *Dialogues*, however, have not proven to be the key to the riddle of David Hume. On the contrary, they have themselves posed a riddle: who speaks for Hume? Unless this question can be answered, Hume's last philosophical testament provides us with no clue to his own religious convictions" (Noxon, "Hume's Agnosticism," 375). Norman Kemp Smith, perhaps the finest Hume scholar of our century, stated his answer to this question unequivocally: "Philo, from the start to finish, represents Hume" (*D*, 59). But others have seen more justification for claiming that Hume's spokesman is in fact Cleanthes, the less radically skeptical interlocutor whom the narrator of the *Dialogues*, Pamphilus, declares at the end to have espoused principles "still nearer to the truth" than those of Philo.

12   Yandell, "Hume on Religious Belief," 111. An important contrasting view is to be found in Mossner, "Hume and the Legacy of the *Dialogues.*" Yandell argues that once one sees that no *character* is Hume, one must turn to the *NHR* to see his real views, which are represented more accurately there. (Why Hume lavished such care on the *Dialogues* is not explained.) Yandell believes that in both works together Hume is explaining why men believe what they believe even though it is not philosophically justifiable, and thus showing man's predicament. "Either blind belief which is destructive of morality or blind belief which is not: such is man's destiny with respect to religious belief" (Yandell, 120).

13   Cicero, *De Natura Deorum*, 5.

14   Of course it is necessary to acknowledge that Hume also seems to hold such a view. In one famous passage he says that "reason is, and ought to be the slave of the passions, and can never pretend to any other office than to serve and obey them" (*T*, 415). As Hume himself notes, however, this view may appear "somewhat extraordinary," and we have already considered it sufficiently for our purposes here.

15   See Danford, *Wittgenstein*, chapter 2.

16   See Hobbes, *Leviathan*, chapter 46; Hobbes, *Elements of Law, Epistle Dedicatory*.

17   Hume's extensive references to Plato's *Laws*, as well as to the works of Xenophon and Cicero, contribute to the surmise that he grasped this implication of the classical author's reflections. The most copious use of ancient writers seems to be in the *NHR*, especially 36, 50–52, 63–64.

18   In the prologue to the *Dialogues*, in fact, Pamphilus, the narrator, suggests that a philosophic (and inconclusive) dialogue "carries us, in a manner, into company and unites the two

greatest and purest pleasures of human life—study and society" (*D*, 4). We should recall here Aristotle's treatment of friendship, in connection with his portrayal of the philosophic life, in books 9 and 10 of the *Nicomachean Ethics*.

19 In fairness, Noxon's argument seems to point in this direction, although he does not draw out its implications. After showing persuasively that Hume believed the "question of natural theology" to be unanswerable, Noxon goes on: "If, then, Hume's opinion was that theological argument is futile, why did he write the *Dialogues*, keep them by him for twenty-five years, revise them in the year of his death, and take such anxious precautions to ensure their publication?

I am sure, that Hume wrote the *Dialogues* precisely in order to reveal the futility of such theological argument, and to show that the only sensible course is to abandon such topics for what he calls 'the examination of common life.' It is obviously not futile to show that a certain kind of argument is futile, and I daresay that Hume himself thought it was very useful" (Noxon, "Hume's Agnosticism," 378–79).

20 On the status of this note, see Norman Kemp Smith's introduction to his edition of the *Dialogues*, 94–95.

21 For example, each work presents a conversation among three interlocutors, conversing in private before a witness who narrates, representing roughly the same philosophical sects (with the exception treated below). Many of the same arguments from the natural philosophers are presented, and even some examples are identical (see Cicero, *De Natura Deorum*, 6, 16). The same anecdote about Simonides is mentioned in both (*De Natura Deorum*, 2.23; *D*, 149).

22 Harris, *Cicero as an Academic*, 21. Cf. Henry David Aiken's introduction to the Hafner edition of the *Dialogues*, xiii.

23 Of course this advice from his friends suggests they believed the *Dialogues* went *beyond* the already published views excoriating popular religions in some way. It is not at first glance easy to see how. Perhaps Hume's friends only wished to protect Hume from additional vilification, or perhaps they believed the *Dialogues* more subversive of all religion than this reading takes them to be.

24 See, for example, Hume's note, in the *Essays*, to his discussion of the priestly life as a distinctive way of life: "Though *all mankind have a strong propensity to religion at certain times and in certain dispositions;* yet there are few or none, who have it to that degree, and with that constancy, which is requisite to support the character of this profession" (*E*, 199n; emphasis added). This footnote—running several pages—is an essay in itself, and a brilliant one. I will cite it below.

25 Cf. Aristotle, *Nicomachean Ethics*, books 9 and 10.

26 The words "while you opposed" would seem to preclude Mossner's claim that Hume is speaking ironically and that we are supposed to take the *opposite* of every utterance of Pamphilus. Mossner argues unconvincingly that these characterizations are wrong in each

case: "As a sheer matter of fact they are all designedly misconceived. For Cleanthes' 'philosophical turn' is not *accurate* (it is *muddled*); Philo's 'skepticism' is not *careless* (it is *disciplined*); Demea's 'orthodoxy' is not *rigid inflexible* (it is *politic expedient*)" (Mossner, "Hume and the Legacy of the *Dialogues*," 7). Since the judgments of character expressed here are those of someone else, and *not* made on the basis of what is said in the *Dialogues*, it is difficult to accept Mossner's view; the characterizations seem to me to be not so far wrong, and in any case our attention is directed at the *characters* as an important element in the *Dialogues*.

27 See Cotta's summary of Epicurus's views at 2.1 and 1.24–28.

28 For an excellent discussion of the similarities, see Noxon, "Hume's Agnosticism," 368–72.

29 Hobbes, *Leviathan*, chapter 3, 99.

30 See, for example, the passages in part 10 of the *Dialogues* where Demea presents an especially Hobbesian view of the "natural condition" of man: "A perpetual war is kindled amongst all living creatures. Necessity, hunger, want stimulate the strong and courageous: Fear, anxiety, terror, agitate the weak and infirm" (*D*, 194; cf. *D*, 196–97).

31 See *E*, 199n, cited above, in note 24.

32 See the passage in part 3 where, after Cleanthes upbraids Philo for his "affected skepticism" which goes beyond "reasonable" skepticism, Philo is described as "a little embarrassed and confounded" (*D*, 154–55).

33 For classical political philosophy, philosophy also presented a double danger to healthy civic life. But one of the dangers (as seen in the intransigent questioning of accepted opinions by Socrates) *saw* itself as a danger precisely because it was political, and so took on the task of supplying a defense against the other danger (natural philosophy). By making itself useful, it could give itself a sort of a home in the city.

34 We may cite in this connection a passage from the *EHU*: "And, those, who attempt to disabuse them of such prejudice, may, for aught I know, be good reasoners, but I cannot allow them to be good citizens and politicians; since they free men from one restraint upon their passions, and make the infringement of the laws of society, in one respect, more easy and secure" (147). Cf. Adam Smith's quotation from volume 4 of Hume's *History*, in regard to the political effects of certain theological views. Part of that quotation runs as follows: "because, in every religion except the true, it is highly pernicious, and it has even a natural tendency to pervert the true, by infusing into it a strong mixture of superstition, folly, and delusion. Each ghostly practitioner, in order to render himself more precious and sacred in the eyes of his retainers, will inspire them with the most violent abhorrence of all other sects, and continually endeavor, by some novelty, to excite the languid devotion of his audience" (*The Wealth of Nations*, 5.1.3.3). Cf. the long footnote to "Of National Characters" (*E*, 199–201), cited above.

Chapter 10: Conclusion

1   Rorty, *Consequences of Pragmatism*, 140.
2   Ibid. Of course, Thomas Kuhn should be cited. Also see Rorty, Schneewind, and Skinner, *Philosophy in History*.
3   Livingston offers an excellent account of what Hume means by this term and the use he makes of it (*Hume's Philosophy of Common Life*, 20–33; see also 272–84). But we disagree, at least to some extent, about where Hume locates the difficulty. I believe Hume is reacting mostly to Hobbes and Descartes, whereas Livingston sees the tendency to "false philosophy" as characteristic of the whole Western rational tradition. He is thus closer to the views of Nietzsche.

    On the other side, the always provocative Antony Flew, in his recent book on Hume, maintains that Hume himself uncritically took over a whole set of Cartesian assumptions, specifically those iterated in the opening paragraphs of part 4 of the *Discourse of the Method*. See Flew, *Philosopher of Moral Science*, 12–17.

Selected Bibliography

Anderson, Robert F. *Hume's First Principles*. Lincoln: University of Nebraska Press, 1966.

Ayer, A. J. *Hume*. Past Masters Series. New York: Hill and Wang, 1980.

Bacon, Francis. *The Great Instauration and New Atlantis*. Ed. J. Weinberger. Arlington Heights, Illinois: AHM, 1980.

———. *Of the Dignity and Advancement of Learning*. In *Francis Bacon: A Selection of His Works*. Ed. Sidney Warhaft. Toronto: MacMillan, 1965.

Beauchamp, Tom L., and Alexander Rosenberg. *Hume and the Problem of Causation*. New York: Oxford University Press, 1981.

Bongie, Laurence L. *David Hume: Prophet of the Counter-Revolution*. Oxford: Clarendon Press, 1965.

Braudy, Leo. *Narrative Form in History and Fiction: Hume, Fielding and Gibbon*. Princeton: Princeton University Press, 1970.

Capaldi, Nicholas. *David Hume: The Newtonian Philosopher*. Boston: Twayne, 1975.

Cavell, Stanley. *The Claim of Reason: Wittgenstein, Skepticism, Morality, and Tragedy*. New York: Oxford University Press, 1979.

Chappell, V. C., ed. *Hume: A Collection of Critical Essays*. New York: Anchor, 1966.

Cicero. *De Natura Deorum*. London: George Bell and Sons, 1876.

Condorcet. *Selected Writings*. Ed. Keith M. Baker. Indianapolis: Bobbs-Merrill, 1976.

Danford, John W. *Wittgenstein and Political Philosophy*. Chicago: University of Chicago Press, 1978.

Davie, George. "Husserl and 'the as yet, in its most important respect, unrecognized greatness of Hume.'" In *David Hume: BiCentenary Papers*. Ed. G. P. Morice. Austin: University of Texas Press, 1977.

Descartes, René. *Discourse on the Method*. Trans. and ed. Elizabeth Anscombe and Peter Thomas Geach. Edinburgh: Thomas Nelson and Sons, 1962.

Duhem, Pierre. *The Aim and Structure of Physical Theory*. Trans. P. P. Wiener. Princeton: Princeton University Press, 1954.

Ferguson, Adam. *An Essay on the History of Civil Society.* Edinburgh: Edinburgh University Press, 1966.

Flew, Antony. *David Hume: Philosopher of Moral Science.* Oxford: Basil Blackwell, 1986.

Forbes, Duncan. *Hume's Philosophical Politics.* New York: Cambridge University Press, 1975.

Gillespie, Michael Allen. *Hegel, Heidegger, and the Ground of History.* Chicago: University of Chicago Press, 1984.

Grave, S. A. *The Scottish Philosophy of Common Sense.* Oxford: Clarendon Press, 1960.

Haakonssen, Knud. *The Science of a Legislator: The Natural Jurisprudence of David Hume and Adam Smith.* Cambridge: Cambridge University Press, 1981.

Harris, Bruce Fairgay. *Cicero as an Academic: A Study of De Natura Deorum.* University of Auckland, Bulletin No. 58, Classic Series No. 2.

Harrison, Jonathan. *Hume's Moral Epistemology.* Oxford: Clarendon Press, 1976.

Hiley, David R. *Philosophy in Question: Essays on a Pyrrhonian Theme.* Chicago: University of Chicago Press, 1988.

Hirschman, Albert O. *The Passions and the Interests: Political Arguments for Capitalism before Its Triumph.* Princeton: Princeton University Press, 1977.

Hont, Istvan, and Michael Ignatieff, eds. *Wealth and Virtue: The Shaping of Political Economy in the Scottish Enlightenment.* Cambridge: Cambridge University Press, 1983.

Husserl, Edmund. *The Crisis of European Sciences and Transcendental Phenomenology.* Trans. David Carr. Evanston: Northwestern University Press, 1970.

Huxley, T. H. *Hume.* English Men of Letters Series. Ed. John Morley. New York: Harper and Brothers, n.d.

Jones, Peter. "Strains in Hume and Wittgenstein." In *Hume: A Re-evaluation,* ed. Donald Livingston and James King. New York: Fordham University Press, 1976.

Kuhn, Thomas S. *The Structure of Scientific Revolutions.* 2d enl. ed. Chicago: University of Chicago Press, 1970.

Laird, John. *Hume's Philosophy of Human Nature.* London: Methuen and Co., 1932.

Letwin, Shirley Robin. *The Pursuit of Certainty.* Cambridge: Cambridge University Press, 1965.

Livingston, Donald W. *Hume's Philosophy of Common Life.* Chicago: University of Chicago Press, 1984.

Livingston, Donald W., and James T. King, eds. *Hume: A Re-evaluation.* New York: Fordham University Press, 1976.

MacIntyre, Alasdair. *After Virtue.* Notre Dame, Indiana: University of Notre Dame Press, 1981.

McCracken, Charles J. *Malebranche and British Philosophy.* Oxford: Clarendon Press, 1983.

Miller, David. *Philosophy and Ideology in Hume's Political Thought.* Oxford: Oxford University Press, 1981.

Moore, James. "Hume's Political Science and the Classical Republican Tradition." *Canadian Journal of Political Science* 10 (1977).

Morice, G. P., ed. *David Hume: Bicentenary Papers*. Austin: University of Texas Press, 1977.

Mossner, Ernest Campbell. *The Forgotten Hume: Le bon David*. New York: Columbia University Press, 1943.

————. "Hume and the Ancient-Modern Controversy, 1725–1752: A Study in Creative Scepticism." University of Texas. *Studies in English*. 28 (1949): 139–53.

————. *The Life of David Hume*. 2d ed. Oxford: Clarendon Press, 1980.

Norton, David Fate. *David Hume: Common-Sense Moralist, Sceptical Metaphysician*. Princeton: Princeton University Press, 1982.

————. "History and Philosophy in Hume's Thought." In *David Hume: Philosophical Historian*, ed. David Fate Norton and Richard Popkin. Indianapolis: Bobbs-Merrill, 1965.

Norton, David Fate, and Richard Popkin, eds. *David Hume: Philosophical Historian*. Indianapolis: Bobbs-Merrill, 1965.

Norton, David Fate, Nicholas Capaldi, and Wade L. Robison, eds. *McGill Hume Studies*. San Diego: Austin Hill Press, 1979.

Noxon, James. *Hume's Philosophical Development: A Study of His Methods*. Oxford: Clarendon Press, 1973.

Pangle, Thomas. *Montesquieu's Philosophy of Liberalism*. Chicago: University of Chicago Press, 1973.

Pocock, J. G. A. *Virtue, Commerce and History*. Cambridge: Cambridge University Press, 1985.

Popkin, Richard H. "David Hume: His Pyrrhonism and His Critique of Pyrrhonism." In *Hume: A Collection of Critical Essays*, ed. V. C. Chappell. Garden City, N.Y.: Anchor, 1966.

Price, John Valdimir. *The Ironic Hume*. Austin: University of Texas Press, 1965.

Quinton, Anthony. *The Politics of Imperfection*. London: Faber and Faber, 1978.

Reid, Thomas. *Essays on the Active Powers of the Human Mind*. Cambridge: MIT Press, 1969.

————. *Inquiry and Essays*. Ed. Ronald E. Beanblossom and Keith Lehrer. Indianapolis: Hackett, 1983.

Richetti, John J. *Philosophical Writing: Locke, Berkeley, Hume*. Cambridge: Harvard University Press, 1983.

Rorty, Richard. *Consequences of Pragmatism*. Minneapolis: University of Minnesota Press, 1982.

————. *Contingency, irony, and solidarity*. Cambridge: Cambridge University Press, 1989.

Rorty, Richard, J. B. Schneewind, and Quentin Skinner. *Philosophy in History*. Cambridge: Cambridge University Press, 1984.

Rotwein, Eugene. *David Hume: Writings on Economics*. Madison, Wisconsin: University of Wisconsin Press, 1970.

Russell, Paul. "Hume's *Treatise* and Hobbes's *The Elements of Law*." *Journal of the History of Ideas*, 46 (1985).

Smith, Adam. *An Inquiry into the Nature and Causes of the Wealth of Nations*. Ed. Edwin Cannan. New York: Modern Library, 1937.

Smith, Norman Kemp. *The Philosophy of David Hume*. London: Macmillan, 1941.

Stewart, John B. *The Moral and Political Philosophy of David Hume*. New York: Columbia University Press, 1963.

Stockton, Constance Noble. "Economics and the Mechanism of Historical Progress in Hume's *History*." In *Hume: A Re-evaluation*, ed. Donald Livingston and James King. New York: Fordham University Press, 1976.

Strauss, Leo. *Natural Right and History*. Chicago: University of Chicago Press, 1953.

Stroud, Barry. *Hume*. London: Routledge and Kegan Paul, 1977.

Thomas, David. *Naturalism and Social Science: A Post-Empiricist Philosophy of Social Science*. Cambridge: Cambridge University Press, 1979.

Todd, W. B., ed. *Hume and the Enlightenment*. Edinburgh and Austin: University Press of Edinburgh and the Humanities Research Center, Texas, 1974.

Vyverberg, Henry. *Pessimism in the French Enlightenment*. Cambridge: Harvard University Press, 1958.

Winch, Donald. *Adam Smith's Politics: An Essay in Historiographic Revision*. Cambridge: Cambridge University Press, 1978.

Winch, Peter. *The Idea of a Social Science and Its Relation to Philosophy*. London: Routledge and Kegan Paul, 1958.

Index